T0382199

The Governance Cycle in Parliamentary Democracies

Parliamentary democracy involves a never-ending cycle of elections, government formations, and the need for governments to survive in potentially hostile environments. These conditions require members of any government to make decisions on a large number of issues, some of which sharply divide them. Officials resolve these divisions by "logrolling" – conceding on issues they care less about, in exchange for reciprocal concessions on issues to which they attach more importance. Though realistically modeling this "governance cycle" is beyond the scope of traditional formal analysis, this book attacks the problem computationally in two ways. Firstly, it models the behavior of "functionally rational" senior politicians who use informal decision heuristics to navigate their complex high stakes settings. Secondly, by applying computational methods to traditional game theory, it uses artificial intelligence to model how hyperrational politicians might find strategies that are close to optimal.

SCOTT DE MARCHI is Professor of Political Science and Director of Decision Science at Duke University. He is a principal investigator for the National Science Foundation's Empirical Implications of Theoretical Models program, and his research focuses on decision-making in contexts that include Congress, coalition and crisis bargaining, and interstate conflict.

MICHAEL LAVER is Emeritus Professor of Politics at New York University. He has published 20 books, including *Multiparty Government: The Politics of Coalition in Europe* (1991), *Making and Breaking Governments* (1996), and *Party Competition: An Agent-Based Model* (2014).

CAMBRIDGE STUDIES IN COMPARATIVE POLITICS

GENERAL EDITOR

KATHLEEN THELEN *Massachusetts Institute of Technology*

ASSOCIATE EDITORS

CATHERINE BOONE *London School of Economics*
THAD DUNNING *University of California, Berkeley*
ANNA GRZYMALA-BUSSE *Stanford University*
TORBEN IVERSEN *Harvard University*
STATHIS KALYVAS *University of Oxford*
MARGARET LEVI *Stanford University*
MELANIE MANION *Duke University*
HELEN MILNER *Princeton University*
FRANCES ROSENBLUTH *Yale University*
SUSAN STOKES *Yale University*
TARIQ THACHIL *University of Pennsylvania*
ERIK WIBBELS *Duke University*

SERIES FOUNDER

Peter Lange, *Duke University*

OTHER BOOKS IN THE SERIES

Christopher Adolph, *Bankers, Bureaucrats, and Central Bank Politics: The Myth of Neutrality*
Michael Albertus, *Autocracy and Redistribution: The Politics of Land Reform*
Michael Albertus, *Property without Rights: Origins and Consequences of the Property Rights Gap*
Santiago Anria, *When Movements Become Parties: The Bolivian MAS in Comparative Perspective*
Ben W. Ansell, *From the Ballot to the Blackboard: The Redistributive Political Economy of Education*
Ben W. Ansell and Johannes Lindvall, *Inward Conquest: The Political Origins of Modern Public Services*
Ben W. Ansell and David J. Samuels, *Inequality and Democratization: An Elite-Competition Approach*
Ana Arjona, *Rebelocracy: Social Order in the Colombian Civil War*
Leonardo R. Arriola, *Multi-Ethnic Coalitions in Africa: Business Financing of Opposition Election Campaigns*

Continued after the index

The Governance Cycle in Parliamentary Democracies

A Computational Social Science Approach

SCOTT DE MARCHI
Duke University

MICHAEL LAVER
New York University

CAMBRIDGE
UNIVERSITY PRESS

Shaftesbury Road, Cambridge CB2 8EA, United Kingdom

One Liberty Plaza, 20th Floor, New York, NY 10006, USA

477 Williamstown Road, Port Melbourne, VIC 3207, Australia

314–321, 3rd Floor, Plot 3, Splendor Forum, Jasola District Centre, New Delhi – 110025, India

103 Penang Road, #05–06/07, Visioncrest Commercial, Singapore 238467

Cambridge University Press is part of Cambridge University Press & Assessment, a department of the University of Cambridge.

We share the University's mission to contribute to society through the pursuit of education, learning and research at the highest international levels of excellence.

www.cambridge.org
Information on this title: www.cambridge.org/9781009315470

DOI: 10.1017/9781009315449

First published 2023

A catalogue record for this publication is available from the British Library

A Cataloging-in-Publication data record for this book is available from the Library of Congress

ISBN 978-1-009-31547-0 Hardback
ISBN 978-1-009-31548-7 Paperback

Contents

Figures

Tables

Acknowledgments

This was a terrifically long project to complete and was only made possible by the support we received at every step of the research. We received much-deserved criticism and advice from Michael Alvarez, John Brehm, Corwin de Marchi, James Fowler, Max Gallop, John Gerring, Libby Jenke, David Laitin, Arthur Lupia, Lanny Martin, Shahryar Minhas, Massimo Morelli, Michael Munger, Scott Parris, John Patty, Zeynep Somer-Topcu, Georg Vanberg, Erik Wibbels, and Steven Wilkinson. Parts of this work were presented at Bocconi University, Nuffield College, and the University of Texas, and the resulting discussions helped us clarify our ideas. Informal discussions with Sean Gailmard, Maggie Penn, and Rocío Titiunik at various Empirical Implications of Theoretical Models workshops contributed more than they know. Daniel de Marchi helped enormously with implementing the Monte Carlo Counterfactual Regret code in Chapter 4. Ken Kollman, John Miller, and Scott Page not only read the manuscript but also inspired our approach to computational social science.

Introduction

The field covered in this book is very limited, and we approach it in this sense of modesty .... Its first applications are necessarily to elementary problems where the result has never been in doubt and no theory is actually required. At this early stage, the application serves to corroborate the theory. The next stage develops when the theory is applied to somewhat more complicated situations in which it may already lead to a certain extent beyond the obvious and the familiar. Here theory and application corroborate each other mutually. Beyond this lies the field of real success: genuine prediction by theory. It is well known that all mathematized sciences have gone through these successive phases of evolution.

(Von Neumann and Morgenstern 2007: 8).

We started this three-year project motivated by a long-standing puzzle in the literature on parliamentary democracies. Governments are responsible to parliaments and must maintain the support of a majority of legislators. The social choice tradition of theoretical work on this subject implies that governments should have a hard time not only getting into office but also staying there – because some legislative majority can always find a "better" alternative. We do sometimes see this type of instability – historically in Italy and recently in Israel, for example. Typically, however, governments do form and do stay in power, sometimes for quite a long time. In a nutshell, despite what some theorists have called "the generic instability of majority rule" (Schofield 1983), why do we not tend to observe this instability in a real world populated by living, breathing, politicians? And why does this stability sometimes vanish, flipping the world into a state where it becomes difficult to build and maintain a government?

Work in the tradition of noncooperative game theory attacks this puzzle by describing it in terms of a radically simplified bargaining environment and making restrictive assumptions about actions

1

available to senior politicians.[1] We ourselves have a hard time, however, imagining that highly motivated, successful, and seasoned senior politicians – playing for the very highest stakes in the business – are bound by the assumptions found in these models. To take just one example, the most influential approach to this problem (Rubinstein 1982, Baron and Ferejohn 1989, Baron 1991, Ansolabehere, et al. 2005, Snyder, et al. 2005) simplifies the bargaining environment by assuming that some exogenous mechanism allows one, and only one, politician at a time to make a take-it-or-leave-it offer. Given an exogenously imposed sequence of offers, the implication is that the first proposer (*formateur*) has a substantial advantage.

We do not, however, think it is in any way reasonable to assume that the most seasoned and sophisticated politicians in the business, doing the thing they most care about, sit quietly on their hands waiting for the talking stick to be passed in their direction. In contrast, we believe that – whether this happens in the cold light of day or in the dark shadows of what we think of as "backstage" – no senior politician can be banned from making any proposal to anyone at any time. Not only will several proposals typically be under consideration at the same time, no exogenous mechanism can dictate the order in which these are considered. In short, assuming that an exogenously imposed *formateur* sequence exists might *theoretically* address the generic instability of majority rule, but does this at the cost of a model that does not *realistically* apply to the world we live in. Our approach here is to privilege the level of realism needed for a plausible description of government formation, recognizing that this will result in complex theoretical models that may well be analytically intractable using traditional deductive methods. In doing this, we leverage two strands of previously published work.

The first strand implies that more realistic and complex strategic contexts are, perhaps counterintuitively, more likely to produce structure and thereby prevent chaotic outcomes (Kollman, et al. 1992, 1998, Miller and Page 2009). In very simple settings, the intuition is that human actors will quickly see all possible courses of action and act in their own self-interest. In the context of majority voting over the making and breaking of governments, this underlies predictions of multiple

---

[1] In the last few years, a number of very interesting studies have been conducted in this tradition, with a focus on providing an explanation for the empirical regularity of Gamson's law (Martin and Vanberg 2020, Cox 2021).

equilibria and cyclical majorities. Complex and difficult environments, in contrast, typically mean that it is hard for people to identify and evaluate every conceivable possibility in real time. This forces them to search for "good" solutions that are not provably the "best" and limits their ability to find counter-proposals, thereby enhancing stability.

The second strand flows from this and puts much more emphasis than many formal theorists on actual human behavior. In complex games, it can be difficult or impossible for real humans to figure out the perfectly optimal strategies assumed by most formal theoretic models. Canonical examples of such games – including bridge and poker – resist these purely deductive approaches. As a result, formal theorists often simplify games, thereby making it possible to assume that behavior consists of straightforward deduction. Recent advances in reinforcement learning in artificial intelligence (AI), however, allow researchers to attack complex games, in many cases achieving performance better than that of expert humans (Billings, et al. 2003, Brown, et al. 2017). Rather than simplifying the game of democratic governance so radically that it can be solved by backward induction, therefore, we set out here to explore effective – though not provably optimal – behavioral rules that scale to complex games.

Populating a more complex and realistic game with agents using behavioral rules that mimic those which might be used by expert humans, we find that in many settings, our model produces stable outcomes – Condorcet winning cabinets – not generic instability. This approach had been proposed, but not previously completed, by other scholars as a potential answer to similar puzzles in the social sciences. Douglas North emphasized the central role of behavior and complexity in his later work and saw this as one answer to the question of how institutions emerge (Denzau and North 2000, Munger 2020). Similarly, Elinor Ostrom focused on the use of heuristics to solve common-pool resource problems in complex environments (Ostrom 2010). Increased availability of computation and advances in reinforcement learning have now made this approach much easier to implement.

We were encouraged from our early work as part of this research program (de Marchi and Laver 2020) that not only showed that stable governments were possible but also allowed us to predict the length of negotiations – bargaining delays – during government formation. We took this as quite strong support for our approach. While there are *empirical* accounts of the duration of government formation negotiations in parliamentary systems, there is no rigorous theoretical model explaining the empirical findings.[2] In our research, we took a direct output of our theoretical model – the likelihood of finding a Condorcet winner in each empirical setting – and used this as a measure of bargaining complexity to predict the length of negotiations. A purely analytical output of our theoretical model thus predicts a real-world dependent variable, providing evidence for our causal mechanisms.

The motivation for this book was to extend our model and use it to predict other important real-world outcomes that have resisted prior efforts. In particular, we were interested in predicting, on a case-by-case basis, which coalition is likely to form after elections in parliamentary systems. This is hard, given the huge number of different possible proposals for government. While making predictions is not the current fashion in political science, it is our belief that this is the best way to test the main implications of any theory. Predict an outcome of substantive interest and, as new data arrives, continually expose the theory to new tests. The composition of governments that form in parliamentary systems is a nearly perfect dependent variable in this sense. It is of enormous substantive interest and easily observable. There are a relatively large number of cases and new data are generated by every new election.

Even better for our purposes, government formation in parliamentary democracies is a complex strategic game played by highly motivated politicians. Our expectation is that if we can successfully analyze this, we most likely will be able to apply our model to other contexts in which bargaining occurs. Examples include alliance formation in the international system and intraparty bargaining in the US Congress.

Complex strategic models of the sort we investigate in this book, along with the behavioral algorithms we use to describe the decisions made by senior politicians, involve a large number of modeling choices. The choices could, in principle, limit the generalizability of our model and produce "curve-fitted" results. By focusing on predicting a real-world outcome such as government formation, we can, however, see if our model is general and examine the impact of different parameter values. *Theoretical* generalizability is increased by committing to an

[2] The main arc of empirical work on the duration of negotiations starts with Diermeier and Van Roozendaal (1998) and continues with Martin and Vanberg (2003) to Golder (2010). On the general difficulty in linking theory and empirics in this area, see Diermeier, et al. (2003).

empirical target. Simply put, we are trying to fulfill Von Neuman and Morgenstern's original goal: "genuine prediction by theory." Of the universe of formal models we could write down about government formation, we are interested here in those that have a direct mapping to real-world political phenomena.

In this book, we describe both the methodology we used and the substantive results we derived. Methodologically, there are several good treatments on how to build computational social science models in the area of *empirical* work (Alvarez 2016). At present, however, there are few treatments of computational social science applied to *theory*.[3] We hope this book, and the availability of our code and data, will help to fill that gap.

Substantively, we are happy to report that our initial results are encouraging; we feel we have achieved our main goals. The models we present here are able to predict: which governments form after an election, how long negotiations take during this process, and how long these governments are likely to last. One issue that deserves attention is that we, unfortunately, do not have other existing research with which to compare our findings. Prior theoretical work has not typically aimed at these targets. It is our hope, however, that by providing a first step in prediction, other researchers will build new models, improving on what we have done here and measuring their progress against our baseline. One way in which science progresses is when a community of researchers uses common benchmarks to compare the performance of models, linking theory to empirics.[4]

In addition to success at prediction, we also have a set of substantive insights that are distinct from earlier research. Loosely, earlier work typically argues that government formation:

i. is led by a proposer with considerable advantages in bargaining;
ii. involves short negotiations where the first proposal is accepted;
iii. tends to result in minimum winning coalitions (not single-party, minority, or surplus governments);[5] and
iv. at most considers government policy on one or two latent "dimensions."

---

[3] The exception is Laver (2020a, 2020b), which is focused on agent-based models.
[4] For an overview, see www.nsf.gov/sbe/ses/polisci/reports/pdf/eitmreport.pdf.
[5] A minimal winning coalition has enough members to exceed the winning threshold (e.g., a simple majority) but without any surplus members.

Our results on the birth and death of governments in parliamentary democracies show that:

i. senior politicians make and are aware of multiple proposals;
ii. negotiations may be lengthy, depending on the modeled complexity of the strategic environment;
iii. negotiations may result in minority, minimum winning, or surplus governments; and
iv. policy matters a great deal and parties negotiate over high-dimensional joint policy programs. Logrolling is a central part of this, and parties with negatively correlated saliences over policy have an advantage in forming coalitions.

Crucially, we link the endless "governance cycle" of elections, government formation, and government survival into an integrated modeling architecture and show that even when governments form, they are not all equally successful in negotiating a joint policy program. Salient and contentious issues may be left unresolved (tabled) and may, at some point in the future, be forced onto the agenda by an exogenous shock. Since such shocks cause legislators to think again about whether they prefer some alternative to the incumbent, the survival of governments refers directly to the (implied) process of government formation. This allows us again to connect a key output of our formal model directly to an empirical model of government durations. This expands on an approach pioneered by Lupia and Strom (1995) in two ways: It generalizes from three to any number of parties and multiple issue dimensions; it models an explicit mechanism that explains the role of unanticipated shocks in bringing down governments.

Finally, we show that the behavior of senior politicians is not only quite complex but poorly described by backward induction (the algorithm employed by noncooperative game theorists). We explore the strategic capabilities of senior politicians by building two quite different types of models, grounded in different behavioral assumptions. The first is an agent-based model, which uses relatively sophisticated rules of thumb – heuristics – to model behavior. The second is an AI approach based on reinforcement learning, which allows agents to teach themselves how to play the game and find "near-Nash" strategies. We find that the performance of both models is similar, which indicates that senior politicians – even though they are experts in their domains, have access to professional staffs, and are playing for high stakes – may not be fully strategic and instead use sophisticated heuristics to make decisions.

We, therefore, model senior politicians as people who, if they wish to be successful while playing a complex game, are what we call "functionally" rational. They are clearly very good at finding *effective* strategies. Given the enormous complexity of their strategic environment, however, being successful also means recognizing that it makes no sense – indeed is functionally *irrational* – to obsess on finding *perfectly optimal* strategies.

We have left many questions on the table for future work. For example, we are able to "back out" from our model unobservable features of decision-making by party leaders, including their relative taste for the perks of office or the policy outputs of government. We also hope to explore which empirical settings have more policy-motivated party leaders given that this is a crucial link in a representative democracy between elected officials and the constituents they represent. In this book, we avoid detailed case-specific work and focus on general results, but differences surely exist between settings. An alternative use of our model is to calibrate it closely to some particular setting of interest and use it to power a theoretically structured case study. This could, for example, help us understand why some countries – Greece during the debt crisis or Israel today – enter into periods of instability.

How to Use This Book

We intend this book to serve two purposes. The first is substantive: We investigate the governance cycle in parliamentary democracies and provide a new benchmark for understanding which types of cabinet are likely to form after elections. The second is methodological: We provide a computational social science approach to building complex games and the reinforcement learning algorithms necessary to play them.

To present this in a readable format, we confine technical details (and some philosophical asides) to *Technical Appendices* at the end of the book, referring to most chapters. Readers interested in the nitty-gritty of our models, replicating what we have done, or the detailed motivation behind some of the choices we have made, will hopefully find answers here.

Different readers may, therefore, choose to take different paths through the Chapters (C) and Technical Appendices (T) of this book.

Readers interested in substantive findings: C2, C3, C5, C6, C7.
Readers familiar with the literature on government formation: T2, C3, T3, C4, T4, C5, T5, C6, T6.
Readers interested in reinforcement learning applied to complex games: C2, T2, C3, T3, C4, T4, C5, T5, C6.

Finally, readers can find all our code and data online at *https://github .com/stormslayer*.

1 | *Governance, Complexity, Computation, and Rationality*

In a referendum held on June 23, 2016, a majority of British voters chose to leave the European Union (EU): "Brexit." This was a big political shock. David Cameron, pro-EU Prime Minister of a Conservative majority government, who had called the referendum confidently expecting to win, resigned. He was replaced on July 13, 2016 by Theresa May, who pledged to lead Britain out of the EU: "Brexit means Brexit." The Conservative Party, however, was deeply polarized over EU membership. May encountered vigorous internal opposition from a minority faction of hard-line "Spartans" to her proposals for a negotiated settlement with the EU. The Spartans preferred to walk away from the EU, with no deal, on World Trade Organization terms.

Vexed and frustrated by the Spartans, encouraged by a substantial opinion poll lead over the opposition, and against much of the advice she was receiving, May called a snap election on June 8, 2017, a mere two years after the previous election had given the Conservatives a majority. Her hope and expectation were for a Conservative majority large enough to destroy the leverage of the Spartans. The result was another shock ... and a catastrophe for May. The Conservatives, far from gaining seats, lost thirteen seats and their legislative majority. May was forced to negotiate terms with the Democratic Unionist Party (DUP) of Northern Ireland for their support of a minority Conservative government. This was a particularly fraught option, since trade across the land border between Northern Ireland and the Republic was of extraordinary concern to the DUP, yet perhaps the most contentious aspect of Brexit. The leverage of the Spartans, furthermore, was increased rather than diminished. May was unable to win approval for *any* deal with the EU and resigned with effect from June 7, 2019.

She was replaced as Prime Minister by Boris Johnson. Johnson, however, did no better than May at getting a Brexit proposal through the House of Commons, and his government was subjected to a series of humiliating legislative defeats on the issue. In response, he called another snap election on December 12, 2019. The Conservatives won this with a comfortable majority, allowing Johnson to form a single-party majority government and, finally, drive through a Brexit settlement with the EU.

This book is about what we call the *governance cycle* in parliamentary democracies, illustrated in striking terms by the recent British political history we summarized. This is a never-ending cycle consisting of elections, followed by government formation, followed by the need for governments to sustain themselves in office in what is typically a hostile environment, followed eventually by the resignation or defeat of the government, and ultimately by more elections. The cycle then repeats itself in an environment subjected to a continuous stream of unanticipated shocks.

The governance cycle takes a particular form in parliamentary democracies, where the executive serves at the pleasure of the legislature. New governments can form only with the explicit or implicit consent of a majority of legislators. Incumbent governments fail if a majority of legislators withdraw this support. The crucial political consequence of this type of constitutional regime is that voters choose legislators, who in turn choose, support, and can dismiss the executive, including a chief executive typically known as Prime Minister.[6] There is no practical separation of powers between the legislature and a directly elected executive as there is, for example, in the United States. Parliamentary democracies are democracies because people indirectly choose their governments when they vote in legislative elections – choosing legislatures that make and break governments.

Most European countries are parliamentary democracies, and most of these use some form of proportional representation for legislative elections. It is rare for any one party to win more than half the popular vote. Thus, it is also rare for a single party to command a legislative majority and so be in a position to make and break governments unilaterally. All of this means that the making and breaking of governments in parliamentary democracies *typically requires negotiations between senior members of different political parties.*

The governance cycle in parliamentary democracies, therefore, involves an endlessly iterating sequence of three key processes,

---

[6] In a bicameral legislature, it is the lower house, elected on the principle of one person, one vote, which chooses and supports the executive. The prime minister is sometimes called chancellor (as in Germany and Austria).

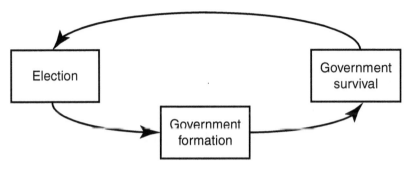

Figure 1.1 The governance cycle in parliamentary democracies

sketched in Figure 1.1. There is an election. This is followed by government formation, followed by a process underpinning the continuing survival of the incumbent government, and eventually followed by another election … and so the cycle continues.

While we can describe the three key processes in the governance cycle separately, they obviously interact with each other, as our Brexit example illustrates. During government formation, negotiating politicians must anticipate how likely it is that any putative government can maintain the support of a legislative majority. When deciding whether to support the incumbent government in office, legislators must anticipate the potential electoral consequences of bringing it down. In turn, these electoral consequences have obvious effects on subsequent government formation. And so on, *ad infinitum*. We set out here to model the full governance process sketched in Figure 1.1. We do this by specifying three interlinked models, each of which builds on existing literatures. Anticipating the integrated model of the entire system, and unlike stand-alone models of these processes taken separately, our models of government formation, government support, and general elections take inputs from, and pass outputs to, each other. These inputs and outputs chain the models together into a unified model of the governance cycle.

Modeling Complex Political Processes

The governance cycle sketched in Figure 1.1 is a complex system at the beating heart of all parliamentary democracies (Miller and Page 2009). A long and excellent tradition of formal modeling has analyzed *parts* of this complex system using purely deductive models.[7] Notwithstanding steady *theoretical* progress within this tradition, however, it is fair to say that the *substantive* understanding of democratic governance has advanced only modestly over recent decades. This is because theoretically analyzing a substantively plausible model of the governance cycle overwhelms the deductive methods of traditional formal theory. We therefore use a different approach in what follows, developing computational, as opposed to deductive, analyses of complex social processes.

We use two quite different computational approaches. One is "top-down" and very similar to traditional noncooperative game theory. We describe the governance cycle as a well-specified extensive form of game, albeit a game somewhere on the spectrum from "extraordinarily difficult" to "formally intractable" when using traditional pencil and paper methods. We then deploy an artificial intelligence (AI) algorithm to crack the game for optimal or near-optimal play. Exploiting reinforcement learning from massively repeated self-play, the algorithm starts with random choices of actions and then continually updates the probability of choosing particular actions in light of counterfactual regret over other strategic choices that could have been made. Recent AI models in this tradition have been extremely effective at beating world-class human players in a number of complex games. Of particular note is recent work on *n*-player Texas Hold 'em poker (Billings, et al. 2003, Brown and Sandholm 2017). The AI model we develop in this book might, therefore, be thought of as "computational game theory" and is, to the best of our knowledge, the first application of AI to political games, such as party competition and government formation.

Our other approach is "bottom-up." Individual decision-makers – for example, party leaders negotiating over government formation – are modeled as "autonomous artificial agents." We assume these agents choose actions in any given situation using

---

[7] This literature is vast. Examples include Rubinstein (1982), Baron and Ferejohn (1989), Laver and Schofield (1998b), Laver and Shepsle (1996a), Fréchette, et al. (2005a), Ansolabehere, et al. (2005), Snyder, et al. (2005), Warwick and Druckman (2001, 2006), Strøm, et al. (2008), Martin and Vanberg (2011), Martin and Vanberg (2020), Cutler, et al. (2014), de Marchi and Laver (2020).

tried and tested rules of thumb or "heuristics," which encode decision processes of living and breathing senior politicians.[8] While these heuristics are in our opinion plausible representations of how real humans make decisions, they are not formally provable best-response strategies since they cannot tractably be derived in complex settings. A simple but realistic example is the "ain't broke, don't fix it" rule – used by decision-makers in complex and hard-to-understand settings for millennia. In the world of government formation and survival, for example, this implies that the members of an outgoing coalition government that wins a new majority in an election will likely choose to go back into government together rather than reopening the whole can of worms and renegotiating a new coalition from scratch.

Different agents may well use different decision rules in the same setting. A given rule, furthermore, may have agent-specific parameters – risk tolerance to take an example we return to below – which can mean that the same rule has different implications for different agents in the same setting. Describing an environment, a set of interacting agents, and the decision rules agents use when interacting with this environment specifies an *agent-based model* (ABM) of the problem under investigation. This is an evolving complex system that can be analyzed computationally using carefully specified suites of Monte Carlo experiments.

Notwithstanding the fact that computational modeling can handle far more realistic assumptions about human behavior than purely deductive models, computational models are also rigorously formal, specified in a series of logical statements that are expressed in computer code. Running the code maps inputs into outputs – exactly the same objective as the "pencil and paper" methods used to resolve models using deductive logic.

Computational models do, however, present us with an important new modeling decision. The fact that we can now handle far more complex models using computational methods means that we face a trade-off. On the one hand, we have the possibility of building models with much more realistic empirical detail. While models like this may be very useful formal representations of some important empirical

---

[8] More commonly, heuristics have been used to study voters and are relatively simple – but empirically fruitful – rules of thumb (Fortunato, et al. 2021).

reality, they are often harder for us to understand intuitively, given the huge parameter spaces involved.[9]

On the other hand, simpler models are easier for us to understand but inevitably tend to be further removed from the real-world phenomena that interest us. Some of the more famous early ABMs were very simple indeed. A canonical example is Thomas Schelling's original model of the evolution of socially segregated neighborhoods (Schelling 1971). This deployed a very simple checkerboard model of the environment and very simple behavioral rules for agents to generate the influential and nonobvious conclusion that people typically live in far more segregated neighborhoods than they prefer. The original model conveys a striking intuition and now has over 5,500 citations on Google Scholar. Yet, it was so simple that the "computation" was executed by physically moving pieces around on a large checkerboard. The Schelling segregation model is an excellent aid to intuition precisely because it is very easy to see how it works. It helps us think about social segregation in general but cannot be used in its simple form to inform public policy about social segregation in particular cities, such as Paris, London, and Chicago. A computational model of social segregation underpinning policy interventions in some specific setting would need to be far more detailed, complex, and "realistic" – but might then be a poorer source of general intuition.

The ever-increasing firepower of computational methods, therefore, confronts us with a question – why are we modeling? – which was of course always implicit but now confronts us with explicit modeling decisions. There is obviously no correct answer to this question. We may above all else want the best possible rigorous underpinning for crucial public policy decisions. Alternatively, we may have a burning desire to understand the workings of some complex social process. We develop very different types of models, depending on our objectives.

Our aim in this book is to *understand* things better. Like traditional formal theorists, we want a model of the governance cycle that allows us to draw general lessons for the general class of parliamentary democracies. For scientific reasons, we expect our model to make good predictions across the full set of parliamentary systems, even

---

[9] Models may become more complex as a result of adding realism to the specified substantive context or because they model more realistic human behaviors.

though we do not make the very detailed and case-specific assumptions that would be needed to optimize its predictions of outcomes in, for example, Germany in 2021. We are engaged, in effect, in theoretical comparative politics.[10]

Our core argument is that computational methods such as those we deploy here are part of the future of political science in general and comparative politics in particular. *Empirical* research in political science has already been transformed by heavy-duty computational methods (Alvarez 2016). The time has come for our *theoretical* understanding of important political processes to be enhanced by computational modeling.

Modeling the Governance Cycle

The governance cycle in parliamentary democracies is self-evidently important substantively and of central concern to social scientists. After government formation is eventually successful, this is followed by an era in which the government must survive in a turbulent environment, which we can think of as a continuous stream of potentially fatal critical events. At some point, the government is either defeated, resigned, or terminated by a scheduled election. With or without an intervening election, the government formation process is restarted. And so on, *ad infinitum*, until a *coup d'état* or a revolution.

We set out here to model this complex process of democratic governance. This is a difficult challenge that nobody, to our knowledge, has attempted before. There is certainly a voluminous and long-standing modern literature on *government formation* in minority legislatures,[11] treated as a stand-alone process. This is conventionally traced back to early work by Riker (Riker 1962) and remains a very active field of research (Martin and Vanberg 2020, Cox 2021). Most of this

---

[10] This is a relatively subtle point. While our model, like any theoretical exercise, simplifies reality, we are demanding that it produce an output that matches something of empirical interest in the real world: Which governments form in parliamentary democracies. Thus, while we have made many simplifying assumptions – for example, we assume well-disciplined parties rather than modeling each individual legislator – we are, however, producing results that map directly to something we are interested in and can measure empirically. This allows us to examine how well our model helps us understand the governance cycle in parliamentary democracies.

[11] Legislatures in which no single party controls a majority of seats.

literature treats government formation as a discrete event focused on bargaining by party leaders. Inputs are party seat shares and possibly policy on one dimension of ideology. The output is a new government. "Payoffs" are immediately distributed, and the game is over. There is a much smaller empirical literature on *bargaining delays*. This recognizes the plain fact that government formation is often a difficult and complicated process, even for seasoned and rational politicians (e.g., Diermeier and Van Roozendaal 1998, Golder 2010, de Marchi and Laver 2020). There is a modest empirical literature on *government survival* that models the durability of governments in terms of features that help them survive a stream of potentially destabilizing critical events (see Browne, et al. 1986a, b, King, et al. 1990, Diermeier and Stevenson 1999, 2000, Chiba, et al. 2015).[12] These discrete topics, however, have never been treated as component parts of a unified process of governance.

As we noted earlier, there is a good reason why canonical approaches to formal theory in political science have hitherto side-stepped this challenge. A typical research program has been to specify a model, however unrealistic, and then attack this using noncooperative game theory – by default ignoring important problems that are known to be analytically intractable. Our approach is different. We specify a problem that is important, but intractable using conventional deductive methods, and then attack this computationally. Analytical and computational approaches both specify formal models of politics. The former uses *deductive logic* to map model inputs into model outputs. The latter *computes* the outputs logically implied by any given set of inputs. There are, however, two key differences between these approaches. One is *method* – how model inputs are mapped into model outputs. And the other is *scope* – computational models allow researchers to study more complex strategic environments.

We find the computational approach intellectually liberating because, among many other things, it allows us to model preferences of living and breathing politicians as a trade-off between two quite different features. The first concerns the perquisites (perks) of public

---

[12] There is obviously also an immense scholarly literature on elections. As will be seen further, however, we treat elections as black boxes, so do not engage with this literature.

office. Some of these perks, like seats at the cabinet table, represent the pinnacle of many politicians' ambitions. The second concerns public policy. On this, we are informed by the long periods of intense negotiations that often characterize government formation. Government formation in Germany after the 2017 election, for example, began on September 24, 2017, and ended on March 4, 2018. On almost any account, government formation negotiations such as these are mostly about the fine details of reaching agreement on a government policy program and reconciling conflicting positions on a large number of discrete issues set out in lengthy party manifestos. In short, forming a government is about a meeting of minds that must simultaneously agree on a joint position in a high-dimensional issue space and how to divide up the valuable perks of office that are typically the pinnacle of a political career.

Another benefit of the computational approach is that it allows us to move beyond the conventional approach of characterizing government survival as a black box process generating shocks that, for largely unmodeled reasons, sometimes cause the government to fall. Rather, we model government survival in terms of a continuous reevaluation by legislators of decisions they might make over government formation (Lupia and Strom 1995). The essence of parliamentary democracies is that the legislature sits in permanent judgment on the executive. Legislators continually ask themselves the following question: "Knowing what I now know (but did not know at the moment of government formation), do I now prefer some alternative government?" We address this by modeling shocks as perturbing key model parameters, which in turn modify legislators' perceptions of the relative merits of the incumbent government. We use our government formation model to map the effects of these shocks into estimates of the extent to which legislators now prefer some specific alternative government to the incumbent. The more our model tells us that the incumbent government is vulnerable to such shocks, the less stable we predict it to be. In this way, our models of government formation and government survival are intimately linked together into a single coherent process.

In what follows, we specify a deductively intractable model that synthesizes all this, and then we resolve this model computationally. We *specify the logic* of our models in formal terms, exactly as in the conventional formal modeling literature. We *implement* these models using computational algorithms, specified unambiguously in code.[13] These algorithms are logically equivalent to the systems of equations associated with formal deductive models. Rather than "solving" these equations by hand, which is impossible for the deductively intractable processes that interest us here, we resolve our model computationally, using carefully designed suites of Monte Carlo experiments.

We describe these experiments in much more detail in the following text. Briefly, though, each involves many thousands of trials of the computer code expressing our model. Over the course of these trials, we systematically vary model parameters, carefully sampling values of these from empirically plausible distributions when possible. For each trial, the model tells us the logically implied values of outputs of theoretical interest, conditional on the parameters of the model. (The computer is above all else a relentless logic engine, much less likely to make a mistake than most human analysts.) Each experiment creates a huge volume of model-generated artificial data on the governance process, mapping values of key inputs onto logically implied values of outputs. Given this mapping, we use conventional methods of applied statistics and machine learning to analyze and describe systematic relationships between model inputs and model outputs. Uncovering these relationships is, of course, the point of any modeling exercise, whether resolved deductively or computationally.

Our approach is a different way of doing theory compared to existing formal analyses. If our code correctly expresses the model and we design the computational experiments meticulously, then we can attack complex problems yet still generate results that rigorously express key logical implications of the model. These results are directly equivalent to those generated by a logical resolution of the model, had this been feasible (Miller and Page 2009, de Marchi and Stewart 2020, Laver 2020a, b).

Intractable Problems and "Functional" Rationality

The fact that the complex processes we model are analytically intractable has two important consequences. We just noted the first, which

---

[13] We will use python code throughout. This has many advantages, including readability, good libraries (e.g., numpy, pandas, and scikit-learn), and broad support by the machine learning community.

is a technical matter of method. Theoretical models of intractable processes cannot be resolved using deductive logic, but can still be resolved computationally. The second is a matter of behavior: Real humans on the ground are continuously navigating analytically intractable processes. Traditional formal models in political science assume that ideal-type "rational" humans use deductive logic to solve analytically tractable problems. Real humans faced with analytically intractable problems, however, do not behave like many theorists, giving up and moving on to another problem. One way or another, they roll up their sleeves and get on with the problem at hand.

The governance cycle we sketch in Figure 1.1 is a complex system; outputs feed back into the system as inputs. More important for our purposes, it is also "difficult" (Page 2008).[14] Among other things, this difficulty arises because the state space – the space of possible outcomes the system might visit – is gigantic. As a consequence, what is often referred to as the strategy space – the space of possible programs of action for moving from one state of the system to another – is also gigantic.

To get a sense of the scale of this problem, consider a simple setting. Imagine a 100-seat legislature with 7 legislative parties and 20 salient issues. Ignoring party labels, there are 407,254 "non-equivalent distributions" – different ways to allocate 100 seats between 7 parties (Laver and Benoit 2003). Adding party labels multiplies this number by 7! = 5,040. The result is over two billion different election results. For each of these election results, each party has 2^{20} possible binary issue position vectors – over one million – and a much larger number of possible issue salience vectors. A complete analysis of this environment would defeat the world's fastest supercomputer. It would of course never be attempted by a "rational" human.

Yet, rational humans routinely operate quite effectively in environments with huge state spaces such as this (de Marchi 2005, Laver and Sergenti 2012). How do they manage? They deploy what we call "functional" rationality. In simple contexts, this means relying on efficient, relatively simple heuristics. As you walk through a supermarket filling a shopping trolley, for example, you make many rough and ready decisions about what to put into the trolley and what to leave on

---

[14] A complex system need not be difficult; a difficult system need not be complex (Page 2008).

the shelf. You don't pull out your smartphone and pore through hundreds of reviews of every single item you might consider buying, each of which has a huge number of features – cost, quality, nutritional value, ingredients, and so on. Indeed, were you to do this for each of the fifty items in your trolley, well-adjusted people would consider you downright irrational. Why? Because they'd think you have much better uses for your fixed budget of time and energy. In contrast, in more complex contexts such as buying a house or playing poker for high stakes, most people would think it perfectly rational for you to spend a lot of time and effort on your decisions.

What is crucial to understand is that humans, faced with complex choice contexts, depend on heuristics. These heuristics, especially for expert human actors, may not be terribly simple and could involve a good deal of computation. We do know, however, that people in such settings will not act according to traditional rational choice for the simple reason that it does not work in complex environments.[15] Trying to play poker using backward induction would result in a very, very slow game! Thus, in *both* simple and complex decision contexts, functional rationality is relied on by human actors, though the exact algorithm and computational demands will vary.

Before setting out our detailed argument, therefore, we take time out to think about functional rationality, and what this might mean in complex political settings. We do this because we want to be crystal clear about why we depart in this book from the approach that characterizes much of modern political science. The governance process we describe is not only complex but also difficult to analyze with conventional formal approaches. The mainstream theoretical approach to attacking such a problem would be to progressively and radically simplify the description of the problem to a point at which it can be analyzed using traditional formal methods.

To take a very simple example, if we want to know the volume of a perfect sphere with radius r, we use classical formal analysis. It would be irrational, on almost any definition, to do anything else.

---

[15] Diermeier and Krehbiel's recommendation to essentially ignore behavior and focus instead on institutions is unworkable in complex choice environments (Diermeier and Krehbiel 2003). While they are correct that modeling behavior explicitly adds substantial complexity to models, there is really no other game in town if we want to understand real-world poker or the governance process in real-world parliamentary systems.

If we want to know the volume of a lumpy boulder, on the other hand, formal analysis is of little use. Nonetheless, functionally rational humans would not be stumped by this problem because perfectly efficient and functionally rational *behavioral* rules are available to them. High school science classes, for example, likely taught them to submerge the boulder in a tank of water and measure the volume of water displaced. Simple, scientific, very accurate, and – on almost any definition – eminently rational.

This example allows us to distinguish what we call "functional" rationality from the similar (but different) notion of "bounded" rationality associated with the Nobel Prize winner Herbert Simon (Simon 1955). A boundedly rational agent tasked with estimating the volume of a lumpy boulder might first accept the fact there is no perfect analytical solution and then specify a "good enough" (satisficing) solution that is for practical purposes acceptable. Some consciously imperfect assumptions might be made (for example, assuming the boulder is a perfect sphere), and some rough modifications made to these (about the size and shape of the lumps, for example). This would give a boundedly rational (analytical) estimate, explicitly known to be "acceptably" suboptimal, of the volume of the boulder. This is quite different from the (behavioral) functionally rational scientific method of submerging the boulder in a tank of water, which gives an estimate as close to perfect as the quality of the measurement instruments available. Bounded rationality involves imperfect, but "good enough," *analysis*. What we call functional rationality involves imperfect, but good enough, *behavioral rules*. In the case of the lumpy boulder, functional rationality will almost certainly yield a much better result and in this sense be "more rational."

Many theorists working in the mainstream of political science choose to analyze complex political interactions by simplifying the game that is being played. They keep simplifying important but intractable problems until these games become tractable using the methods of traditional formal analysis. In effect, they assume that lumpy boulders are perfect spheres. Unfortunately, they may end up "solving" the wrong problem, since a perfect sphere always rolls down a gentle slope, while a lumpy boulder often does not. In our view, the real world of politics is more like a lumpy boulder than a perfect sphere. Functionally rational politicians navigate this world using behavioral rules, not formal analysis.

An illuminating example of how functionally rational humans attack intractable problems is the classic Travelling Salesperson Problem (TSP). This is easy to state, well-specified, deductively intractable, yet "solved" every day by ordinary civilians. The traveling salesperson, in today's terms a driver delivering a truckload of internet orders, is given a long list of addresses scattered all over the map. The problem is to find the shortest route that visits every address. It is intractable in the sense that there is neither a deductively provable nor a feasibly computable best strategy for an arbitrarily large number and scatter of addresses. The problem can be computationally "smashed" by calculating the length of every possible route and picking the shortest, but this solution is not scalable, given the spectacular increase in the number of different possible routes as the number of addresses increases. For n locations, there are n ways to pick the first stop, then $n-1$ ways to pick the second stop, and so on. The total number of different routes is $n \times (n-1) \times (n-2) \ldots = n!$. With a modest 100 packages to deliver in a day, for example, the number of possible routes has 157 digits and takes two lines of text in this book to write down. Even with the world's fastest computer, there is zero chance of computing the length of each route, and finding the shortest, before the next day's work comes in. However, while they can neither solve this problem deductively nor smash it computationally, untold thousands of delivery drivers nonetheless solve it *functionally* every day, finding a "pretty good" route, even if nobody can prove it's the very best route.

This impressive feat of functional rationality is achieved by using decision-making *heuristics*, programs of action which work both well and fast, respecting the maxim that "the best is the enemy of the good." While there is only one "best" solution, however, there are many different "good" solutions, and different people may well settle on different programs of action for finding these. One that works quite well for the TSP, given most address lists, is the following "greedy" program of action: visit the closest unvisited address; iterate until you have visited all addresses. It is "greedy" because, myopically, it chooses the best option considering only the immediately proximate decision of where to go next, ignoring the possibility that the full sequence of future choices might imply a different choice for the next visit. However, we know from easy TSPs with short address lists, where we can compute every possible route and smash the problem, that while this greedy algorithm by no means always finds the best route, it typically comes close.

A self-employed delivery driver with one truck working an eight-hour day might well find this an effective program of action. Amazon, however, seeking to save a penny off the cost of each delivery because it delivers billions of parcels a year, might invest a lot of money in developing slightly better (and secret) programs of action for the TSP to gain an edge over competitors. Crucially, Amazon would not make any progress by assuming away the complexity of the problem to allow them to use a deductive rational choice approach – they would develop a computational algorithm instead. In doing this, Amazon would be deploying what we call functional rationality to develop effective behavioral rules for attacking the actual problem at hand, in all its gnarly complexity. Traditional bounded rationality, on the other hand, typically involves analytically solving a known-to-be sub-optimal simplified version of the problem.

Functionally Rational Politicians

Just as no one seriously proposes to "solve" the TSP analytically by assuming the addresses to be visited are all arranged on a straight line, we do not propose to analyze the governance cycle by making assumptions that the problem becomes deductively tractable but substantively irrelevant. Like delivery drivers and traveling salesmen, functionally rational politicians inhabit a world that, while complex, they successfully navigate every day. They develop their own heuristics – functionally rational programs of action – for attacking complex decision problems. They do this partly by trial and error and partly by learning from others.

The fact that the acquisition of decision heuristics by functionally rational politicians likely results from some type of reinforcement learning process suggests that at least some of these heuristics will incorporate the "Pavlovian" *win-stay, lose-shift* rule. This rule is the subject of a large research program in the vast reinforcement learning literature (Nowak and Sigmund 1993, Page and Nowak 2002, Nowak 2006, Shu 2020, Guo 2019). In the setting of government formation, this "ain't broke, don't fix it" rule implies that the members of an outgoing administration that has maintained its legislative majority, or gained support, may well simply choose to reconstitute the incumbent government: "win-stay." If, on the other hand, an outgoing majority government loses its majority, or an outgoing minority government loses seats in the legislature, then something is broken and we have "lose-shift": Negotiating politicians are likely to use more complicated decision rules to find a new government.

At the heart of our approach, therefore, is the desire to *model behavior* from the bottom up – from the perspective of living, breathing humans on the ground (Bendor and Swistak 2001, Miller and Page 2009, Bednar and Page 2018). This is quite distinct from the more conventional approach in political science, which takes the perspective of the all-seeing outside observer, and tries to analyze how institutions and the preferences of idealized decision-makers map into equilibrium outcomes. Indeed, we do not embark on this enterprise with the expectation of being to identify "equilibrium" outcomes in any formal sense.

Choosing Modeling Assumptions: "Realism" versus Generality

A model is a simple representation of the real world, with moving parts designed to help us to understand how the world works. This is of course valuable in and for itself, but good models also allow us both to predict future events and to make effective policy interventions.[16] Good modeling always involves a trade-off, however. This concerns how we choose which features of the world to build into our model and which to exclude.

The most "realistic" model imaginable includes every single feature of every real-world setting of interest – thousands, even millions, of features. As an example, imagine we want to build a model of a city that allows a delivery driver to navigate this efficiently. A hyperrealistic model would describe in great detail every road, traffic signal, road sign, and building. It would forecast the weather and traffic volume at every moment of the working day. It would also forecast the behavior of every human or animal who might run out into the road in front of the delivery truck, even every puddle or banana skin

---

[16] We subscribe to Friedman's belief that theorists should be allowed to make simplifying assumptions and that "falsifying" assumptions does not, in most cases, challenge the implications of the model (Friedman 1953). Crucially, however, Friedman does believe that as a consequence of allowing theorists free reign to choose assumptions, the proof of the pudding of a model is to expose it to empirical tests.

on the sidewalk on which the driver might slip when making a delivery. Google Maps comes as close as we are likely to find in practice to this sort of ideal-type ultra-detailed model for guiding real-world drivers. Its underlying model involves a huge number of features and uses massive computational firepower to analyze an immense pipeline of data, continually adapting predicted optimum delivery routes in real time. Impressive and practically useful as this modeling achievement undoubtedly is, however, it is too detailed and granular – paradoxically, *too close a fit* to the particular empirical reality it models – to be much help if we want to *understand* the complex dynamics of traffic flow in general, perhaps to change speed limits or introduce new one-way systems.

At the other end of the spectrum of practically useful models is one that describes the city using a simple street map and list of addresses. If the problem is to find the shortest route for a delivery driver to visit each address, because the driver wants to complete the job as fast and cheaply as possible, then it would hinder rather than help the analysis to model the location of every banana skin on the sidewalk – even though it is *just possible* that on some routes the delivery driver might slip on a banana skin and break a leg.

A fundamental contradiction affecting all serious modeling is that, while any good theorist rightly emphasizes the logical rigor of deriving implications from a model given its assumptions about the real world, *there is no logically rigorous way to determine what those assumptions should be*. An example of direct relevance for parliamentary governance concerns whether we include the head of state as a decisive actor in this process. We face a tough modeling choice. There is no doubt, based on reading constitutions and political histories, that heads of state, whether presidents or monarchs, often have a formal role in the governance cycle. Some can choose whether or not to dissolve parliament after a government has lost a confidence vote or to ask existing parliamentarians to form a new government. Some can ask a particular politician to lead government formation negotiations – to become what political scientists call a *formateur*. The detailed political role of the head of state, however, differs in material ways from country to country. In some countries, such as Ireland, this role is almost completely nominal. In others, such as France, the head of state may be a significant political actor (Gallagher, et al. 2012 provide a summary of country-by-country differences in the role of the head of state in government formation). It is clearly a reasonable project, therefore, to model the role of the head of state in the governance cycle of parliamentary democracies. We could identify a number of features of this role that vary from country to country, model the potential impact of these features on the governance cycle, and then take the logical implications of this model to data. While we would have no criticism of someone who did this, we do not do it ourselves. Why?

This is a good practical example of the important substantive modeling choices that every good theorist must make. These choices are guided by why we build a model at all. Do we want to make detailed predictions, precisely calibrated to particular countries? Or do we want to make general statements that apply to a large class of parliamentary democracies, setting aside detailed differences between these? If we want to predict whether Party A will get more than 50 percent of the popular vote in the next general election in Country X, for example, then we are in a very specific forecasting mode. This requires us to calibrate our model as precisely as we can to the here and now of Party A and Country X. We are not, in this context, overly interested in a general model of party competition that tells us what will happen "on average" across all parliamentary democracies.

If, on the other hand, we have a general intellectual interest in understanding the governance process in parliamentary democracies, then we don't want to get bogged down in the minutiae of particular cases. *The whole point of the exercise is to generalize across cases, not to predict what will happen in some particular case.* This is the position we ourselves start from, and this in turn informs our substantive modeling choice – for this particular example – to ignore the potentially partisan political role of the head of state. Our modeling architecture is flexible enough that others can add this as an extension. Our core objective is to understand the governance cycle in a heterogeneous set of parliamentary democracies. We therefore calibrate and evaluate our model in terms of how well, on average, it helps us make general predictions for the full set of cases, as opposed to how well it makes more precise predictions calibrated to some specific case. There is no "correct" answer to this trade-off. We want our model to be detailed enough to be informative. Indeed, the whole point of this book is to build and interrogate a more realistic model of the governance cycle than those that precede it. We also want our model to be general. We want to learn lessons about postwar governance in a range of parliamentary democracies, not just about Sweden in 2020, for example.

Our Argument in Context

Like everyone who sets out to analyze political and social interaction, we stand on the shoulders of those who have come before us. There is an immense literature on the various stages of the governance cycle in parliamentary democracies. A large part of this concerns the formation of government coalitions, stretching back several decades to the work of William Riker (Riker 1962). The dominant stream in this work is set in the traditions of neoclassical economics, which assumes that all key political actors are sophisticated strategic agents with perfect information and unbounded analytical power. Research in this tradition evolved into a highly productive subfield within political science, as a result of which we now understand the bargaining over government formation much better than we did before.

There is, however, much we still do not understand and on which the mainstream modeling tradition offers little hope of making progress. Negotiating a new government is self-evidently a high-dimensional problem, different in crucial ways from the low-dimensional simplifications of mainstream theoretical accounts. Consider, for example, the German government formation process that unfolded between September 24, 2017, and March 4, 2018. The outcome was a coalition between Social Democrats and Christian Democrats. Forming a new coalition involved not only agreeing on how to allocate a set of cabinet positions, each of which is valued intensely by senior party politicians, but also agreeing to a joint policy program. The starting points for the policy negotiations were a 76-page manifesto published by the Christian Democrats as their offer to voters in the 2017 election, along with a 116-page manifesto published by the Social Democrats. Each manifesto set out distinctive positions on a very wide range of policy areas, specifying very different high-dimensional policy positions for the two negotiating parties. Given these two opposing positions, the job of the negotiators was to come up with an agreed joint program of government. Six months after the election, the end point of long and tortuous negotiations was an agreed 177-page joint policy document, specifying common positions in 59 different policy areas.

Traditional analytical approaches, understandably, do not come close to telling us how negotiators for two parties would somehow forge two quite different high-dimensional party manifestos into a single high-dimensional joint program for government. Nor would they tell us why government formation in this setting was such a long and tortuous process. These key features of government formation arise from processes too complex to be resolved using traditional deductive analysis. We attack this problem by modeling the effect of behavioral rules for "logrolling" between negotiating parties, whereby an actor concedes on issues of less concern in exchange for reciprocal concessions on issues of more concern. These rules include the possibility of "tabling" issues, on which negotiating parties agree to disagree. This allows them to form governments on the basis of incomplete policy agreements and gets around the possibility that government formation may founder as a result of irreconcilable differences on a small number of the many important issues at stake.

In parallel with the development in political science of analyses grounded in the notion of theoretical ideal-type strategic rationality, a research tradition stretching back to Simon's (1955) bounded rationality and drawing on work in cognitive psychology evolved into the vibrant and productive subfield of behavioral economics (Kahneman and Tversky 2000, Gigerenzer and Gaissmaier 2011, Gigerenzer and Selten 2002). This approach assumes, as we do here, that real humans do not conform to an ideal type of perfect strategic rationality, instead using informal decision heuristics rather than backward induction.

It should by now be clear that our argument here is much more in the behavioral than in the neoclassical tradition, augmented by a fundamental reliance on computational as opposed to deductive analysis. This allows us to take on hard but realistic problems that we know are analytically intractable. As theorists, we find this liberating. Rather than anticipating analytical intractability when we specify a model and trimming our theoretical ambitions to match what we expect to be achievable, we specify what we think is the "right" model of the process under investigation. We do this because, if the model is well specified, then we can express it in code. If it is coded, then we can manipulate it computationally. And if we manipulate it computationally in a carefully defined and rigorous way, then we can systematically map model inputs into model outputs. When all is said and done, this is what theoretical modeling is all about.

Plan of Campaign

In Chapter 2, we describe the institutional environment for the governance cycle in parliamentary democracies. This is an infinite loop involving three interconnected processes. Each process feeds outputs into, and takes inputs from, the others. While all three processes are interconnected, we see the core process as government formation. On our account, the role of legislative elections in any parliamentary democracy is to generate a new legislature and thereby change the inputs for government formation. The government survival process involves legislators continually anticipating the government formation process, should this be triggered in light of unanticipated shocks to their expectations. Once we have an effective model of the government formation process, therefore, modeling government survival and elections is relatively straightforward.

Chapter 3 populates this environment with functionally rational negotiating politicians. The combination of the institutional environment and behavioral rules used by politicians to navigate this generates our baseline models of government formation and survival. These substantially extend and refine our published model of "government formation as logrolling in high dimensional issue spaces" (de Marchi and Laver 2020). We take as our starting point the observation that negotiations over government formation between senior politicians from different parties typically involve reconciling detailed party manifestos setting out substantially different policy positions. Party manifestoes are long statements of multidimensional policy platforms.[17] Each, as in the German case we just described, may well run to over 100 pages and stake out party positions on many different issues. Senior politicians negotiating to form a new government, however, must either agree to a common position on each issue in their respective manifestoes or "table" some issues on which they agree to disagree.[18] When they table an issue, they effectively hope that unanticipated events do not force it onto the public agenda during

---

[17] A number of empirical studies demonstrate that high-dimensional policy spaces are important features of legislatures and should serve as a baseline assumption in formal models (Aldrich, et al. 2014, de Marchi, et al. 2021).

[18] Note that we talk about "tabling," an issue in the American sense – meaning to take it *off* the agenda. This is almost completely the opposite of the meaning in English, where to table a proposal is to put it *on* the table for discussion.

the lifetime of the government, thereby dividing coalition members and potentially destabilizing their administration. A natural, and indeed common, way for negotiating politicians to reconcile two or more detailed policy documents such as this is to logroll (Carrubba and Volden 2000, Aksoy 2012, Ecker and Meyer 2019). Politician A concedes to Politician B on an issue that is important to B but less important to A. In exchange, B concedes on an issue that is important to A but less important to B. The logroll means that neither politician gets exactly what they want, but both get their way on the issue most important to them.

Having nailed down the core model in the complex governance cycle, which concerns the government formation process, we turn to the intimately related matter of government survival. In essence, we see the "life and times" or, more starkly "survival," phase of democratic governance in terms of a question continually before every legislator. "Do I prefer the incumbent government, or some alternative government reasonably likely to command majority support in the legislature?" By construction, a majority of rational legislators did prefer the incumbent government at the moment of its formation. But things change in unexpected ways. Exogenous shocks to the political environment force a decision on an issue that has been tabled by the partners in government, destabilizing an existing coalition deal. Such shocks may also change expectations about the result of the next election, reducing incentives of those who expect to gain from this to support the incumbent government. Exogenous shocks may in effect change key parameters of the governance process, thereby causing legislators to revisit the government formation process and reconsider how they might now vote, given new parameter values. We therefore model government survival by probing the robustness of the existing government to shocks forcing decisions on issues that were tabled when the government was formed and shocks to the preferences of negotiating politicians.

Having set out our baseline models, we resolve these computationally in two quite different ways. The first, which we elaborate in the second half of Chapter 3, explores the types of behavioral rule that functionally rational politicians might use to navigate this complex setting. This involves what has come to be known as "agent-based modeling" – ABM (see de Marchi and Page 2014 for an overview and Laver 2020a, b for an introduction to designing, building, and exercising ABMs). Both the environment for social interaction and the

behavioral rules used within this environment by the different interacting agents are precisely described in computer code. (One of the
great advantages of computational analysis over verbal reasoning is
that imprecise computer code crashes in flames for all to see, whereas
imprecise verbal reasoning is often overlooked by the unwary.) Monte
Carlo experiments then unpack the implications of these behavioral
rules in multiple model trials for each case under investigation, each
with a different random specification of model parameters.

The second type of computational resolution of our model, set out
in Chapter 4, involves an AI approach. This is, to the best of our
knowledge, one of the first applications of AI to theoretical modeling in political science, but its potential applications in this context
are considerable. The "governance game" set out in Figure 2.2 is
deductively intractable – as are the well-known games of Go or Poker.
Nonetheless, recent advances have allowed AI models to beat world-
class players at both Go and Poker. In essence, the AI approach we uti-
lize has substantial similarity to noncooperative game theory. It starts
by specifying the problem under investigation as an extensive form
game, albeit one that is intractable. It then incessantly plays against
itself, systematically and relentlessly learning, and never forgetting,
what works and what does not. In Chapter 4, therefore, we apply AI
to the problem of "winning" the governance game in parliamentary
democracies and compare the results to our ABM. Putting forward
both types of model – an ABM with more constrained heuristics and
an AI leveraging enormous amounts of computational power to focus
on strategy – allows us to examine which approach best describes elite
human actors such as party leaders.

We interrogate our models of government formation and government survival in two quite different ways. First, wearing the hats of
pure theorists in Chapter 5, we investigate how various moving parts
of our ABM connect to each other. In relation to government formation, for example, how does being the largest party, or a party whose
legislators hold relatively extreme political views, affect the prospect
of being a member of the eventual government? For a model that has
been resolved analytically, such investigations take the form of analytical "comparative statics." Solving a system of equations generated
by the model, how does such-and-such change in input X affect output
of interest Y? This type of analysis proceeds differently for computational models, which are interrogated using carefully designed suites

of numerical experiments. As noted above, these involve Monte Carlo trials of the computational model, repeated many times, whereby random values of input X are generated, with the logic embedded in the model's code used to derive the implied value of output Y for each. This allows us to map out the relationship between X and Y. The level of detail in this map increases with the number of independent trials. With careful design and powerful computational resources, we can vary several key model inputs simultaneously to map out the resulting multivariate relationships, as well as associated interaction effects.

We want our models to say something useful about the real world, however. This means that we are not interested in their implications for all logically possible parameter settings but only for those we're likely to encounter in the real world. For example, one important model parameter is the number of legislative parties. We are certainly not interested in what the model says when this is a negative number, neither are we much interested in what the model says about 250-party, or even 50-party, systems. We are beginning the process of *calibrating* the model to empirical settings of interest to us, placing limits on the ranges of input parameters in light of our knowledge of the empirical world. We will not raise too many eyebrows in the comparative politics community, for example, if we confine the interrogation of our models to political systems with between two and twenty legislative parties. We do not do this for theoretical reasons. It's simply a pragmatic decision to make efficient use of our finite research resources by not spending these on investigating the 99- and 100-party systems we know full well we'll *never* encounter in the real world. *This is not empirical research,* but empirically calibrated theoretical analysis, which we report in Chapter 5.

We turn in Chapter 6 to empirical research because we want to assess whether our theoretical analyses of both the ABM and AI models have real-world relevance as opposed to being purely self-referential constructs. Put another way, there are *many* theoretical models we could write, but we are most interested in the *much smaller* subset of models that has a demonstrable mapping to real-world political outcomes. We therefore use our model to generate propositions that are both uniquely attributable to the model and predict empirically observable political outcomes. We assess the model by carefully comparing its predictions with the empirical record. This general statement of scientific principle sounds nice in theory, but it is difficult to achieve in practice. There are two main reasons for this: one deep and difficult and one shallow and difficult.

The deep and difficult problem arises from the requirement that predictions be "uniquely attributable to the model." This requires demonstrating there is no other model that might make the same predictions, a demonstration which is of course logically impossible. Your theory might be that the Sun revolves anticlockwise around the Earth, and a prediction from this theory would be that the Sun appears to rise in the East and set in the West. You can observe real sunrises and sunsets in many different parts of the world until the cows come home, but even a billion observations supporting this proposition would not make your model true. Presenting your lifetime's research at a scientific conference, some young upstart will stand up and point out an alternative theory – the Earth rotates around the Sun in a clockwise direction – that predicts precisely the same observations. In this sense, science is always imperfect. What we do as scientists is to do our honest but imperfect best, with careful research design and statistical analysis, to rule out every rival explanation of the set of empirical facts we claim as evidence in support of our theory.

The shallow and difficult problem concerns data. Actually, there are two problems here. One is that many of our theoretical constructs are fundamentally "latent" and unobservable, even if we have perfect data. The other is that we never have perfect data – nor can we measure everything we might want as inputs to our theoretical model.

As it happens, we are actually better off in terms of data when investigating the governance cycle in parliamentary democracies than scholars in many other subfields of political science. Reliable and authoritative data on many crucial matters are easily available in the public record. These matters include: who are the prime minister and members of the cabinet; when were they installed in, and removed from, office; which party do these people belong to; which cabinet portfolio does each control; how many legislative seats does each party control; and how many people from each party voted for and against each motion put to the legislature. Even on these "objective" matters, a dirty secret of the profession is that different "authoritative" datasets rarely agree on everything and that merging datasets can force the analyst to make difficult substantive decisions. For example, a small breakaway faction from some party votes as a block, defies the former party line, has a name, but does not register as a political party or contest elections. Is this a party or not? Should we increase the number of legislative parties? These matters of interpretation can cause different datasets to diverge. Such divergences are rarely mission critical, however, and can be handled by meticulously recording the inevitable decisions on them in footnotes or appendices.

The more difficult problem concerns the measurement of latent concepts, strikingly in our case legislators' preferences. While these preferences are on most reasonable interpretations "real," and critical to the analysis, they are fundamentally unobservable, even to legislators' own (conscious) selves. We can observe the *consequences* of these preferences, such as legislators' voting behavior on particular bills or the election addresses they write, but these are all endogenous to politics and are precisely the sort of thing we are trying to predict. Nonetheless, it is conventional in political science to "measure" the preferences of key politicians in one of a number of different ways. Two very different methods are commonly used to do this. This first depends on content analyses of party manifestos, legislative speeches, and other political texts. These texts may be labeled for policy preferences by human experts (Budge, et al. 1987, Klingemann, et al. 1994, Budge, et al. 2001, Klingemann, et al. 2006), crowd workers (Benoit, et al. 2016), or machines (Laver, et al. 2003, Slapin and Proksch 2008, Benoit, et al. 2009, Lowe, et al. 2011). The other main method, which for reasons we elaborate below we use here, relies on "expert surveys" (Laver and Hunt 1992, Benoit and Laver 2006, Bakker, et al. 2015, Bakker, et al. 2020) that ask large numbers of country specialists to rate party positions on key issues or policy dimensions.

While there are widely accepted sources of information on politicians' "latent" policy preferences, other key features of our analysis are even more fundamentally unobservable. These include, for example, the relative preferences of politicians for the perks of office and public policy outputs, and the tolerance of politicians for leaving government policy on key issues undecided at the moment of government formation. Not only are there no data sources on these matters, but there likely never will be. In Chapter 5, therefore, we also use our Monte Carlo experiments, with their randomly chosen values of key unobservable parameters, to "calibrate" our model for the empirical analyses in Chapter 6. We do this by "backing out" ranges of values for unobservable model parameters that are associated with successful model predictions in the training data. We then use these ranges of parameter values in our out-of-sample empirical analysis.

A key feature of the empirical work we report in Chapter 6 distinguishes us from much mainstream empirical work in comparative politics. We evaluate the empirical performance of our models by making out-of-sample predictions, on a case-by-case basis, of observed political outcomes. Many published papers in empirical comparative politics start, as we do, with a theoretical model. This may be a rigorously specified and analyzed formal model, or some informal theoretical conjectures. The model is used to derive predictions about how a vector of inputs, $X_1 \ldots X_n$, maps into some output of interest, Y. Empirical data on $X_1 \ldots X_n$ and Y are collected. The conventional approach in political science is then to use some form of regression model to assess whether, *in the dataset on average*, $X_1 \ldots X_n$ map into Y as predicted. Victory is declared when regression coefficients on $X_1 \ldots X_n$ are both in the predicted direction and statistically significant. This is quite similar to what we did in Chapter 5, when *calibrating our model in-sample*. We go a step beyond this in Chapter 6, however. We take our calibrated model and use this to *predict case-by-case observed outcomes in new, out-of-sample, data*. The empirical metrics for evaluating our model thus involve case-by-case predictive success in out-of-sample data. This approach, common in modern data science, is still rare in political science. As a result, we do not know how far many of the widely cited empirical "findings" in political science would be robust to testing on a completely new dataset (King 1995, 2003).

Chapter 7 reviews what we feel we have achieved in this book and maps out the possible ways forward for the future. We conclude by stating the obvious. We have picked an important but previously intractable problem at the heart of democratic politics and set ourselves a task in which we are bound to fail. We do not regard this as a pointless exercise, however. Science never definitively *succeeds* but *advances* by failing in interesting and informative ways. Our job in what follows is to fail in interesting and informative ways that take us at least one small step closer to understanding the governance cycle in parliamentary democracies.

2 | *The Governance Cycle*

Constitutional Setting

The constitutional setting that interests us here is a "fusion of powers" regime where the executive is chosen by, and is responsible to, the legislature. Constitutions in such settings invariably mandate that the incumbent chief executive remains in place until replaced by an alternative who is (tacitly or explicitly) supported by a majority of legislators. This support is demonstrated by a (potential) legislative vote of confidence or investiture. The qualifications in parentheses are added because there are parliamentary democracies (e.g., the United Kingdom) in which an *explicit* investiture vote is not a constitutional requirement and legislative support is *tacitly* demonstrated by the ability of the incumbent government to survive legislative votes of no confidence. Surviving an actual vote of no confidence explicitly demonstrates the incumbent's legislative support. The *absence* of a motion of no confidence, given that proposing such a motion is open to legislators who want to replace the government, *implicitly* indicates the incumbent's legislative support. The bottom line is that a new government cannot replace the incumbent if it cannot win a legislative investiture vote and/or survive an immediate no-confidence vote. A new executive, therefore, takes office with either the explicit or the tacit support of a majority of legislators. This is a universal and constitutionally binding feature of parliamentary governance. It is one of the exogenous and immutable rules of the game.

We assume a "government" in this environment comprises a prime minister (PM), constitutionally appointed by the head of state, and a "cabinet" (roomful) of government ministers who collectively comprise the formal government. Cabinet ministers are bound by a constitutional requirement for *collective cabinet responsibility*. They must resign or be sacked from the government if they cannot publicly defend cabinet decisions, however acrimonious the private discussions leading up to these decisions might have been. Constitutionally, the resignation of any minister or ministers, however politically damaging this might be, leaves the incumbent government in place. The only resignation causing the government to fall is that of the PM.

The division of administrative responsibilities within the executive places each cabinet minister at the head of a civil service department. Each department is responsible for both developing and implementing public policy in important areas, such as defense, economic policy, education, foreign affairs, and justice. These policy areas define the relevant minister's policy "portfolio." There are typically also "junior" ministers. These are political appointees responsible for more specialized policy briefs within a department's broad portfolio – for example, European affairs or overseas aid within the department of foreign affairs. Other coveted senior positions may be in the gift of the government, ranging from legislative committee chairs to ambassadorships to positions chairing various state bodies. The further we move away from the cabinet, however, the more the list of government patronage appointments varies from country to country. Since our objective is to compare the making and breaking of governments in different countries, we use a narrow definition of "government" – the PM and cabinet – as a common denominator. This narrow definition follows the prior literature and is widely portable between different countries, all of which have a chief executive and a "cabinet" of senior political appointees.

Politicians' Preferences

Given this definition of parliamentary democracy, the voting decisions of legislators make and break governments. These decisions are ultimately determined by legislators' private preferences. We see the preferences of negotiating politicians in terms of two basic components. The first concerns the government policy program. The second concerns the distribution of government offices – perquisites or perks as we'll call them. We follow convention and describe the perks of office essentially as a fixed set of prizes to be distributed between the winners of the government formation game. We assume each element in this bag of swag has the same value, no matter how its contents are distributed. For example, when we assume, as do most other models of government formation, that the set of perks consists of cabinet portfolios, we also assume that each politician attaches the same value to the same portfolio. In other words, we assume two politicians cannot increase their combined satisfaction by exchanging their portfolios. This is a significant simplifying assumption, particularly since different cabinet portfolios are always associated with different policy areas, and in our models, different politicians attach different levels of importance to different policy areas. Without it, the possibility exists that a minister for agriculture and a minister for defense, for example, would both feel better off if they were to swap portfolios.

There has been considerable empirical research over several decades on the allocation of portfolios between parties in coalition cabinets. This has resulted in a substantial consensus on the empirical relationship between the legislative seat shares of the parties in government and their shares of cabinet portfolios – though there is no consensus on the theoretical explanation for this relationship. This has been striking and robust enough to have been accorded the rare status of a "law" in political science: Gamson's law, named after the sociologist who first reported it (Gamson 1961, Browne and Frendreis 1980, Fréchette, et al. 2005b, Warwick and Druckman 2006, Laver, et al. 2011a, Cutler, et al. 2016). This law summarizes the striking empirical pattern that parties' shares of cabinet portfolios are sharply proportional to the seat shares they contribute to the government's seat total. Assuming that different portfolios have different values for different parties does not substantially improve this relationship (Warwick and Druckman 2001, Druckman and Warwick 2005).

Our simplifying assumption describes negotiating politicians' preferences in terms of two *separable* components, however. These are: the value of government offices, in and for themselves; and the value of the government policy program. We, therefore, set aside the *policy implementation* aspects of holding a particular cabinet portfolio. We focus instead on what partners in government *agree to do* when they negotiate a joint policy program, not on what they *actually do* when in government. This sets our approach apart from so-called "portfolio allocation" models (e.g., Laver and Shepsle 1996b, Dragu and Laver 2019) which focus on policy implementation and assume that *implemented* government policy is to a large extent determined by the allocation of cabinet portfolios between politicians with different policy preferences.

Turning from the perks of office to the other separable component of politicians' utilities, public policy, we adopt the standard convention of describing politicians' policy preferences in spatial terms. Departing from convention, we describe these preferences in terms of high-dimensional manifest issue spaces rather than low-dimensional summaries of these. We do this because we want to keep our assumptions about legislators as close as possible to the bare metal of actual legislative *behavior*. The convention in political science is to summarize politicians' policy preferences using one or at most a tiny number of "latent" dimensions. These summary dimensions are not "real"; they are not actually discussed in real political negotiations. Rather, they are assumed by political scientists to be reasonable and simple summaries of the actual policy environments manifested in the real world, which are always complicated and messy. The best known of these latent dimensions is a general left-right dimension of "socioeconomic" policy, typically deployed in one-dimensional spatial accounts of political competition. More detailed accounts deploy additional latent dimensions: economic left-right, social "liberal-conservative," pro- or anti-environmentalism, "hawk-dove" on foreign policy, and so on. These latent dimensions can be seen as summaries of positions on large numbers of correlated and much more detailed *manifest issue dimensions* that describe the actual concerns of real politicians on the ground (Stokes 1963, Converse 1964). Figure 2.1 shows an example of a summary "liberal-conservative" dimension of social policy. Knowing Amy's position on abortion and gay marriage, for example, it is relatively easy to predict her position on immigration and gun control. Her positions on these four *manifest* issue dimensions are correlated, and the same can be said of Bob. This means that a single *latent* liberal-conservative policy dimension can be thought of as summarizing their positions on these four issues.

While such summaries make it much easier to specify and analyze simple models of politics, they do not describe politicians' policy preferences *in relation to the actual decisions they must make*. Latent policy dimensions are artifacts of political science. They are in no way the stuff of real politics. While we can as a convenience summarize legislators' positions on particular issues in terms of a small number of latent "policy" dimensions, these summaries are always imperfect. There are two important reasons for this.

First, even if the positions of different politicians on a cluster of manifest issue dimensions are correlated, in the way illustrated in Figure 2.1, those same politicians may differ hugely on the importance,

Figure 2.1 Four manifest issue dimensions summarized using one latent dimension

or salience, attached to different dimensions. For example, Amy may care much more about gun control than Bob, and Bob may care much more about gay marriage than Amy. If Amy and Bob are forced for some reason to agree to a common position on both gun control and gay marriage – as they would be if they planned to go into government together – then this might seem a very difficult task if we simply look at the *positions* on these issues set out in Figure 2.1. However, taking account of the very different *saliences* they each attach to the two issues, the task may actually be much easier. If Amy gets her way on gun control and Bob gets his way on gay marriage, they might both be fairly satisfied. This would be what both political scientists and real politicians call a "logroll." A logroll takes place on two issues when both sides concede on the issue they feel least strongly about. What this example in particular, and the possibility of logrolling in general, shows us is that simply summarizing the correlated positions of politicians on a set of manifest issues using some latent policy dimension(s) can hinder rather than help our understanding of the real world of bargaining and negotiation.

Second, while the preferences of the set of politicians as a whole on a cluster of issues may seem to be correlated, the preferences of two particular politicians engaged in government formation may still differ quite a bit. Two party leaders on the "left" of a latent economic policy dimension, for example, may well differ sharply on the balance of taxation between income, wealth, and corporate profits. Two legislators on the liberal end of a social policy dimension may well differ sharply on the legalization of heroin or voluntary euthanasia.

Governance in the real world involves making decisions on a large number of manifest issue dimensions. The actual decisions politicians face, whether in government or in the legislature, do not concern whether to move toward the liberal end of some latent social policy dimension. They concern specific issues such as whether or not to legalize marijuana, or heroin, or voluntary euthanasia. When it comes to writing a party manifesto, negotiating a program of government, or drafting legislation, it is self-evidently necessary to state positions on manifest issues, not latent dimensions. No actual political party writes an election manifesto announcing that their social policy will be one standard deviation left of center on the liberal-conservative policy dimension. They say they favor legalizing marijuana, for example. We therefore describe politicians' policy preferences in terms of high-dimensional manifest issue spaces, as opposed to the low-dimensional latent summary spaces typically deployed by theoretical models in political science, which in effect ignore what actually happens in the bargaining process.[19]

We simplify these policies somewhat by assuming that positions on each manifest issue dimension are *binary*.[20] We feel this is behaviorally realistic. Policy-making in the real world involves changing the *status quo* which means implementing a particular decision. It is not a general aspiration, objective, or policy. "Lower taxes," for example, is a general policy aspiration. To implement an actual policy in this area on the ground, concrete actions have to be specified – for example, "lower the base rate of income tax by one percent" or "increase the threshold at which income tax becomes payable by $5000." Not taking the proposed action leaves the *status quo* in place, while taking it changes the *status quo* in a precisely specified way. We therefore describe politicians' policy preferences in terms of high-dimensional binary issue spaces.[21] Specifically, we assume an m-dimensional discrete space of binary positions on each of a large set of issues expected to require action by any incoming cabinet. Politician i's ideal position

---

[19] There is also a technical reason why we pursue a multidimensional policy space: The behavior of formal models when only perks are at stake or there is just one left-right policy dimension is quite different from the multidimensional setting (Aldrich, et al. 2014, de Marchi, et al. 2021).

[20] While we do consider the assumption of binary issue positions to be substantively realistic, this is an example of a decision rule that would become computationally expensive if we chose to model issue positions as real valued rather than binary. As we will note in Chapter 4, "coarsening" the policy space is a necessary part of reducing the size of the extensive form game such that it can be studied using computational methods.

[21] Note that, as we will shortly see, the *salience* attached to each issue by each politician is real valued. Therefore, while we do feel that individual *positions* on each issue are best described in binary terms, we assume the *utility* derived from individuals' issue positions is real valued.

is given by an issue vector p_i of size m, each element, p_{ij}, of which is a binary number reporting i's preference on issue j. Positions on each issue describe whether i supports (1) or opposes (0) a specific proposed change to the *status quo*.

As we have noted, it is also very likely that politicians differ quite a bit in how strongly they feel about different issues. Some may feel very strongly about the environment, for example, while others care more about national defense. As we discuss in the following text in more detail, such variations between politicians in the relative saliences they attach to the same issues are central to our account of government formation negotiations. This focuses on logrolling, whereby politicians trade positions on issues on which they disagree, but to which they also attach differing levels of importance.

Logrolling may not always be possible. Two negotiators may disagree on an issue about which they both feel strongly, yet have opposite preferences. An extreme example of this would arise in negotiations between two politicians for whom there is a perfect rank-order correlation between relative issue saliences. Both negotiators agree perfectly on which are the high and low salience issues, so they have no incentive to trade positions on any issue. It will be next to impossible for them to agree on a joint program of government. On the other hand, a distinctive implication of our approach, which sets it aside from previous work on government formation, is that the more *inversely* correlated the relative issue saliences of negotiating politicians, the easier it is for them to agree on a joint policy program by trading issue positions on which they disagree. Disagreement between negotiators on key issues is not necessarily, therefore, a barrier to agreeing on a joint policy program, as long as negotiators attach different relative saliences to the same issues.

The relative *salience* of each issue for politician i is given by a vector s_i of size m. The element s_{ij} shows the relative salience of issue j to politician i: $0 \leq s_{ij} \leq 1$ and $\Sigma_j(s_{ij}) = 1$. We talk about *relative* saliences, summing these to unity for every politician, because we model individual behaviors, specifically the trade-offs each politician might make when balancing a loss on some issue against a win on another. If our intention was to model the aggregate social welfare of outcomes from the governance cycle, then we might adopt a different approach.

As noted earlier, we assume that politicians derive values both from agreed government policies and from the distribution of government perks. Different politicians trade off the relative values of perks and policies in different ways, treating these as "separable" components of their utility. In other words, the value they attach to a particular policy position does not depend on how many perks they have. Specifically, we assume that politicians' utility functions involve a convex combination of separable utilities derived from policies and perks. The utility of politician i for cabinet c, U_{ci}, is

$$U_{ci} = \alpha_i \left(g_{ci} \right) - \left(1 - \alpha_i \right) \left(\sum s_{ij} \left| p_{ij} - p_{cj} \right| \right)$$

where g_{ci} is i's proposed share in cabinet c of the fixed set of government perquisites.[22] In what follows, we take these perquisites to be cabinet portfolios. Furthermore, since the proportional allocation of cabinet portfolios is such a robust and pervasive empirical pattern, we take this to be common knowledge among negotiating politicians, so that they expect cabinet portfolios will be allocated according to Gamson's law. The relative salience of, and preferred position on, issue j for politician i are s_{ij} and p_{ij}, respectively. The proposed position of cabinet c on issue j is p_{cj}. The trade-off rate α_i measures the relative importance of perquisites and government policy for politician i.

Finally, we follow almost all existing formal models in assuming that information about politicians' issue preferences is also common knowledge. Our model, like almost all before it, therefore, assumes complete information.[23] The alternative assumption, that politicians' preferences or value for perks versus policy are private information, is clearly a possible extension to our model. We caution, however, that an incomplete information extension will add considerable complexity and difficulty to the modeling endeavor. We reserve it for future work after our complete information model has been resolved.

Agreeing to Disagree: Tabled Issues

The number of issues potentially requiring action by any government is vast. It is extraordinarily unlikely that negotiating politicians will be able to agree to a joint position on every single one of these. Failure to agree on a joint position on every issue that might conceivably arise

---

[22] We present the utility function and some notation here to motivate the narrative. For full details, see Technical Appendix A2.

[23] For an exception, modeling coalition governance with incomplete information, see Dragu and Laver (2019).

need not, however, stop parties from going into government together. Negotiating politicians may resolve disagreements on many issues, but may still set aside some issues about which they all feel strongly, yet disagree. They can "agree to disagree" on these hard-to-resolve issues, leaving these out of the joint policy program. In this event, we say they "table" these issues. Returning to Figure 2.1, for example, it may be that Amy and Bob both feel *very* strongly about abortion, but disagree fundamentally on abortion policy. If they are able to logroll an agreed position on most other issues, they can decide to table the issue of abortion, completely leaving it out of their set of agreed issue positions. What is important here is that, in a substantial departure from almost all previous work on government formation, we assume that the set of agreed issue positions in the joint policy program of any cabinet is *endogenous*. There is no exogenously fixed set of issues on which agreed positions must go into the joint government policy program. The set of issues covered by the joint program *is itself a product of government formation negotiations*.

Tabling salient issues during government formation negotiations does however come at a cost for the politicians involved. When coalition partners go into office with tabled issues in their agreed joint program, they do so in the hope that unanticipated shocks will not force these issues onto the government agenda. But a global pandemic may confront partners in government with divisive choices on civil liberties. An unexpected war in Europe may drive a wedge between members of a coalition cabinet on defense policy. If an exogenous shock forces a tabled issue onto the government agenda, then the partners in government must come up with a joint position on an important matter about which they have explicitly agreed to disagree. For this reason, as we discuss in much more detail in the following text, the more there are tabled issues in an agreed coalition policy program, the more vulnerable is the government to random shocks that perturb the political environment.

Tabling a salient issue in an agreed joint policy program generates uncertainty about what might happen if an exogenous shock were to force partners in government to confront the issue. Politicians may be more, or less, tolerant of such uncertainty. The possibility of tabling issues, therefore, adds another feature to our description of politicians' preferences. We capture this with a parameter τ_i ($0 < \tau_i < 1$), which reflects the attitude of politician i to the uncertainty associated with tabling an issue. When $\tau_i \approx 0$, we model an extremely "optimistic," or risk tolerant, politician who expects no policy loss to arise from tabling an issue. On the other hand, when $\tau_i \approx 1$, we model an extremely "pessimistic," or risk averse, politician who *always* expects a tabled issue to turn out as badly as possible, yielding the maximum policy loss. The parameter τ_i reports the expected policy loss for politician i arising from tabling any given issue. The salience-weighted expected value of a tabled issue, $|p_{ij} - p_{cj}| = \tau_i$, appears in each agent's utility function in precisely the same way as for any other issue. When politicians consider a coalition proposal, the expected policy loss arising from tabling any issue is, therefore, weighted in their utility functions by the relative salience of the issue.

Politicians and Political Parties

The defining feature of the governance process, as we model this, is that it takes place in a parliamentary democracy where the executive is responsible to the lower house of the legislature. This is at once a simplification. Some parliamentary democracies are bicameral, and some upper houses can have an important impact on the governance cycle. Article 94(1) of the Italian constitution, for example, states that the government "must enjoy the confidence of both Chambers" and this is indeed very relevant to government formation in Italy. In other bicameral systems, such as Ireland, the constitution gives the upper house no power whatsoever over the fate of the government. Rather than model particular powers of upper houses in particular bicameral systems, we focus instead on the universal power of *lower* houses to make and break governments in all parliamentary democracies, whether bicameral or unicameral. We thereby lose some of the detail of particular cases, but gain much in the increased generality of our model. Further, if Italy is a systematic exception when we test the empirical implications of our models, for example, we could take a closer theoretical look at the potential political implications of Article 94(1).

We describe the lower house of the legislature as a set of popularly elected legislators, each affiliated with one of n disciplined (or coherent) parliamentary parties.[24] Each parliamentary party has a leader. We model the discipline (or coherence) of parliamentary parties by

---

[24] The difference between discipline and coherence is that members of a *disciplined* party may well have diverse preferences but nonetheless always obey their leader, whereas members of a *coherent* party all have substantially the same preferences.

assuming that each party's legislators can be treated "as if" they all have the same preferences – and, therefore, the same preferences as their party leader. This assumption sets aside intraparty politics and is of course a considerable simplification. While we feel sure that intraparty preference diversity and the intraparty politics that arise from this are important features of the governance cycle, we leave this for future work. On a related matter, we also set aside the *endogeneity of parliamentary parties*, the processes by which they form, fuse, and split. For now, we stay within the mainstream of modern political science and hope to make at least some progress in understanding the governance cycle by treating an exogenously given set of *n* legislative parties as if these are either disciplined or coherent. Finally, we do not consider "pre-electoral coalitions." This is in part because, while these do sometimes exist, they are more a feature of electoral competition than of the governance process. Pre-electoral coalitions are neither formally binding nor officially recorded and, from a practical point of view, are not always authoritatively documented.[25]

Components of the Governance Cycle

Having been more precise about the preferences of negotiating politicians and the political parties they belong to, we are now in a position to be more specific about the three phases of the governance cycle – government formation, government support, and elections – sketched in Figure 1.1. The flowchart in Figure 2.2 unpacks these.

The *government formation process* is described inside the upper dashed box. Once triggered by a government defeat, resignation, or an election, it iterates until the legislature approves a new executive. The *government support/survival process* is set out inside the central dashed box. Once initiated by the formation of a new government, it iterates continuously until the government resigns, is defeated, or there is a scheduled election. The *general election process* is set out in the lower black box. Since our substantive focus here is on elite governance rather than popular elections, we do not model the systematic evolution of public opinion between elections, leaving this interesting and important process to others. We therefore model elections

---

[25] If anything, not recognizing pre-electoral coalitions will hurt the empirical performance of our model when we turn to such matters in Chapter 6.

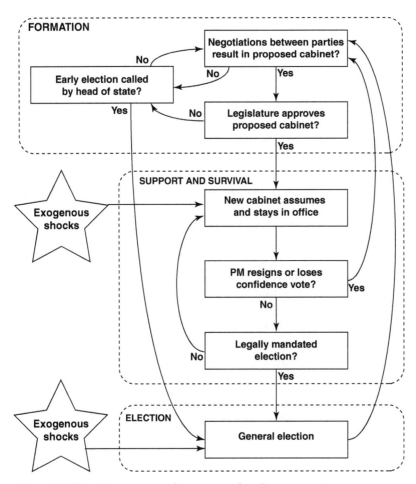

Figure 2.2 Three interconnected processes of parliamentary governance

in terms of a series of random shocks to public opinion, which affect voters' support for the various political parties on offer.

Figure 2.2 not only sets out the component parts of the governance process but also shows these to be intimately connected. Outputs of one process, such as elections, feed directly as inputs into other processes, such as government formation. Anticipations of election results affect government survival. For ease of exposition, we first describe each process separately, briefly sketching these links. We return to discuss them in more detail as the book unfolds.

Government Formation

The logical engine at the heart of our model of the governance process is a model of government formation. Our model of elections serves to generate inputs to the government formation process. Our model of government survival describes this as continuous re-evaluation by legislators of what might happen if the government formation process were to be re-triggered. Government formation has been the subject of an enormous and widely reviewed literature over the past six decades. We refer readers to selected overviews of this, returning to cite particular contributions when these have direct relevance for our argument (Laver and Shepsle 1996b, Laver and Schofield 1998a, Müller and Strom 2003, Strøm, et al. 2008, Martin and Vanberg 2011, Martin and Vanberg 2015, Martin and Vanberg 2020).

Three types of event trigger the government formation process in parliamentary democracies. The first is a constitutionally mandated general election. The second is the failure of an incumbent government without an election. This may be caused by a loss of legislative support for the government, resulting in its defeat on a legislative vote of (no) confidence. It may also be caused by the resignation of the incumbent PM in anticipation of such a defeat. The third is an election provoked by the resignation of an incumbent PM who anticipates a favorable result.[26] The government formation process is, therefore, triggered by, and takes inputs from, the government support and election processes. Once triggered, the government formation process continues until one of two outcomes is achieved. The first is the installation of a new government at which point the governance cycle moves to the "support/survival" process. The second is a new general election resulting in a new legislature. This can happen *in extremis*, if no government can be found which commands majority support in the current legislature.

What Is Being Formed, and When?

We define a "government" as a PM and a cabinet of ministers, subject to a constitutionally binding rule of collective cabinet responsibility. To increase comparability across parliamentary democracies, we do

[26] This can arise in countries where the constitutional convention is that the Head of State will not deny a request from the incumbent PM for an early election.

not consider junior ministerial or other patronage appointments, since these vary so much from country to country. As set out above in our specification of politicians' utility functions, therefore, we see a government as a cabinet, c, defined by a vector g_c of perks allocations between parties (according to Gamson's law) and a joint policy vector, p_c, that specifies government positions in a high-dimensional discrete issue space.

Government formation involves negotiations between senior politicians. There may well be some superficial structure to these. For example, the leader of the largest party, or the incumbent PM, may be designated as *formateur*, with the "exclusive" right to make offers to others. Notwithstanding what we might see on the surface of the government formation process, it surely has hidden depths. Under the surface, there is a complex web of informal discussion and communication between politicians from different political parties. These people are mostly seasoned and sophisticated political operators. It seems to us inconceivable that they would sit back as passive spectators of the crucially important business of government formation – the most important game in town. Much of what is most interesting about politics goes on behind closed doors where *multiple* proposals are considered *simultaneously*.

Once negotiations, both those that are visible and those that are invisible to outside observers, result in a proposed government *with terms agreed by all participants*, this is put to the legislature. If a majority of those voting approve, then this becomes the new incumbent government.[27] Successful government formation, therefore, involves more than a legislative majority. It does require a legislative majority but is also *subject to a veto* by any member of the proposed government. Politicians who disagree with any proposal cannot be dragged into some putative government against their will.

When it comes to our empirical work, we follow the convention in both political science and real-world politics, treating any of the following as triggering government formation:

---

[27] As we noted above, legislative approval in many countries involves an explicit investiture vote. When it does not, legislative approval is implicit, in the sense that any new government is immediately subject to legislative defeat in a motion of no confidence. In what follows, we generalize the precise procedural details of legislative approval for a new government, which vary from country to country, and treat explicit and implicit legislative approval as equivalent.

- the PM dies, resigns, or is defeated in a legislative vote of (no) confidence;
- there is a general election;
- a party whose members hold cabinet portfolios withdraws its members from the cabinet.

As noted previously, a binding constitutional feature of all parliamentary democracies is that the death, resignation, or defeat of the PM triggers the government formation process. Some might say, however, that there is not a change of government if, following a general election, the same PM forms a government with the same partisan composition. For example, Helmut Kohl was German Chancellor (prime minister) continuously from 1982 to 1998. He took office and formed a government between elections, but went on to fight and win four general elections in 1983, 1987, 1990, and 1994. After each election, he formed coalition cabinets with precisely the same partisan composition, of Christian Democrats (CDU/CSU) and Free Democrats (FDP). With the benefit of hindsight, there might be a view that there was only one long-lasting German government throughout this entire period.

Science is not about analyzing things with the benefit of hindsight, however. Kohl never won a parliamentary majority in any of the elections he fought; following each election, the *option* was always on the table of forming a cabinet with a different partisan composition. Indeed, Angela Merkel subsequently exercised this option on three occasions by forming "grand coalitions" with the Social Democrats. The fact that five Kohl governments in succession had the same partisan composition is an empirical observation, an *ex post* outcome of government formation, not part of an *ex ante* definition of this. The real world of politics, furthermore, follows the same convention. In the case of the Kohl government(s), for example, these are always treated as five different administrations: Kohl I, Kohl II, Kohl III, Kohl IV, and Kohl V.

The same argument applies when one of the government parties leaves the incumbent coalition, but there is no general election and the same PM continues in office. In this somewhat uncommon event, there *must* be a change in the partisan allocation of cabinet portfolios. There is also the *option* to change the joint government policy program, which was a product of negotiations with a party that is no longer part of the government.

The government formation process in a parliamentary democracy may, therefore, be triggered both after and between elections. There are differences in these two types of settings, which might cause us to analyze them in somewhat different ways.

Government Formation Immediately after an Election

Most scholarly accounts of government formation in parliamentary democracies implicitly assume that this is taking place immediately after a general election, starting with what is in effect a clean slate. Each of the parties has had the opportunity to publish new issue positions adapted to current circumstances or to reaffirm old positions. The election has likely generated new seat shares for the various legislative parties.

A general election, therefore, generates a new setting for government formation. We follow this convention. While the heart of our model concerns short-run adaptive behavior by politicians engaged in the governance cycle, we do not model long-run "learning" from the history of government formations – for example, taking account of the stability of all previous governments and their subsequent electoral success. This would certainly be an interesting avenue of investigation to pursue in future work once our baseline model is nailed down.

Government Formation between Elections

When government formation is triggered between two elections, however, the situation is quite different. A government that was in some sense in equilibrium has failed.[28] This equilibrium might be in accord with some explicit model of government formation, or arise from some unmodeled process we can neither observe nor understand. Either way, the outgoing incumbent government was the equilibrium outcome of some formation process. The legislative arithmetic has not

---

[28] We are using the term "equilibrium" loosely here. Given the complexity of the process detailed in Figure 2.2, it is unlikely that a government is an equilibrium in a strict sense. While this could be the case – see Proposition 5 in Chapter 5 – it is more likely that a government is the end result of a comprehensive search by party leaders. If one thinks of this as the outcome of an optimization process rather than a Nash equilibrium, that would be closer to the truth.

necessarily changed, but *something* has changed to modify the incentives of legislators to support the incumbent government. Some shock to the parameters of the parliamentary system has brought this about.

This might be a shock to anticipations of the results of an early election conveyed by opinion poll findings. It might be a shock to the issue agenda or to politicians' ideal policy positions arising from some unanticipated event. While we can observe the *effect* of such shocks in destabilizing an incumbent government, it is rarely possible to measure *ex ante* the extent to which they shift the parameters of the government formation process. In terms of what we can measure, therefore, interelectoral government formation may look like a rerun of the previous government formation process, though we know this cannot in fact be true since, if it were, the outgoing government would not have fallen. No scholar to our knowledge has explicitly tackled this problem, and we have no good solution to it. In our empirical work later in this book, therefore, we concentrate on government formation immediately after an election.

Government Support and Survival

Constitutional Causes of Government Failure

The life and times of any government in a parliamentary democracy involve many different types of activities, which can be difficult to disentangle given the fusion of powers between legislature and executive. We simplify here by dividing what incumbent governments can do into either *legislative* or *executive* actions.

The practical political reality is that most of what governments actually do involves *executive* actions. Most policy changes enacted by governments are achieved without passing new laws. This is not least because most legislation explicitly provides for, or is silent about, the possibility of detailed interpretation and implementation of the law by the relevant cabinet minister. Going beyond this, we may exaggerate somewhat but are not far short of the truth if we assume that the minister with jurisdiction over a particular issue area may enact any policy that is neither illegal nor unconstitutional. The ultimate formal arbiters of this are the courts, in a process of judicial review.

Substantially changing the incumbent government's policy program, therefore, typically involves changing the government. This is because even if government-sponsored legislation is defeated in the legislature, this has no legal or constitutional effect on the government's ability to continue in office. This may be embarrassing, even humiliating, and in certain political circumstances might provoke a government resignation, but the incumbent government may, if it chooses, continue in office regardless of such a defeat. For these reasons, we do not model the process of "ordinary" legislation when we model the governance cycle in parliamentary democracies. We focus instead on three key types of legislative votes, each of which can cause an incumbent government to fail, and all of which are, from our perspective, functionally equivalent.

The first is a motion of no confidence. The defining constitutional feature of a parliamentary democracy is that the executive must maintain the "confidence" of the legislature. If the incumbent government loses this, then it falls. The second is a motion of confidence. The government may propose such a motion at any time, and, once proposed, this has the same constitutional status as an opposition motion of no confidence. A common use of this procedural device arises after the government has lost a key vote on an important piece of substantive legislation. In effect, the government can put it up to those who just voted against it, who are often rebels from government parties, to go ahead and bring down the government. The third key legislative vote is on the government's annual budget. In all parliamentary democracies, this must, as a "money bill," be approved by the lower house of the legislature. Losing the vote on final passage of the annual budget legislation is equivalent to losing a vote of no confidence.

The bottom line in all of this is that the binding constitutional constraints in the government support process do not concern the ability of the government to pass primary legislation, but do concern its ability to win votes in the lower house on motions of confidence or no confidence, and on its annual budget. These constraints structure our model of government survival.

Government Survival and Unanticipated Shocks

The government support and survival process is triggered as soon as government formation successfully concludes. Its input is the government that has just formed. Legislators approve this new government based on what they know, or can reasonably anticipate, *at the moment the government forms.* At that instant, the government is an "equilibrium" outcome of *some* formation process, whether this process was explicit or implicit, modeled or unmodeled, and whether we understand it or not.[29] Any change destabilizing this equilibrium, therefore, must be an unanticipated shock. What motivates a sufficient number of legislators in a parliamentary system to bring down a government they previously supported? Since they presumably factored *everything they could anticipate* into their previous decisions to support the government, their changing preferences for different governments must arise from *unanticipated shocks.*

There is a substantial literature on government survival. Much of this research consists of purely empirical research on government durations. This literature uses censored Poisson regressions to model the effect of random shocks on government durations, conditional on certain observed features of each government (King, et al. 1990, Warwick 1994, Diermeier and Stevenson 1999, 2000).

There is a much smaller theoretical literature on government survival. This derives from Lupia and Strom, who modeled the effects of shocks to electoral expectations for a simple setting with two government parties and a single outside option (Lupia and Strom 1995, Diermeier and Merlo 2000). They exercised their model to identify circumstances in which the government parties would renegotiate their deal following the shock, and those in which a new election was likely.

Laver and Shepsle (1998) built on this work to model the effects of shocks on government stability of four different types of shocks. First, there are "public opinion shocks." While politicians may extrapolate from past experience to anticipate that the new government will lose support in the interelectoral period, events may happen which push such changes beyond expectations. There may be a scandal, or the bungling of a crisis, causing public opinion to shift unexpectedly

---

[29] Imagine, to take a perhaps far-fetched example, that the two leaders of ideologically quite different parties are firm friends because they are fanatical supporters of the same soccer team. The bonds of trust and friendship between them might make it more likely they would go into government together, even given the policy differences between them. No general model, of course, either could or should comprehend this – even though it might be an anecdotally correct account of some particular government formation process. Some observers did claim that British party leaders David Cameron and Nick Clegg found it easy to negotiate, successfully, over government formation because they had similar privileged backgrounds and private education.

against one or more government parties. This alters expectations about the outcome of the next election, thereby changing the incentives of legislators to maintain the incumbent government in office. Second, there are "policy shocks" that perturb ideal policy positions of senior politicians. For example, the world financial crisis of 2008 likely changed the preferences of many politicians about the desirability of government intervention to support large financial institutions. Third, there are "agenda shocks" that perturb saliences of particular issues. For example, a hurricane or tsunami may suddenly raise the political importance of government spending on environmental protection, even if preferred policies on this do not change. Last, Laver and Shepsle discuss "decision rule shocks." These are more arcane, arising when there is an unexpected change to the decision rule for how the legislature approves proposals. One example is a shock generating the need for a constitutional amendment, which might change the relevant decision rule from a simple to a qualified majority.

Of these, two types of shocks are directly relevant to our model of the governance cycle. *Policy shocks* change the policy preferences of key politicians. These can arise when unanticipated events change legislators' preferences. Excellent examples of policy shocks arose during the COVID-19 pandemic of 2020–2021. The huge shocks generated by this caused preferences to change in many policy areas. For example, constraints on civil liberties and dramatic injections of public money into the private sector were approved by politicians who had formally been deeply opposed to such policies. Similarly, the Russian invasion of Ukraine in 2022 caused politicians in many Western states to change their preferences on defense spending and energy policy, putting the unity of the Spanish coalition cabinet, to take just one example, under severe pressure.

As we will see, our model has a more detailed description of politicians' preferences than that of Laver and Shepsle and involves four different preference parameters. These refer to: preferred issue positions, relative issue saliences, trade-offs between perks and policy payoffs, and tolerance for leaving contentious issues out of the agreed government program. As we explain in much greater detail in the following text, we simulate the noisy environment in which any incumbent government must survive by systematically perturbing these preference parameters and observing the relative frequency with which such perturbations cause legislators to prefer an alternative to the incumbent. This has the effect of simulating what we can think of as *policy shocks*.

Agenda shocks affect tabled issues. While the entire space of conceivable policies is immense, any agreed program of government typically deals with only a small part of this. As we have seen, negotiating politicians may well agree to disagree on particular issues, tabling these and excluding them from their agreed joint program of government. The dimensionality of this agreed program is thus endogenous to political negotiations. In tabling some contested issues and leaving these out of the agreed policy program, the partners in government are in effect gambling that unanticipated events will not force such issues onto the government agenda and cause a ruckus. But sometimes an agenda shock does indeed happen. We model this as forcing a previously tabled issue onto the agenda, potentially destabilizing an incumbent government. We have specified the payoff to party i for having a tabled issue in the joint program of government as τ_i ($0 < \tau_i < 1$). A shock forcing tabled issue j onto the agenda means that the authors of the joint program must now set a position, whether 0 or 1, on issue j. If the previously tabled issue resolves after the shock at 0, for example, then parties preferring position 0 on the issue gain from this shock; parties preferring position 1 lose.[30] Any party that loses utility as a result of an agenda shock may now prefer some alternative government, thereby destabilizing the incumbent. For this reason, the more tabled issues there are in an agreed program of government, the more vulnerable the government is to agenda shocks.

The General Election Process

Figure 2.2 shows that the governance cycle in parliamentary systems triggers a general election in two possible situations. The first is exogenous to the political process: the end of the constitutionally mandated period between elections. This type of election can be fully anticipated, even if its actual outcome cannot. The second election trigger is endogenous and arises from a failure of the government formation process. This failure can happen either following an election or between elections after the incumbent government has lost its legislative support base. Some constitutions formally mandate a period of

---

[30] Recall that the policy component in politicians' utility functions is measured as distance between the ideal point and the agreed policy, and hence is always either zero or negative.

time, or a number of failed attempts, after which government formation is deemed to have failed and a new election is triggered. Much more commonly, the decision to declare government formation a failure and trigger an early election is a formal responsibility of the head of state, typically based on the advice of senior politicians. If the head of state holds, and acts upon, strong partisan preferences, this adds further complexity to the governance cycle. We could in theory model this feature but it is not our primary interest. We therefore assume that the head of state will declare the government formation process to have failed and trigger a general election after a specified number of failed formation attempts, where this number is an exogenous feature of the political environment which varies from country to country. As noted, in some countries, the head of state may also decide to bypass the government formation process and dissolve the legislature, if asked to do so by a resigning PM. The results of elections feed directly into the government formation process, and so the cycle continues.

We face important decisions about how to model elections. The most important is whether to model the behavior of individual voters in large electorates, and/or vote-seeking position-taking by senior politicians. Our prime substantive concern here is not with these key features of electoral competition (which are very important but very different scholarly projects), but with the impact of actual and expected election results on the governance cycle. We, therefore, simplify here, given our core focus on understanding the governance cycle, by treating elections as black boxes, which take inputs from the governance cycle and output exogenous random shocks to party seat shares, generating a new party "weight" vector, w. This leaves open the possibility of subsequent model extensions that capture the inner workings of the electoral black box.

We model electoral shocks to seat shares as being drawn from a normal distribution with a mean of zero and a variance parameter measuring electoral volatility. Since, surprisingly, the observed variance in party seat shares does not vary very much from country to country in postwar Europe, we used the same parameterized distribution of electoral shocks for all countries.[31] We could in theory add

---

[31] Interestingly, the variance parameter for this distribution is nearly constant across parties in post–World War II PR systems and is a linear function of the pre-election size of the party.

more structure to these shocks. For example, we might see the scale of electoral shocks as a function of how parties locate along a set of dimensions, which might represent policy positions or indeed any other feature, perhaps demographic, which conditions electoral support. Electoral shocks might then be biased, and we can model this by using a biased normal distribution of electoral shocks. We could add party-specific biases to electoral shocks, basing these on information from recent public opinion polls. Finally, we could envisage taking a step toward making election results endogenous to the governance cycle by conditioning the parameters of the distribution of electoral shocks on theoretically meaningful outputs of the governance process.

To a large extent, our decisions on these matters will be affected by whether we seek a general analytical model of the governance cycle in parliamentary systems, or a more predictive model, calibrated to the details of some particular political setting. We can calibrate our model to fulfil either task, but our primary concern here is to understand the governance cycle in parliamentary democracies as a whole, rather than to make predictions about some specific political setting. We begin, therefore, by modeling election results as unstructured and unbiased random shocks to the preexisting seat distribution.

In modeling shocks to the distribution of *seats won rather than votes cast*, we are making an important assumption about the role of electoral systems. When political events have an impact on election results, they do so by changing the behavior of voters. The underlying shocks are to the distribution of votes between parties. This is transformed into a distribution of seats by the electoral system. Every country that interests us has a different electoral system. There are: different electoral formulae, different popular vote thresholds for legislative representation, different distributions of district sizes, different laws about registering to vote, different laws about registering political parties, different campaign finance laws, and so on.

For example, the Netherlands has a highly proportional electoral system, and the entire country is a single 150-seat district. There is no legal threshold, so any party winning enough support for a seat, which requires less than 1 percent of the national vote, is represented in the legislature. In a system such as this, shocks to the distribution of votes between parties translate fairly precisely into changes to the distribution of legislative seats. In stark contrast, the simple plurality system used for parliamentary elections in the UK, with 650 single-seat districts, is highly unpredictable in how it transforms votes cast into seats won. This is especially true when there are more than two parties and strong regional variations in levels of partisan support, as has always been the case in the postwar era. Depending on the precise distribution of votes between parties *in each individual district*, big shifts in the distribution of votes between parties can have little effect on the distribution of seats, or small shifts in the distribution of votes can have a big effect. On several occasions since World War II, indeed, the party winning the most seats and forming a government was not the party winning the popular vote.[32]

Since every parliamentary democracy of interest to us does indeed have a different electoral system, and since we want to make statements about the governance cycle in the general class of parliamentary democracies, we abstract from the electoral system and focus in our theoretical work on shocks to the distribution of legislative seats, however these might have been caused. Having made this important theoretical decision, we model electoral shocks as unbiased random draws from a normal distribution of possible seat perturbations, with a mean of zero and a variance calibrated to the observed variance of seat shares in postwar European parliamentary democracies.

The body of this chapter verbally outlined the various component parts of our model of the governance cycle. This sets the scene for the next chapter (Chapter 3), in which we discuss how functionally rational politicians might behave in this complex environment. Technical Appendix A2 elaborates on our verbal arguments in greater detail. This allows readers more interested in substance than in technical detail to move ahead to the next chapter, consulting this Appendix if the need arises.

---

[32] There is an obvious analogy with the Electoral College system for choosing a chief executive in the United States.

3 | An Agent-Based Model of Government Formation and Survival

Seasoned politicians negotiating over government formation have both private preferences and publicly stated positions on a very wide range of issues, any of which an incoming government may be called on to resolve. Different politicians typically attach different levels of relative importance to each of these issues. They also have different preferences about the intrinsic value and prestige of simply being part of the government. Government formation, therefore, is about politicians, who value both the perks of office and public policy outcomes to different degrees, agreeing on a proposal for government that involves both a distribution of perks between them and a joint public policy program located in a high-dimensional issue space. This explains the plain fact that the formation of real governments often takes days, weeks, or even months of difficult negotiations. If these negotiations are "difficult" for seasoned and rational senior politicians, they are also difficult, indeed deductively intractable, for scholars trying to model them.

We said in Chapter 2 that we choose not to take the conventional route of assuming away this difficulty so we can specify a simple model that is amenable to deductive analysis. Rather, we attack this difficult problem in two quite different ways. One way, set out in the following chapter, is focusing on artificial intelligence. The other, set out in this chapter, is focusing on how functionally rational seasoned politicians navigate the complex world of government formation using decision rules and heuristics. None of these politicians, to our knowledge, has ever given up trying to form a government – giving up the biggest prize in the political game – because the problem is difficult and/or deductively intractable. Complex wheeling and dealing is what seasoned politicians do for a living. They do this using sophisticated rules of behavior that, over the course of their careers, they have found to serve them well. In this chapter, therefore, we model interactions between senior politicians who rely on *behavioral* decision rules and heuristics to make key decisions, as opposed to *theoretical* best-response strategies derived from a formal model deductively resolved using backward induction.

When we focus in this way on human behavior, we model the political world from the bottom up. Traditional formal models of government formation, in contrast, model the world from the top down – from the god-like perspective of an omniscient analyst. Recall from Chapter 1 how human delivery drivers behave on the ground when faced with the intractable problem of finding the shortest route between 100 addresses. They use heuristics that cannot be proved to be the *best* solution to their problem but work pretty well in most circumstances. Untold millions of parcels are delivered successfully every day, notwithstanding the deductive intractability of the problem. Human politicians engaged in the intractable problem of government formation almost certainly behave in the same way. Having learned from experience that the perfect is the enemy of the good, they develop heuristics to navigate the difficult process of government formation toward a good outcome for themselves.

We therefore consider heuristics that functionally rational seasoned politicians might use when trying to form governments in high-dimensional issue spaces. Our behavioral model of government formation takes the difficult institutional environment set out in Chapter 2 and explores what happens when functionally rational politicians navigate this using the behavioral rules we set out in this chapter. This approach has come to be known as agent-based modeling. Agent-based models (ABMs) are typically exercised computationally. The essence of agent-based modeling is not computation, however, which is simply a method. It is bottom-up modeling of the interaction of agents using decision-making heuristics of some kind. Indeed, one of the seminal ABMs – of housing segregation – was originally exercised physically on a large checkerboard (Schelling 1971).

We use the ABM of government formation that we develop in this chapter for two quite different intellectual tasks. The first is essentially theoretical. Our formal model maps key inputs into outcomes of substantive interest. In our case, inputs include issue positions and seat shares of the legislative parties. A key outcome of analytical interest is the partisan composition of the cabinet likely to emerge from the process of government formation. The model, when it maps theoretical relationships between inputs and outputs, allows us to make sound predictions about outputs, conditional on inputs. How much does a lower seat share, or a more extreme position on key issues, affect a party's chances of being a member of the government that eventually forms? Our core aim in doing this is to *understand* government formation a little better. Obviously, this is a key motivation for all good theorists.

The second task is essentially *empirical*. Our model, by design, makes predictions about real-world government formation. Predictions, of course, can be of immense practical use. If we systematically out-predict the market on the share price of Tesla in a year's time, then we can become very rich by going long or short on Tesla stock. The *scientific* reason to make predictions is not to become very rich, how-ever, but to evaluate the accuracy and utility of the models that make the predictions. As it happens, social scientists almost never use their models to make what most civilians think of as *predictions* – which concern what will happen in the future. Instead, social scientists typi-cally "predict history." In our case, actual government formations are rather rare. This means we would have to wait a long time to observe a large enough number of government formations to allow us to make reliable statistical inferences about the quality of our model. We're interested in about twenty-five parliamentary democracies, which on average have a government formation every couple of years – some more frequently while some less. If we make predictions now and wait for history to unfold, it will be 10 years before we have a sample of 125 observations.

Fortunately, we already have easy access to the past thirty years' worth of government formations in the same set of countries. Some might think we are cheating if we "predict" what we already know. Scholars call this "curve fitting." We do not do this. Rather, we use an approach now standard in machine learning. We split our historical data into "training" and "test" sets. We use the training set to both exercise our model theoretically and calibrate key model parameters, in particular those that are fundamentally unobservable empirically. We then set aside our training set and use our calibrated model to make empirical predictions for the "out-of-sample" test sets that played no part whatsoever in calibrating the model. Comparing model predic-tions with observed outcomes, the success rate of our out-of-sample model predictions helps us evaluate the usefulness of the model itself. In this way, we apply standard scientific methods to the social science problem of evaluating theoretical models of government formation. This process, while more involved than most theoretical and empirical enterprises in the social sciences, allows us to have confidence that our model of government formation is not simply logically true but also has something to say about real-world government formation.

In Chapter 2, we set out our baseline model of the governance cycle in parliamentary democracies. This specifies:

- the institutional environment for the governance cycle;
- key decision-makers and their utility functions;
- three core phases of the governance process, repeated endlessly: government formation, government survival, elections; government formation ...

In what follows, we discuss how functionally rational senior politicians might use behavioral decision rules and heuristics in this environment during their negotiations over government formation and survival. When we populate the environment described in Chapter 2 with politicians using well-specified decision rules and heuristics, we have built an ABM of the governance process.

How to Choose from an Infinite Number of Possible Heuristics?

There is no single correct answer to the question of which particular decision rules to select, from the infinite number of possibilities, for the modeling of any decision problem. Viewed under a high-powered microscope, every human on the planet attacks the same problem in a slightly different way. As we saw in Chapter 2 when discussing the TSP, the very fact the problem is intractable means there is no way to *prove* that some particular decision rule for navigating this is "best" in every context. The heuristics of interest to us concern human behavior, so our initial criterion must be behavioral. Does this particular decision rule reflect the behavior we observe, or might reasonably expect to observe, in real humans?

As a directly relevant example, consider how party leaders might choose other party leaders with whom to negotiate over government formation. They might write the names of the other leaders on slips of paper, arrange these in a circle, spin a bottle, and negotiate with the leader chosen by the bottle. They might sort the names of the other

parties in alphabetical order and start with the first (or last) party on
the list. They might sort other parties in size order and start with the
first (or last) party on the list. They might only negotiate with other
leaders of the same height. Or they might sort other parties in terms of
the similarity of their members' preferences on the important issues of
the day, approaching the leaders of the parties with the most similar
preferences.[33]

These are all rules for picking coalition partners. We can choose
between them in three quite different ways. Assuming they would tell
us the truth, we could ask past and present party leaders who have
been involved in coalition negotiations how they picked their partners.
Most politicians who engage with us would probably tell us the truth
as they see it, but many might not even be consciously aware of the
precise rules they use to choose actions. On a more pragmatic level,
this method is unlikely to succeed because elite surveys of senior politicians have woefully low response rates – so much so that those politicians who do condescend to respond to inquisitive political scientists
are wildly unrepresentative.

A second approach to evaluating behavioral rules is to conduct a computer "tournament" that pits decision rules against each
other, observing which rules perform best in the tournament. This
approach was famously pioneered by Axelrod for Prisoners' Dilemma
(PD) games and adapted by Fowler and Laver for party competition (Axelrod 1980a, 1980b, Axelrod and Hamilton 1981, Axelrod
1997, Hoffmann 2000, Fowler and Laver 2008). The essence of this
approach is that state-of-the-art practitioners in the field are asked to
submit decision rules that they expect to be successful in navigating a
well-specified problem. These rules are then pitted against each other
in a computer simulation and scored in terms of their success. The
highest scoring rule is the winner. The winning rule is not the *provably* best rule for the setting at hand and may even be provably *not* the
best rule (Binmore 1998). It is simply the best rule *in the tournament*,
the context of which is defined by the finite set of other submissions.
But if the people submitting rules to the tournament are all experts in
the field, as they arguably were in Axelrod's tournaments, then the

---

[33] It is also plausible that historical interactions might play a role in who negoti-
ates with whom. We do not account for history in this way given our desire to
build a general model of government formation. Case-specific details, like the
prior electoral history, are an interesting avenue for extending our research.

winning rule is at least the best of those submitted by experts – which is by no means nothing.

PD tournaments have been repeated numerous times since Axelrod's work, for the most part appealing to computer scientists interested in computational intelligence. An issue that has arisen with these has been the extraordinary success of "teams" of decision rules – an approach pioneered by computer scientists from the University of Southampton. Members of the same team "sign on" to the game with a distinctive sequence of initial moves, so that each can recognize the others. Using a handshaking approach, whenever the designated leading member of the team meets other members, the leader defects and the followers cooperate (Rogers, et al. 2007). The leader consequently makes huge profits and wins the tournament. The lesson that cooperating teams can very successfully navigate PD-like settings is an important one – it may well underlie the essential logic of both political parties and organized crime syndicates. For our purposes, however, we already noted that we take political parties as given and our model will focus on decision-making by individual party leaders or their proxies, not on teams of politicians.

In order to run a computational tournament such as this, we would need a well-specified game with a robust computational implementation – both of which we have built here. But, we would also need a set of expert practitioners to submit rival decision rules. This existed for the PD game at the time of the Axelrod tournaments and to a lesser extent for the Fowler–Laver tournament. It does not yet exist for the governance cycle we model here. While we by no means rule out the possibility of informative computer tournaments in the future, we are not currently in a position to run one.

This leaves the third general method for selecting decision rules to model, which is to work from first principles. Thinking about the environment described in Chapter 2, there are four key decision points for politicians engaged in government formation. They need to consult their decision rules at each of these points. The first decision is to pick potential partners in government. The second is to propose a new coalition, c. This involves proposing a vector of perks shares between parties, g_c, and a vector of proposed cabinet policies on salient issues, p_c. Parties receiving nonzero perks are the partners in the proposed governing coalition. The third decision point affects these parties' inclusion in the proposed coalition. No party can be forced into government against its will, so actors can unilaterally veto any proposal that involves them. Nonvetoed proposals for government are put to the legislature. The fourth decision point involves party leaders deciding whether to support a proposed new government or to retain the *status quo*. A decision rule for politicians engaged in government formation involves specifying a course of action at each of these four decision points.

In what follows, we begin by specifying what we take to be a "natural" program of action at each decision point. This is based on our own reading of the literature, both formal and informal, on government formation. The result is but one of very many possible sets of decision rules, and our modeling architecture is open enough to implement any of these. We start with what we take to be reasonable and uncontroversial rules, in tune with existing work, however, so we can specify and analyze a baseline model upon which we and others may subsequently build.[34] The rules we, or anyone else, might choose to investigate in no sense exhaust the range of possibilities. We can, however, gain some encouragement that we have made appropriate choices if the decision rules deployed in our model generate accurate predictions of outcomes in the real world – a matter to which we return in Chapter 6.

The "Reversion Point" in the Event of Failed Government Formation

Before we specify negotiating politicians' behaviors at various decision points, we must specify what they expect to happen if bargaining fails and no new government wins legislative approval. This outcome is usually referred to as the "reversion point" of government formation and is specified as one of the rules of the game. This is a crucial assumption for all bargaining models, and the intuition is straightforward. The deals that decision-makers will approve depend critically on what happens if bargaining fails and no deal is reached. Most existing government formation models have a reversion point, whether this is explicit or implicit, of zero for all players. No one gets anything at all

---

[34] Of course, human behavior also evolves. For example, social media have radically transformed how humans, including human politicians, interact with each other. There is no "one true set" of decision rules for us to investigate.

unless a government is formed. Once a government is formed, payoffs are distributed instantaneously and everyone goes to the beach. This does not, however, reflect the endlessly cycling process of governance outlined in Figure 2.2.

As we noted in Chapter 2, the binding constitutional rule in the event of a failure of the government formation process is unambiguous. The incumbent prime minister continues in office, albeit in a "caretaker" capacity, until replaced by a new prime minister. No parliamentary democracy is ever left without any government at all, with the doors of government buildings swinging in the breeze. *Constitutionally*, therefore, the reversion point, *R*, for the government formation process in parliamentary democracies is the incumbent government.

Behaviorally, however, there is a persuasive argument that negotiating politicians should look forward to the ultimate possibility of new elections in the event of chronic failure to form a government. This is provided for in the process outlined in Figure 2.2 and means that the ultimate reversion point is a new election, rather than indefinite continuation of the caretaker incumbent. As noted in Chapter 2, we model such elections as unbiased random shocks to the *status quo* seat vector and do not model any endogenous evolution of party policy positions between elections. This implies that, in expectation, the outcome of a new election would result in a new government formation process with identical parameters to those of the current government formation process, with the same reversion point. In this context, considering the possibility of new elections in the event of a failure of the government process does not change the constitutionally binding rule that the reversion point is either the incumbent government or a new government identical to this in expectation.

While, *constitutionally*, the outgoing incumbent government continues in a caretaker capacity until replaced, most scholars agree that *in practice* a caretaker cabinet typically has much less freedom of action than a freshly installed cabinet that is identical in all other respects (Laver and Shepsle 1994). Cabinet ministers remain in office as caretakers to keep the machinery of government ticking over, but are explicitly or implicitly constrained constitutionally to maintain the policy *status quo* and refrain from significant policy initiatives. The autonomy of any cabinet portfolio, and hence value to its holder, is significantly discounted in a caretaker cabinet. In Chapter 2, we specified the utility of cabinet *c* for politician *i* as

$$U_{ci} = \alpha\left(g_{ci}\right) + \left(1-\alpha\right)\left(\sum s_{ij} * 1_{p_{ij}=p_{cj}}\right)$$

where g_{ci} measures party i's share of the perks of office, p_{ij} measures party i's preferred (binary) policy position on issue j, p_{cj} measures the cabinet's position on issue j, and α_i measures the relative importance for i of perks and policy. In words, actors derive utility from gaining as many perks as possible and by minimizing the policy distance between themselves and the other members of their coalition c. We now clarify that U_{ci} refers to a freshly installed cabinet after an election. The reversion point, R, for a caretaker cabinet, has a utility for each negotiating politician of

$$U_{Ri} = \theta\alpha\left(g_{Ri}\right) + \left(1-\alpha\right)\left(\sum s_{ij} * 1_{p_{ij}=p_{Rj}}\right)$$

where θ ($0 < \theta < 1$) is a country-specific parameter measuring the extent to which being a caretaker cabinet minister is less valuable than being a freshly installed incumbent of exactly the same portfolio. Note that, *for parties which are not cabinet members*, the reversion utility, R, is identical to that of an otherwise identical cabinet. Parties outside the cabinet have no perks utility to be discounted, while the constitutional norm is that caretaker cabinets maintain the policy *status quo*. For parties that are members of the caretaker cabinet, however, the reversion utility R sees the value of perks reduced by a factor of $(1 - \theta)$ compared to an otherwise identical cabinet. Cabinet ministers in caretaker cabinets, as opposed to other politicians, are substantially better off if the caretaker cabinet is explicitly reinstalled as the new incumbent.

Having specified the reversion point, R, for failed government formation negotiations, we can now specify a decision heuristic for negotiating politicians. We do this by specifying the actions this indicates at each of the key decision points identified earlier.

A Greedy Proposal Heuristic for Government Formation

We set out here to be as systematic and modular as we can when describing programs of action, which from now on we call decision rules. For example, consider decision rules for formulating proposals for new governments. We can think of three basic modules in this class of rules: (1) find potential coalition partners, (2) propose a joint issue position, and (3) propose an allocation of cabinet portfolios.

Picking Partners in Government

One possible rule for picking potential coalition partners focuses on the anticipated complex *policy* negotiations involved in forming a government, which as we know from empirical observation can take weeks or even months:

min-distance: using some measure of inter-party proximity on issue positions, pick coalition partners in order of the proximity to you, adding partners until the combined seat share of the proposed coalition exceeds the winning threshold (typically, 50 percent).

Another rule for picking partners focuses on the perks of office assuming that, according to Gamson's law, these will ultimately be shared in proportion to the seat shares of the parties in government:

min-size: pick coalition partners such that the combined seat share of the proposed coalition exceeds, but is as close as possible to, the winning threshold.

A third rule for picking partners might favor incumbency, using the "ain't broke, don't fix it" approach to cracking the complex problem of government formation in multiparty systems. This is based on the "win-stay, lose shift" logic set out in the following section.

win-stay: If you are a member of the incumbent government, and the seat share of the government parties exceeds the winning threshold, pick the incumbent coalition.

None of these potential rules for picking coalition partners is pulled out of thin air. Each is derived from an empirical literature that describes government formation in the real world.[35] In this sense, the specification of functionally rational decision rules is a formalization of informally observed empirical regularities in human decision-making behavior. As is clear from the win-stay rule, it is also likely that different parties use different decision rules in different situations. We can, therefore, think of a "rule regime" which specifies: a set of different decision rules for attacking the same problem; and the circumstances in which each rule is likely to be used.

---

[35] This is a large literature, but for exemplars see Laver and Shepsle 1994, 1996b, Müller and Strøm 2000, Martin and Stevenson 2001, Bäck 2003, Strøm, et al. 2008, Spoon and Klüver 2017, Bowler, et al. 2021.

The heuristic we propose here to set the ball rolling is "greedy." It maximizes short-term gains at the current decision point, rather than looking into the future to determine whether the best short term move may be inferior in the longer term.[36] Greedy heuristics are typically easy to understand and generate fast decisions, in comparison to brute force techniques like backward induction. In many real settings where time is of the essence, a faster decision rule may beat a more computationally intensive and, therefore, slower rule, even if the slower rule is "better" in all other respects. It's no good being the world's most accurate gunslinger if you've been shot before you get your gun out of the holster. Greedy rules can be surprisingly successful – we saw this with the well-known nearest neighbor heuristic for delivery drivers. Furthermore, greedy heuristics may be attractive in complex and uncertain settings in which forward-looking strategizing may be impractical, for decision-makers with relatively short time horizons, and those forced to decide under time pressure. For example, office-seeking politicians may be motivated above all else to agree on a coalition *now*, setting aside any consequential future costs of doing this as too uncertain, or too difficult to calculate. Thus, we start with a greedy heuristic for government formation, in a modeling environment that can comprehend many different heuristics. While our greedy algorithm is both straightforward and computationally more efficient than backward induction, however, it is more elaborate than the behavioral rules typically used in ABMs and still requires substantial compute time, given the complexity of bargaining in this context.[37]

The logic of our behavioral model for proposing governments deploys a simple form of reinforcement learning. We first

---

[36] There are, of course, examples where party leaders explicitly consider the future in determining their coalition memberships. For example, the membership of the SPD voted in 2018 on whether or not the party should join Merkel's coalition government. A feature of the intraparty campaigns was a debate about the future of the SPD and concomitant effects of continuing as a junior partner of Merkel's government compared to the immediate payoff of joining the government.

[37] Obviously, current electronic computers are still far less efficient than most human brains, while "substantial" compute time today will hopefully be the blink of an eye in the future. That said, there are examples in the literature of actors using computationally intensive decision rules. Notable examples are Kollman, et al. 1992, 1998.

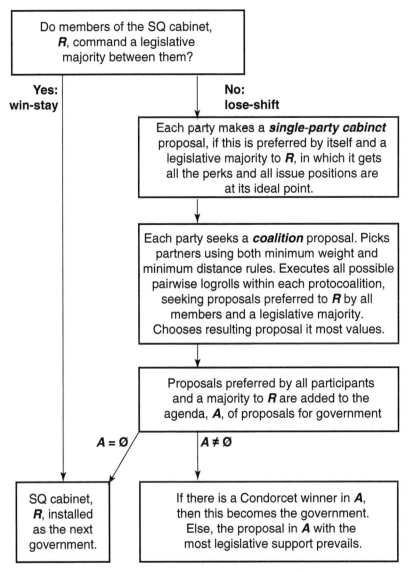

Figure 3.1 Flowchart of the government formation process, once triggered

summarize this as a flowchart in Figure 3.1, before describing it in greater detail.

Once the government formation process has been initiated by one of the triggers described in Figure 2.2, the first question concerns whether the incumbent government maintains its majority:

Win-stay. If you are a member of a *status quo* government that "wins" the election, in the sense its legislative seat share exceeds the winning threshold, then "stay": propose the *status quo* government.

If this is not the case, then "shift": consider alternative options. Assuming that party leaders expect proportional perks payoffs according to Gamson's law, this involves first picking new potential coalition partners and then negotiating an agreed government policy program.

Lose-shift phase 1: single-party search. Leaders of the largest parties explore the possibility of forming a single-party government which both they and a legislative majority prefer to the reversion point, R.

Lose-shift phase 2: coalition search. Party leaders broaden their search to consider various types of minimum winning coalition. In all cases, they eliminate from their consideration proposals that are worse for any proposed coalition member than the reversion point, R. (This takes account of the fact that all members of a proposed cabinet have an implicit veto over this. No party may be marched into the cabinet room against its will.) Since different parties have different values for α, they trade off the payoffs from agreed government policy and the distribution of perks in different ways. We therefore envisage two different rule regimes for this search for coalition partners:

alpha-branch. High-α party leaders like perks more than policy payoffs; they, therefore, use the **min-size** rule to search for minimum weight winning coalitions. Low-α leaders care more about policy than perks and use the **min-distance** rule to search for coalitions that minimize policy differences. In both cases, parties identified as members of the proposed coalition **logroll** to find a policy vector. Logrolling identifies all possible pair-wise trades that increase the utility of all coalition members.

best-rule. Given the complexity of the bargaining environment and the difficulty of determining which rule to use to pick coalition partners, party leaders use both **min-size** and **min-distance**, submitting the proposal they most prefer, if this is also preferred to the status quo by all its members and by a legislative majority.

Proposing an Allocation of Government Perquisites

As we have noted on several occasions, we assume that seasoned politicians are familiar with the extraordinary robustness of Gamson's law (Gamson 1961, Browne and Frendreis 1980, Laver and Schofield 1998a, Ansolabehere, et al. 2005, Warwick and Druckman 2006, Cutler, et al. 2014). We assume this pervasive proportionality norm to be what amounts to "folk wisdom" among negotiating politicians. It may also be a common expectation among both rank and file party members and voters, with real force in constraining bargaining (Martin and Vanberg 2020, Cox 2021). Understood in terms of our account of government formation, complex high-dimensional policy negotiations can proceed more smoothly if negotiators accept that, when it comes to allocating cabinet portfolios after a joint policy program has finally been agreed, these portfolios will be allocated proportionately. Abiding by this norm means that tortuous policy negotiations do not fall apart at the last minute because of a squabble over portfolio shares.[38]

Party leaders, therefore, expect that, at the end of complex government formation negotiations, the numerical distribution of perks will be in proportion to party sizes. A possible extension of the model would allow the allocation of perquisites also to be a matter for unconstrained negotiation. Our preliminary investigations of such a model, however, suggest it generates endlessly cycling results, in essence because it reduces the portfolio allocation component of government formation to a divide-the-dollar game. Behaviorally, it seems likely that real negotiating politicians understand this very well, offering another intuition about why experienced and ambitious politicians seem reconciled to proportional perks allocations.

Making Policy Proposals

The essence of generating a proposal for government, therefore, is not simply allocating perks but finding a successful policy compromise. We assume the leaders of the larger parties begin this process by investigating the feasibility of forming a single-party minority government – in which they would control all of the cabinet portfolios.

When party leaders investigate the feasibility of forming *single-party minority governments*, they start from the position that the best possible outcome is to control all the perks *and* to implement their ideal policy on every single issue. Obviously, if a single-party controls a majority of legislators, then it can make this proposal and succeed. Where our model differs from the mainstream is what we assume happens when

[38] Or, alternatively, that a prior agreement on perks allocation won't be unpicked during subsequent policy negotiations.

no party controls a majority, which is that party leaders first investigate the possibility of a minority government giving them all portfolios and their ideal policy on every issue. Anticipating an upcoming vote in the legislature, party leaders only make such a proposal if it is preferred by a legislative majority to the reversion point, *R*.

Party leaders will often be unable to form a single-party minority cabinet such as this. In this event, we assume they seek to form a coalition cabinet by *logrolling an agreed issue vector* with the proto-coalition identified by the behavioral rules for picking partners. We model the process of logrolling an agreed issue vector with a particular proto-coalition of other parties as looking for pairs of issues where trades can occur. We do not, therefore, model more complex logrolls involving "unbalanced" trades (such as a two-for-one trade of issues).

A more precise description of these rules for picking coalition partners and generating proposed cabinets is in Technical Appendix A3, including a simplified version of the algorithm in pseudo code in Figure A3.2. Two features of these decision rules are worth highlighting. First, each party leader may submit a proposal, raising the possibility that several simultaneous proposals are on the agenda. This amounts to assuming an "open-outcry" regime for making proposals for government, rather than an exogenously imposed sequencing of these. Unlike most recent models of government formation, we assume a setting in which any party leader can make a proposal and in which they are not artificially constrained, for the sake of tractability, to consider only one proposal at a time. Second, party leaders have a right to *veto* any proposal for a cabinet in which they are members. If they prefer the *status quo*, they cannot somehow be *compelled* to join a new coalition. Given the possibility of multiple proposals, by construction all preferred by some legislative majority to the *status quo R*, how do party leaders choose which proposal to support?

Choosing between Proposed Governments

How do legislators compare multiple proposals for government with each other and with the discounted status quo, *R*? There is an *agenda*, *A*, of possible governments, comprising *R* and the list of proposed new coalition cabinets. Given the heuristics for picking coalition partners and making policy proposals set out above, however, and the requirement that any proposal must be not only majority preferred by the legislature but also preferred by all its coalition members to **R** and, therefore, not vetoed, the resulting agenda of proposals is likely to be short.

Traditional bargaining models in political science often assume that negotiators are selected to make proposals by some exogenous automaton, with a probability that is either flat or proportional to party seat shares (Rubinstein 1982, Baron and Ferejohn 1989, Baron 1991, Ansolabehere, et al. 2005, Snyder, et al. 2005). As the authors of such models would be the first to admit, this assumption is a convenient analytical device but is by no means an empirically realistic description of the world. Perhaps not so obvious, however, is that assumptions such as this sharply constrain the sophistication of the behavior of party leaders, in effect forcing them to be far less "rational" than they might be. They cannot consider more than one offer nor do they have any strategic role in the order in which proposals appear on the agenda.

Unlike many other types of bargaining to which such models might be applied, government formation is the biggest game in the political universe. This means that, even if there does happen to be some explicit formal protocol for selecting people to make proposals for government, as for example in Greece, the *realpolitik* of negotiating a new government is extraordinarily unlikely to be bound by any rigid rule that tells seasoned politicians when they can and can't make proposals.

An excellent example of this unfolded after the British Labour government under Prime Minister Gordon Brown lost its majority in the general election of May 6, 2010. The constitutional convention, asserted by Edward Heath in similar circumstances in February 1984, was that the incumbent PM was entitled to the first attempt to form a new government. However, Conservative leader David Cameron blindsided Brown on prime time TV, at a news conference where he looked straight into camera and announced a "big open offer" to form a coalition cabinet with the Liberal Democrats. Notwithstanding ongoing backroom negotiations between senior Labour and Liberal Democrat politicians, and the fact that Liberal Democrat policy positions were on most accounts closer to Labour than to the Conservatives, this unscheduled and unexpected public offer, not part of any government formation protocol, set terms which Brown felt unable to counter. He resigned. Frantic negotiations between Conservatives and Lib Dems resulted in a new coalition cabinet, the first formal coalition in Britain since World War II.

It therefore seems to us eminently reasonable to assume that, when it comes to government formation, *any party leader can make any proposal to anyone at any time*. We assume that all party leaders may make proposals in accordance with the decision rules set out above and that these proposals all appear on the government formation agenda. Given this agenda of proposals, *A*, we assume that the real politics of government formation takes place away from the public gaze, in what was once called a smoke-filled room but in these non-smoking times we can think of as "backstage" – *dans les coullisses* is the French term precisely describing this. Our assumptions about the backstage politics of government formation are as follows.

- If some proposed cabinet c^* $\in$ *A* is majority preferred to every other alternative in *A*, then this prevails and becomes the new government. (Note that c^* has already survived the participant veto stage.) The government is the Condorcet winner *among the restricted set of proposals* in *A*.
- Else, there is a cycle of proposals. For every proposal c $\in$ *A* in the cycle, there is another proposal c' $\in$ *A* which is majority preferred to c.

These assumptions do not describe any politics we can actually observe, but what implicitly happens inside the black box of backstage politics.

From the above, it is possible that no new proposal is preferred by the legislature to the reversion point *R*. We do not regard a model prediction of no new government forming as a failure. On the contrary, we regard it as an important observation about the government formation setting in question. Empirically, of course, most government formations processes do not cycle endlessly. Most cycles are broken when a government is chosen by some exogenous and possibly arbitrary means outside the model (e.g., a new election). But the possibility that a government was imposed by exogenous means, not selected autonomously by the legislature, is clearly significant. Absent detailed knowledge of local "cycle-busting" mechanisms, we make the "brute force" assumption that, *ceteris paribus*, the alternative in *A* (including *R*) with the most legislative support is the most likely to succeed – even if it is part of a cycle.

Completing Our Model of Government Formation

Our baseline model of government formation in high-dimensional issue spaces takes the institutional environment set out in Chapter 2 and populates this with the functionally rational agents described above in this chapter, using the above agenda rule for choosing between proposals.[39] This generates an ABM of government formation which we express in Python code and exercise computationally in Chapter 5, before using it to make empirical predictions in Chapter 6. As shown in Figure 2.2, our model of the government formation process is in effect the logical engine of the entire system. Our black box model of elections feeds into it. Our model of government survival depends on a continual re-evaluation by legislators, following random shocks, of decisions they made on government formation. We now turn to these matters.

Elections as Unbiased Random Shocks to Seat Shares

We model legislative elections at time t as a black box that administers unbiased random shocks to the vector of party seat shares (w_{t-1}) that resulted from an election at $t-1$. The description of elections in terms of unbiased random shocks may raise a few eyebrows. We therefore pause to re-emphasize the distinction between "case-based" models that are empirically calibrated to make precise predictions in some specific setting and "comparative" models calibrated to make general statements, on average, about general classes of cases – which is our concern here. *In some particular case,* politicians may have public or private information that, for example, public opinion is systematically trending in some specific way. If we wish to make predictions precisely calibrated to this case, therefore, we can model a potential future election in terms of shocks to existing seat shares that have anticipated *biases* toward or away from particular parties. We have no expectation of *systemic* electoral biases, however, across the entire universe of cases to which we address our model. Further, we assume that functionally rational politicians will, at the moment they support some proposed government, *take into account any future systematic change*

---

[39] This agenda rule is not a constitutionally binding feature of the environment, but in effect a shared norm or convention used by seasoned politicians to determine when backstage negotiations have reached a conclusion.

which can reasonably be anticipated. It is, therefore, *unanticipated* unbiased shocks that destabilize equilibrium governments.

We therefore model functionally rational politicians' expectations of a potential future election result at t as a new seat vector w_t generated by adding Gaussian noise to each element in w_{t-1}. Specifically, for each element in w_{t-1}, we draw a shock term from a normal distribution with a mean of zero and a standard deviation of σ_i. The parameter σ_i measures the expected size of the unbiased electoral shock to seat shares for party i. In our Monte Carlos, we calibrate σ_i to the observed mean standard deviation in party seat shares in postwar Europe. Finally, we linearly rescale parties' shocked seat shares at t to sum to unity. Interestingly, σ_i across all cases have a very similar value and is equal to $\sim.87(w_{i,t-1})$. That is, the variance of the shock is a fixed function of the number of seats the party had at time $t-1$.

Our open computational architecture allows others who might think that electoral shocks are systematically biased in some precisely specified way, or of alternative distributions of such shocks, to substitute their own assumptions and explore the effect of these. Our approach, following economic intuition about efficient markets, is to assume that, at the moment of government formation, politicians take into account everything which can possibly be anticipated. We therefore treat events which cannot be anticipated, and which potentially destabilize incumbent governments, as unbiased Gaussian noise.

Modeling Government Survival

Most political activity in the real world takes place between the moment a government is born and the moment it dies. During this period, any incumbent government must survive in a more or less hostile environment. Governments survive in parliamentary democracies by maintaining the support of a majority of legislators. There is a substantial scholarly literature modeling government survival as the incumbent's ability to withstand unanticipated shocks. This empirical research program is based on survival analyses, using Poisson regressions and independent variables culled from the scholarly literature, to predict observed government durations – the latter "censored" by the constitutionally mandated maximum interelection period (Browne, et al. 1986a, 1986b, King, et al. 1990, Diermeier and Stevenson 1999, Diermeier and Merlo 2000, Diermeier and Stevenson 2000, Laver

2003, Chiba, et al. 2015). A smaller theoretical literature, which informs our argument in this chapter, models how unanticipated shocks to the expectations of legislative parties change their incentives to support the incumbent government. Most shocks leave these incentives intact. Some, however, provoke a renegotiation between the existing partners in government. Bigger shocks may be too serious to be resolved by such renegotiation, bringing down the incumbent government because a majority of legislators now prefer some alterative (Lupia and Strom 1995, Diermeier and Stevenson 2000, Smith 2004).

As we noted previously, Laver and Shepsle discuss four different types of shocks that potentially destabilize incumbent governments (Laver and Shepsle 1998). Our model deploys two of these. The first are preference shocks, which change preferred issue positions and may undermine legislators' preferences about the incumbent government's agreed policy program. The second are agenda shocks, such as pandemics or hurricanes, which change issue saliences and may force issues up the policy agenda. Return to the model of the governance cycle sketched in Figure 2.2: Both preference and agenda shocks can destabilize an incumbent government.

Preference Shocks

As already noted, an excellent example of shocks that change legislators' policy preferences happened during the COVID-19 pandemic, during which many politicians were forced to change their minds about the desirability of huge constraints on individual liberty, or vast injections of public money into the private sector. In the specific context of our model, such preference shocks may perturb any of our key preference parameters, dealing with: issue positions, p_{ij}; issue saliences, s_{ij}; trade-offs between perks and policy payoffs, α_i; and tolerance of tabled issues, τ_i. These shocks may sufficiently change the utility calculus of some legislators – whether in or out of government – to the extent they now prefer some alternative to the incumbent. They may also undermine the detailed logroll that underpins the incumbent's agreed policy program.

The technology to measure the potential effect of preference shocks is an integral part of our computational experiments, described in detail in Chapter 5. Briefly, for $r = 1,000$ repetitions for each case, we apply parameterized Gaussian shocks to each of the key preference parameters listed above. We then observe the proportion, Φ_P, of preference shocks that cause the model to generate a predicted government, *which is different from the incumbent.* The higher the proportion of predicted alternatives to the incumbent, the more vulnerable we expect this incumbent to be to preference shocks.

Agenda Shocks and Tabled Issues

As we have already seen, governments do not need to make decisions on every conceivable issue. Partners in government, therefore, may agree to disagree on contentious issues and still go into government together. In Chapter 2, we described politicians as "tabling" such issues during government formation negotiations. Agenda shocks result from random events – such as earthquakes, hurricanes, and pandemics. Such shocks push issues, including tabled issues, up the political agenda without necessarily changing politicians' preferences on these issues. They may, therefore, force partners in government to make potentially divisive policy decisions which they have previously chosen to avoid. For example, pandemics force governments to make hard choices balancing disease control against economic activity – as many incumbents painfully discovered during the course of the coronavirus pandemic in 2020. Partners in government may differ fundamentally about this trade-off while managing to govern amicably together if not forced to confront it. An economic shock, pandemic, or war, utterly unforeseen when the partners agreed a joint program, can generate an agenda shock exposing a deep rift in the government coalition.

No other scholar, to our knowledge, has explicitly modeled the effect of agenda shocks. The model of government formation we set out here explicitly incorporates these, however, taking into account the possibility that politicians can table issues on which they agree to disagree. The expected policy loss for politician i arising from tabling any given issue in an agreed joint policy program is τ_i ($0 < \tau_i < 1$). For extremely "optimistic" or risk-tolerant politicians who expect no policy loss to arise from tabling an issue, $\tau_i \approx 0$. For extremely "pessimistic" or risk averse politicians who expect tabled issues to turn out badly and generate the maximum policy loss, $\tau_i \approx 1$.

The hypothetical example set out in Table 3.1 shows how an agenda shock might destabilize an incumbent government. The leaders of

Table 3.1 *Two partners in government table contentious issues in their joint program*

		Issue #							
Party		1	2	3	4	5	6	7	8
A	*Salience*	H	H	H	L	L	L	H	H
	Position	0	1	0	1	0	1	0	1
B	*Position*	1	0	1	0	1	0	1	0
	Salience	L	L	L	H	H	H	H	H
AB deal	*Position*	0	1	0	0	1	0	T	T

two parties, A and B, have negotiated a joint program with agreed positions on eight issues. The binary issue positions of each party are shown as 0 or 1. A simplified representation of the relative saliences of each issue for each party are shown as high (H) or low (L).

To make things clear in this extreme example, the two parties have opposing positions on *every* issue. They can still agree to a joint deal, however, since they have perfectly complementary saliences on issues 1–6. They trade positions on these six issues, in each case, agreeing on the position of the party which values the issue the most. They conclude the deal by agreeing to disagree on issues 7 and 8, tabling these (T) in their joint program. The final agreed joint program is the "AB deal" shown in Table 3.1. Politicians in Party A get policy loss τ_A for each of the two tabled issues; politicians in Party B get τ_B. Despite starting government formation negotiations *disagreeing on every salient issue*, the parties' complementary issue saliences allow them to logroll, *subject to tabling issues 7 and 8*. This deal may be preferred both by them, and by a legislative majority, to any alternative. Parties A and B, therefore, go into government together with a program (0, 1, 0, 0, 1, 0, T, T). This is the essence of our model of government formation.

Our model explicitly describes what happens following an agenda shock that forces a tabled issue onto the government agenda. Instead of an *anticipated* payoff of τ_i ($0 < \tau_i < 1$) for each party, in or out of government, there is now a *realized* payoff of 0 or 1, depending on the particular exigencies of the shock. Say the realized outcome is 0. This is *better* than τ_i for all politicians whose preference on this issue is 0, and *worse* than τ_i for all politicians whose preference is 1.[40] The converse is true if the realized outcome is 1. Crucially, an agenda shock forces politicians to take a position on an issue tabled in the joint program, on which they must have opposing views. *This will always make at least one of the partners in government worse off.* As a result, the partners in government and/or a majority of legislators may no longer prefer the current joint program to any other. Considering the example in Table 3.1, imagine an agenda shock forces issue 7 onto the government agenda, with a realized outcome of 1. This gives a policy loss of 1, instead of τ_a (<1) to Party A, and may cause A to prefer some alternative government deal.

A particular agenda shock may not destabilize an incumbent government. The members may still prefer their existing deal, even after the previously tabled issue position, T, is realized as 0 or 1. However, a stream of agenda shocks cannot strengthen, and can only tend to destabilize, an incumbent government that has tabled issues in its joint program. A simple measure of vulnerability to agenda shocks is, therefore, the number, ϕ_A, of issues in the joint program that are tabled. The higher ϕ_A, the more vulnerable we expect the governing coalition c to be to agenda shocks.

A Model of the Overall Governance Process

We've now written down a model for each of the three phases of the governance process set out in Figure 2.2. These models are interlinked. The election model feeds into the formation model. The formation model feeds into the survival model. The survival model anticipates the new formation process that might be provoked by unanticipated random shocks to model parameters. In the real world, this is a never-ending and, indeed, evolving process. Our black box model of elections does not take inputs from prior government survival and formation phases, however. This allows us to take a first step toward modeling this complex process by treating an actual general election – a realized election shock – as setting in motion a chain of events that begins with government formation and continues into government support and survival, culminating with a random shock or constitutional mandate that triggers another election.

---

[40] Recalling that the policy components in legislators' utilities are negative.

4 | *Artificial Intelligence and Government Formation*

In Chapter 3, we specified an ABM of government formation and survival. We use an ABM to attack this problem because even seasoned and sophisticated politicians who wheel and deal for a living can't analytically "solve" the difficult game of forming a stable government in a high-dimensional issue space – and then maintaining this in office. Our ABM, as we have seen, works from the bottom up. We assume these seasoned politicians are functionally rational, so tackle intractable problems using tried, tested, and above all *implementable* decision heuristics. Having specified both a complex environment and the heuristics used by functionally rational agents to navigate this, the resulting ABM is resolved by *computationally* mapping key inputs into key outputs.

In this chapter, we set out an alternative, "top down," approach. We develop an AI algorithm to solve our analytically intractable game using what we can think of as computational game theory. While AI models have penetrated most aspects of daily life, from diagnosing cancers to powering remarkable video imagery, they have largely been ignored, to the best of our knowledge, by political scientists. Yet formidable successes by AI models in solving games like Chess, Go, and especially a bluffing game like Poker, suggest they also have the potential to attack difficult political games. Before developing our AI model of governance in what follows, however, we pause to consider the relative advantages of the ABM and AI approaches to modeling difficult social and political interactions.

ABM or AI?

The central problem of analyzing government formation in parliamentary democracies concerns how to model the *behavior* of each member of a set of negotiating politicians, given the complexity of bargaining simultaneously over perquisites and agreed high-dimensional joint issue positions. Mainstream scholarship within political science over the last few decades typically sidesteps this behavioral question, playing down individual behavior and radically simplifying the theoretical description of bargaining over government formation. This approach does help clarify what is at stake, who the key actors are, and the effect on political outcomes of simple parameterized features of the environment. But simplifying the game until it becomes deductively tractable has not, over the decades, produced an abundance of hypotheses about real-world government formation. Radical simplifications have come at the cost of external validity.[41]

One of the best-known empirical hypotheses the mainstream approach has generated to date, for example, deduces that the *formateur* (or "proposer") of a government – the person picked by some exogenous process to lead government formation negotiations – has substantial additional bargaining power. The problem with this is that it is nearly impossible in real-world settings to identify the *formateur ex ante*. Indeed, in the replication dataset for the main empirical study of the *formateur* effect (Ansolabehere, et al. 2005), 249 of the 250 people identified as *formateurs* came from the party of the eventual prime minister. What is clearly happening is that the experts and graduate students generating these data are using historical sources *ex post* to identify *formateurs* of *those governments which actually formed*. The consequence is that *formateur* status enters the analysis as simultaneously a cause and an effect, mechanically generating empirically significant findings, while "failed *formateurs*" are systematically under recorded. Even accepting these limitations, furthermore, empirical evidence for a *formateur* advantage essentially disappears once we control for party size (Laver, et al. 2011b, Cutler, et al. 2014).

The decisive argument for us, however, is substantive. On any reasonable empirical account of government formation, it seems to us

---

[41] Typically, concerns about external validity are raised about laboratory experiments (Jenke, 2022). For example, asking undergraduates to play war games may not tell researchers much about real-world leaders engaged in war, who have considerable experience, professional staffs, and play for enormous stakes. We believe the same concern should be raised about formal models. One can write any number of bargaining games, but without any mapping to actual bargaining by humans, it is difficult to distinguish between deductively true but empirically irrelevant models and the smaller set of models that actually tell us something about the real world.

self-evidently true that multiple proposals are simultaneously on the table, at the very least implicitly, in such high-stakes negotiations. It seems inconceivable that sophisticated, ruthless, and highly motivated politicians politely sit around doing nothing until they are handed the talking stick. Even if the public spotlight does happen to be focused on some designated *formateur*, it seems very naïve to deny the near certainty that, in private, in the shadows, other senior politicians are vigorously exploring the options.[42]

To make progress in this endeavor, we must address the issue of how, behaviorally, real negotiating politicians actually play the game.[43] In the last chapter, we proposed one possible solution: ABMs. It is important to note here that our approach to ABM differs substantially from the norm in the social science literature. Typically, the agents modeled in ABMs are endowed with very little computational ability. In the path-breaking work of Schelling, for example, the agents in his models of social segregation examine a handful of neighbors and rely on a simple condition to determine whether they stay put or move to another location. Our behavioral approach, while similar in spirit, characterizes much more sophisticated agents who have considerable computational power at their disposal. These actors look for policy or salience complementarity, make strategic comparisons to the *status quo* government, and search quite exhaustively for favorable coalitions. They are also able to logroll policies with possible coalition partners and compare multiple proposals simultaneously to determine which they prefer. The actors in our ABM are not "simple-minded." Rather, we feel they plausibly resemble experienced party leaders who have considerable resources, including staffs of subject matter experts, on hand (Keohane 1999).

There are, of course, limits to how exhaustive this search can be. Our model of logrolling, for example, confines trades to those involving pairs of issues. By far the largest constraint is the level of strategic

---

[42] An innovative model by Bassi (2013) does build on the possibility that senior politicians negotiate for the right to be *formateur*. Even on this account, however, the *formateur*, once chosen, has the exclusive right to make take it or leave it offers.

[43] Often, the literature offers a contrast between "rational choice" and "bounded rationality," where the former is seen as godlike and the latter as extremely limited. This is a false dichotomy. As noted in Chapter 3, the behavioral algorithm employed in rational choice models only works when the models are quite simple. Put another way, it does not scale to complex games.

behavior present in our ABM. The actors in our models are "greedy" and myopic, not looking forward to considering the best response of others to any proposal they might make, the best response to this ... and so on, *ad infinitum*. It seems reasonable to assume that many seasoned politicians are not as myopic as this and do take at least some account of potential actions by opponents when planning any actions they themselves might take.

In short, game-theoretic models allow for fully strategic actors, but at the cost of limiting the complexity of the game these actors are able to play. ABMs, in contrast, allow for more complex games, but depend heavily on nonstrategic assumptions about the behavior of negotiating politicians. In what follows, we set out an alternative in an attempt to get the best of both worlds – a complex model of a real-world problem that actors attack using AI. For games as complex as n-person Texas hold 'em poker, AI approaches have performed as well or better than expert human poker players (Billings, et al. 2003, Brown and Sandholm 2019).

The AI approach we develop below is very similar in ethos to traditional game theory in how it models strategic behavior. Games are specified using the traditional extensive form approach, though the size of the extensive forms that can be handled is huge. For the game detailed in Figure 2.2, for example, there has never been a piece of paper large enough to show the entire extensive form. Nonetheless, as we will now see, AI approaches can arrive at near-Nash solutions to such complex games by *sampling* from this gigantic extensive form.

Finally, we note that the AI model differs in two key respects from the ABM we developed in Chapter 3. The ABM, by virtue of its decision rules, focuses on whether or not the *status quo* government continues to command support after an election. The AI model, in contrast, ignores this fact and allows all actors to negotiate freely in each case. Where the ABM constrains offers to Gamsonian perk distributions, the AI model allows actors to propose any perk and policy distribution they wish. These are, obviously, important changes, and the AI model is more in keeping with a purely game-theoretic approach.

Monte Carlo Counterfactual Regret

As we noted above, a fatal obstacle to using traditional game-theoretic approaches to model the governance cycle is that the game set out in Figure 2.2 is too complex to resolve deductively. In what follows, therefore, we explore a computational approach to analyzing games using AI that has had great success in the last decade. This depends on the concept of Monte Carlo counterfactual regret (MCCFR). Behaviorally, in contrast to the simple humans typically assumed by ABMs, intelligent agents in this approach are modeled as "superhuman," in the sense that they can deal with the huge number of possibilities involved in bargaining over government formation. They can not only evaluate the *myopic* consequences of each of the huge number of possible actions involved in *n*-party bargaining over government formation, they can also evaluate the *strategic* implications of these actions.

MCCFR (along with Monte Carlo tree search) has emerged within the computer science community as the dominant algorithm for solving extensive form games with a finite set of decisions but a combinatorially intractable game tree (Lanctot, et al. 2009). An actor known as the *traverser* makes decisions in the game tree, initially according to a uniform probability distribution for each action. The game tree is *traversed* in this way a huge number of times and the outcome recorded. The traverser takes a *sample* of traversals of the extensive form game and uses the outcomes of each to update the probability of choosing each action, based on "regret." Regret is the difference between the payoff from the selected action and those from the alternative actions, evaluated according to a payoff function.

Essentially, traversers "learn" how to play the game. The more they play, the more they increase the probability of choosing better actions and reduce the probability of choosing worse actions. This learning continues until a near-optimal strategy is identified. At this point, even with massively repeated self-play, no better strategy can be identified by the algorithm. For two player games, this strategy converges to a Nash equilibrium for the traverser in substantially less time than it would take to iterate through every terminal node of a massive game tree. While MCCFR is not guaranteed to converge to a Nash equilibrium for games with more than two players except in special cases, it achieves high-quality "near-Nash" results and is the dominant AI technique for this type of problem (Johanson, et al. 2013).[44]

---

[44] A related algorithm is Monte Carlo tree search, which also has very good performance. We have implemented both algorithms and results are similar.

This simple algorithm has delivered state-of-the-art performance on otherwise intractable problems, such as poker. MCCFR also benefits in the degree to which expert knowledge can help the algorithm. Clever state encodings, reductions of the search space, and other heuristics can dramatically reduce the size of the tree without hurting performance and in many cases improving results (Waugh, et al. 2009). Also, unlike many other deep learning techniques, MCCFR is fast and relatively easy to train.

The logic of this approach is surprisingly straightforward and involves three main steps: *counterfactual regret*, *regret matching*, and *sampling*. Before getting into the details of each of these steps, it is important to keep in mind that the core of this approach is identical to that of noncooperative game theory. Scholars studying negotiations over government formation must specify:

i. The decisive *actors* in the model. In our case, these are the leaders (or their surrogates) of disciplined legislative parties.

ii. An extensive form game which captures the *actions* available to each actor as well as the *payoffs* for each on completion of the game, contingent on actions taken. As noted in previous chapters, these actions are making, vetoing, and voting on proposals for government. Payoffs derive from high-dimensional agreed government policy positions and allocations of cabinet portfolios (as perks) between parties.

iii. A utility function for each actor. In our case, this is a convex combination of perks received and the policy distance between party policy and the agreed program for government.

Unlike traditional approaches where a researcher solves deductively for equilibria (if they exist), with MCCFR we set up the game and then put the algorithm to work in finding near-Nash strategies for each player. We start with the counterfactual regret (CFR) component of this.

The algorithm plays the game multiple times, continually using information from prior iterations to learn how to improve its performance. To gain intuition about how this works, consider the simple game of rock-paper-scissors[45] with two players, Rachel and Ross,

---

[45] The rules of the rock-paper-scissors game are as follows. The two players simultaneously make a hand gesture signaling the choice of rock (closed fist), paper (open palm), and scissors (two fingers in scissors shape). The players win as follows. Rock beats (blunts) scissors. Paper beats (wraps) rock. Scissors beat (cut) paper. Obviously, therefore, there is no dominant pure strategy.

playing multiple times.[46] In each iteration of the game, Rachel and Ross both have a $1 stake. The winner takes both dollars; if the game is a tie they keep their stake.

At the start of the game, imagine Rachel randomly decides that her strategy (a probability distribution over the three possible actions of playing rock, paper, or scissors) is to always play rock – a probability distribution of (1, 0, 0). In the first iteration of the game, Ross plays paper. *CFR* is an evaluation of how happy a player is, at each information set in the game, compared to the alternative actions that might have been taken. Having lost a dollar, Rachel will clearly be unhappy after the last play. Consider her regret for having played rock, compared to the other actions that were available. If she had played paper, the game would have resulted in a tie and Rachel would not have lost a dollar. Even better, if she had played scissors, Rachel would have won a dollar. Compared to what she did play (rock), she has regrets of $1 for not playing paper and $2 for not playing scissors.

The second step tells Rachel what to do about her regret. *Regret matching* is a function that maps regret from the last iteration of the game into a new strategy for the next iteration. For rock-paper-scissors, which features only one action per player per iteration of the game, this function is quite simple. Rachel uses a mixed strategy with probabilities proportional to her regret from the first iteration of the game. Rock is played with probability 0/3, paper with 1/3, and scissors with 2/3. Clearly, this is better than her prior strategy of playing rock all of the time, but it's not yet an equilibrium solution to the game.[47]

For the next iteration of the game, imagine that Ross plays scissors and Rachel plays the mixed strategy of (0, 1/3, 2/3) and, after suitably randomizing, plays paper. Rachel's regret from this iteration of the game is $2 for not playing rock and $1 for not playing scissors. To determine her mixed strategy for the next play of the game, she looks at the *cumulative* totals of regret for each possible action to determine the probabilities she will select that action in the next iteration. Rachel now chooses rock with probability 2/6, paper with 1/6, and scissors

[46] This section follows the original research by Lanctot, et al. (2009) and the rock-paper-scissors example detailed in Neller and Lanctot (2013).

[47] We run the MCCFR algorithm until strategies deviate less than a fixed threshold. If strategies do not converge, the case is treated as one in which the reversion point is reached.

with 3/6. That is, she has a new mixed strategy of (1/3, 1/6, 3/6) for the third iteration of the game.[48] This is again an improvement over the last mixed strategy. If, the game is iterated many times, and if both Rachel and Ross use CFR to learn the best strategy as described above, the strategies of both will converge, with enough play, to the Nash equilibrium of (1/3, 1/3, 1/3).

CFR and regret matching taken together represent the vanilla CFR algorithm. While it is of course trivial to solve analytically for the Nash equilibrium in rock-paper-scissors, the point of this example is that the algorithm can learn the best strategy *without ever solving the complete game.*[49] This is obviously of crucial value for investigating games that cannot be solved deductively.

We have used the simple game of rock-paper-scissors to illustrate how CFR works, but the great advantage of this approach is when used on deductively intractable games. Deriving effective strategies in most real games, including the government formation process we set out in Figure 2.2, involves searching very large extensive game forms with many information sets and an unmanageable number of possible histories of play. When the extensive game is very large, we might try to apply the CFR algorithm as set out above and span every possible history of play, each iteration of the game. In addition to overwhelming even massive computational capacity, however, this is not the most efficient way to use inherently finite computational resources. Perhaps surprisingly, we can achieve better performance in most cases by *sampling* a single history of the game per player for each iteration, while iterating the game a very large number of times. This is the MCCFR algorithm, compared with CFR for a single iteration of the game in Figure 4.1. The left panel shows a vast number of naturally branching paths through a complex game, and the right panel shows a single path randomly sampled from these. The core point is that since computational budgets are always finite, it is in most cases a more

---

[48] This proportion is based on positive regret only and ignores negative regret. For example, when Rachel and Ross both choose scissors, both would have negative regret for the counterfactual action of choosing paper.

[49] Readers should feel free to compute this for themselves. In addition, it should also be clear that both players need to base their strategies on CFR and regret matching. If Ross never deviated from playing rock, for example, Rachel (following the above algorithm) would end up always playing paper (which is not Nash).

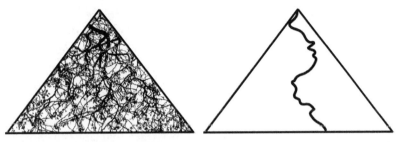

Figure 4.1 Histories of play considered by CFR and MCCFR for a single iteration of the game (from Schmid, et al. 2019)

efficient use of this finite computational budget to randomly sample one history from each of multiple iterations than to evaluate multiple histories from one iteration (Lanctot, et al. 2009, Gibson, et al. 2012).

We leave rock-paper-scissors behind; since each player has only one action in each iteration, no sampling needs to be performed. In other "small" games, we can also traverse the entire tree using CFR for each iteration of the game. However, for an extensive form as complicated as the government formation game we describe, using MCCFR to sample histories of the game at each iteration allows for much more computationally efficient analysis.[50]

Comparing MCCFR with Deductive Models and ABM

As we have noted, AI using MCCFR allows us to analyze our complex government formation game in much the same way as traditional noncooperative game theorists would approach the problem. The key difference is that, for games like this with a very large extensive form (many actions, many information sets, many possible histories), purely deductive approaches are overwhelmed. If theorists do not use an approach like MCCFR, then they must over-simplify games and are forced to draw tenuous analogies between the results of these games and real-world phenomena. MCCFR offers theorists the possibility of specifying more complex games, closer to the real-world phenomena of interest, and solving for near-Nash strategies using self-play.

---

[50] One can employ any sampling scheme by partitioning the set of terminal nodes in the extensive game. Commonly, researchers use outcome sampling, where this each terminal history is an element in this partition.

Behaviorally, however, relying on MCCFR asks quite a lot of human actors. They must engage in massively repeated play of the game and conduct a computationally intensive Monte Carlo analyses to learn "good" strategies. MCCFR thus requires an enormous amount of computation even when the game is simplified via abstraction (see below). This stands in sharp contrast to the ABM approach we set out in Chapter 3. While our ABM uses more computation than is typical in social science research, it still follows rules that are behaviorally plausible in the sense that they could be implemented by a party leader supported by a professional staff.

The reason we use both an ABM and AI approach to studying parliamentary governance is to compare very different behavioral models. Crucially, we can determine whether senior politicians are best described by the relatively parsimonious decision rules used in our ABM or if they have more in common with the fully strategic actors in our AI model. The key point, however, is that in both of these behavioral approaches we remain focused on the outputs of our model: a probabilistic prediction of the partisan composition of the government likely to form at the end of the bargaining process. Thus, while the behavioral assumptions of our MCCFR and ABM approaches differ, both address the same underlying formal model, and both produce results that are testable against observed outcomes of government formation in the real world.

In the remainder of this chapter, we detail the steps we take to apply MCCFR to the government formation process set out in Figure 2.2. While the algorithm detailed above works on very large extensive games, we must take additional steps to improve efficiency, given the exponential growth in complexity as the number of parties increases. Government formation settings with ten or more parties are common in the real world, and these are computationally difficult to solve, even with MCCFR, without additional assumptions.

Simplifying Bargaining via Abstraction

Even an efficient algorithm like MCCFR will buckle under the computational load when confronted with the enormous number of decisions involved in negotiating over government formation in high-dimensional issue spaces. Each party leader can make an offer to form a government, which involves choosing one of 2^n-1 possible coalitions.

For each of these, the offer must include a division of the perquisites among the members of the coalition and a policy offer. If there are twenty cabinet portfolios, for example, there are many different ways to distribute these between the various parties in each possible coalition. If there are twenty binary issue dimensions, for example, there are 3^{20} different agreed joint issue vectors (taking account of the possibilities of tabling an issue) – for each possible perks allocation to each possible coalition.[51]

Following the AI literature, therefore, we coarsen the space of offers to allow for a computational solution. Readers may at this point feel that we are simplifying the game (true!) and that this runs counter to our critique of purely deductive models that also simplify games to reach a solution. We make two brief points on this before proceeding. First, and most crucial, is that while we are simplifying the game, the output of the coarsened game matches the uncoarsened version and maps directly to the empirical target variables of interest (most notably, which governments form and which parties are in them). Tests of the coarsened model are thus directly comparable to nature as well as the tests of the uncoarsened model. Second, there is a "no free behavioral lunch" theorem in play here. Our ABM plays the uncoarsened game but has constraints on behavior such that computation and strategy are limited. Our MCCFR algorithm plays a coarsened game but with considerably greater computation and strategy.

One must choose to simplify somewhere and it is impossible to allow both the behavioral rules and the model to have arbitrary complexity. There is and always will be a trade-off, when modeling real-world settings, between the complexity of the environment as modeled (which can be higher with ABM) and the complexity of agent's modeled responses to this (which can be higher with AI). The important point for us is that both of the approaches we pursue produce results that directly connect to the real-world phenomena of interest.

---

[51] An important difference between the MCCFR algorithm and our ABM is that no *explicit* logrolling occurs here. But, all possible offers are part of the extensive form game and MCCFR actors can "learn" that the policy offers associated with successful logrolling have higher payoffs. In other words, MCCFR can find deals identical to those generated by logrolling behavior. To further simplify the extensive form, we can also eliminate tabled issues – this comes at some price given our knowledge of cases, but substantially reduces the parameter space of the game.

To make analyzing government formation with large numbers of parties and policy dimensions tractable for MCCFR, we first limit the dimensionality, m, of the issue space to be no larger than the fourteen issue dimensions for which we have reliable empirical data on issue positions and saliences. Notwithstanding the availability of real-valued empirical data on issue positions, our assumption for the ABM was that both party and agreed government positions can realistically be treated as binary, an assumption carried through to our AI model. However, unlike the ABM, as a first pass at an AI model, we do not allow for the possibility of tabled issues in joint government policy programs, further coarsening the space and leaving us with 2^m possible policy vectors. This is a purely practical decision based on creating a model that has reasonable computational demands. With more computational power, it would be a straightforward matter to allow the possibility of tabled issues. For the time being, however, since the possibility of tabled issues was a novel, important and distinctive feature of our ABM, this is a clear price in realism for using the AI approach rather than the ABM.

We also coarsen the set of possible allocations of perquisites. We have been assuming that the key perks in government formation are cabinet portfolios, each of which is an indivisible resource, constraining perks allocations to be integer-valued. Countries have different sized cabinets (which can be changed endogenously as an outcome of government formation), generating a huge space of possible perks vectors for any given cabinet. If there are n actors in a particular case, then the total number of possible divisions of r perks between them is:

$$perks\ divisions = \frac{(n+r-1)!}{(r-1)!\ n!}$$

For the AI model, we therefore coarsen the space of possible party perks allocations, binning these to allow only one of eleven possible perks shares: [0.0, 0.1, 0.2, ... 1.0]. This amounts to assuming that the perks allocation problem is one of allocating roles in a ten-seat cabinet – recalling that receiving zero seats in the cabinet means by definition that the party is not a member of the government. We have no *substantive* reason to expect that increasing the size of possible cabinets modeled, thereby increasing the granularity of possible perks offers, would yield additional insights. *Computationally*, however, doing so exponentially increases the size of the game tree and does not lead to better results.

Finally, the last step we take to reduce the dimensionality of the extensive form game is to assume that $\alpha = 0.5$ for all party leaders; that is, that they value policy and perquisites equally.[52] This is another substantial price to pay for moving from our ABM, in which the perks-policy trade-off is not only party-specific but can also take any value, $0 \leq \alpha_i \leq 1$.

Even though we coarsen the game in this way to make it tractable for AI algorithms, it is still much more complex than games that can be solved using a deductive approach. To illustrate these issues, our largest game state in the training dataset is the 2010 Netherlands case containing ten relevant[53] players and a fourteen-dimensional policy vector for each player. Even with aggressive coarsening of the extensive game detailed above, this is still $\dfrac{(10+10-1)!}{(10-1)!10!}$ perks distributions and 2^{14} possible policy outcomes, for a total of 1,513,521,152 possible unique proposals. Across ten players, where each player chooses to either make a proposal (which they are constrained to vote for) or consider the proposals made by others, this is approximately $1.26 * 10^{92}$ states for the full game. Just as with poker, many of these states are irrelevant. For example, it makes no sense for a party to propose a government with a policy position far away from its ideal or one that does not include itself as a member. But this estimate provides a good upper bound for the complexity of the game in cases with many parties and policies.

As with our ABM, we further coarsen the game by excluding the possibility that party leaders, for some devious strategic reason, propose coalitions they have no intention whatsoever of supporting. We constrain politicians who propose a particular government to vote for their own proposal. This constraint significantly reduces the size of the game tree, for a very small substantive price; we are not aware of any real-world case in which some party proposed a government coalition to parliament and then refused to support this. As in our ABM, party

---

[52] At the risk of repeating ourselves, we are obviously not fine-tuning parameters like α or adding case-specific parameters because our goal is not to wring every last ounce out of the predictions of our models. Rather, we want to see how far we can get with a very general scientific model of government formation that applies to all cases.

[53] "Relevant" is defined here as being a pivotal party; having a nonzero Shapley value.

leaders who make no proposal support the proposal that gives them the highest expected payoff.

Even with these simplifications, the tree for this game is still orders of magnitude larger than desirable for a single case. Since we need to solve many cases rather than just one, we rely on the notion of "constrained fictitious play," which replaces a full MCCFR AI for most players. This renders the game tree efficient to solve for our case universe, using a single workstation.

MCCFR with "Constrained Fictitious Play"

An important feature of the government formation process is that the complexity of the strategy space varies sharply by party, as a function of *pivotality* – the probability that a party's legislative seats are essential to minimum winning coalitions (MWCs). Some parties are essential members of *no* winning coalition. This is true, for example, for the two smallest parties in a five-party 99-seat legislature with the following seat vector: (26, 26, 25, 20, 2). Some parties are pivotal in far fewer coalitions than others. For example, after the 1999 general election in Portugal, the raw seat vector in parliament was (115, 81, 15, 15, 2, 2). At first glance the first two parties seem relatively similar in size, compared to the four smaller parties. However, when we look at the relative frequency with which each party is pivotal in a winning coalition, making the difference between winning and losing, we see a different story. The Shapley value measures precisely this probability, and the Shapley values for Portugal in 1999 are: (0.833, 0.033, 0.033, 0.033, 0.033, 0.033). There is a vast difference in pivotality between the first and second largest parties in the extent to which they are essential members of winning coalitions – and no difference at all between the second largest party and the smallest. The plain fact that the largest party is an essential member of many more winning coalitions substantially increases its bargaining leverage.

We exploit this feature of the government formation process using a refinement called constrained fictitious play (CFP) MCCFR, which builds on previous work by Ganzfried and Sandholm (2008) and Heinrich and Silver (2014). Rather than taking account of *fully strategic play by all players*, we rely on a simpler approach in which less pivotal players use a heuristic-based approach to selecting strategies, with a large stochastic component to prevent corner solutions. More pivotal players are modelled as fully strategic, taking up the vast majority of processing time, playing against the expected heuristically generated actions of their less pivotal opponents. For the subset of players with low pivotality, therefore, we model their behavior using very simple heuristics. These behavioral rules, while inferior to those which are fully strategic, are nonetheless quite effective without consuming a huge amount of computational power. Their main job is to provide enough variance to allow the pivotal players using MCCFR to improve their strategies.

Our baseline version of this model classifies the largest party as fully rational and assumes it plays using the complete extensive form game. The $n-1$ less pivotal parties are classified as constrained fictitious (CF) players. These CF players make proposals that: (a) identify as coalition partners one of the MWCs they belong to, picked randomly with uniform probability, (b) propose a joint issue vector that is the median of members' ideal issue vectors for the chosen MWC, and (c) propose a seat-weighted distribution of perquisites, following Gamson's law. The set of proposals for CF players is constrained to include only coalitions better than the reversion value for all member parties. Otherwise, they make no proposal and vote for the proposal, from the set of proposals made by other parties, which maximizes their individual utility. This approach ends up being surprisingly powerful. We refer to it as "Constrained Fictitious Play" because, while it is not fully adaptive for all players like a true fictitious play algorithm – though see the alternating play refinement below – it follows the same logic.

Alternating Play

As a final extension to our AI model of government formation, we specify a method that improves robustness and accuracy in linear computing time. It does this by alternating the strategic roles of the two largest parties, providing a more challenging environment for each. Ranking parties in order of seat share, Party 1 in our core AI model searches the complete extensive form using MCCFR while the other $n-1$ players are heuristic CF players as above. For the alternating play extension, after finding the MCCFR solution for Party 1, exactly as above, we swap the roles of Party 1 and Party 2, allowing us to derive a full MCCFR solution for Party 2, given Party 1's current best strategy. We then switch roles again, so that Party 1 again searches the full game. Crucially, in the new trial, we now use the previous iteration's MCCFR solution (jittered with noise) for Party 2, not its original simple heuristic. In this way, we adhere more closely to logic of alternating fictitious play where the length of play we allow for the model depends on available computation.

Alternating play thus allows players to develop a stronger response based on the best previous strategy from the previous iteration of the game. This approach also avoids over-fit models, as well as cycles in the most common context where no Condorcet winner exists. Alternating CFP MCCFR thus exposes the MCCFR algorithm to a broader set of strategies, so the final result is more robust to strategic play on the part of smaller parties, without exposing the model to situations that could cause nonconvergence.

Finally, a matter of considerable substantive importance is that this technique also allows the second largest party to be the head of the ruling coalition, which is not possible using the basic AI algorithm. Almost all real-world government formation settings, indeed, result in a government led by one or other of the two largest parties (Döring and Manow 2020). For alternating play, we compare the final results of the largest player's best strategy and the second largest player's strategy and assign the winner based on which actor receives the highest average reward.[54] The strategy that offers a higher reward to its coalition leader implies that the player needed to give up less to form a winning coalition, meaning that the resulting strategy is less brittle to counter offers because the members are more closely aligned on policy.

Exercising the AI Model and Making Predictions

The approach we take to exercising the AI model differs from how we exercise the ABM (detailed next in Chapter 5). The AI model takes the

---

[54] One could object to this as an interpersonal comparison of utility. That said, this is more of a decision-theoretic choice for the purpose of making predictions rather than a modeling decision. Utility for each actor in our model depends on policy outcomes and perks, and these have a shared value across parties. Our goal is very limited: If there are two proposals, both of which are preferred by the legislature to the status quo, which should we pick as a prediction? The informal argument we make is that the proposal that generates the most utility for the party leader that makes it allows that leader more "wiggle room" to deal with counter offers. An alternative approach which also works well is to choose the proposal with the greatest support in the legislature (and flip a coin in case of ties).

extensive game form as an input and we search for mixed strategies based on a Monte Carlo approach that depends on CFR. For each case, the AI model generates results that consist of mixed strategies for each player in the game.

Once we have mixed strategies in hand, we play the game 1,000 times using these strategies. Our results from the AI model are the governments (if any) that form on the basis of a majority vote. In simple cases, a very few coalitions are identified as likely outcomes; in others, especially those with a large number of pivotal parties, the mixed strategies produce a range of possible outcomes. We can, of course, specify the probability that each of these coalition outcomes is produced by the model.

In contrast, the ABM has parameters that are used for the behavioral rules detailed in Chapter 3, some of which are fundamentally unobservable – for example, the trade-off rate between perks and policy payoffs. For the ABM, a Monte Carlo is used to perform multiple trials for each case, sampling parameter values from the probability distributions we specify in Chapter 5. In each case, we get a distribution of possible coalition outcomes but the meaning is quite different. In the ABM, the distribution represents the range of possible outcomes given our fundamental uncertainty about the parameters we use in the model. For the AI model, the distribution is a natural consequence of playing the game multiple times with actors that are using mixed strategies.

Given that actors in the AI model are both more strategic and endowed with superhuman levels of computation, it will be no surprise that the AI model does not always generate Condorcet winning proposals. Not only are actors more sophisticated, they are also able to propose any distribution of perks and are not restricted (as they are in the ABM) to follow Gamson's law. When parties are unable to agree on a government, the AI model returns a null result indicating that the reversion point of bargaining has been reached. This happens frequently compared to the results from our ABM.

In making predictions for the AI model, we thus leverage a hard fact about real-world government formation, which is that governments do almost always form. We thus follow the logic of the "brute force" predictions from the ABM. After (mixed) strategies are produced from MCCFR, we generate 1,000 trials of the game and return the most likely coalition across these trials. This is the basis of the empirical tests of the AI model we report in Chapter 6.

Two Contrasting Approaches to Cracking
the Same Difficult Problem

We now have two quite different computational approaches to attacking our government formation game. The ABM approach, set out in Chapter 3, works from the bottom up, focusing on plausible decision heuristics, supplemented by a large amount of computational power to discover "good" coalitions. The strengths of this approach include transparent behavioral rules and relatively fast execution times even for "large" cases with more than ten pivotal parties. The AI approach using CFP MCCFR, set out in this chapter, requires far more computational power, even after considerable simplification of the game tree. The strengths of this approach are that it can model fully strategic actors and generates near-Nash outcomes. This makes it more easily comparable to traditional game-theoretic methods, if these could have been applied to the intractable problem at hand.

We have now specified both our ABM and our AI model and move on to apply these to the real-world politics of government formation and survival. In Chapter 5, we exercise the ABM by systematically mapping inputs into outputs, for empirically plausible parameter settings, in what is in effect the computational analogue of analytical comparative statics. By comparing predictions in our calibration set to observed outcomes, we can also empirically calibrate values of unobservable model parameters (e.g., α and τ). In Chapter 6, we use the ABM, empirically "tuned" in this way on the calibration set, to predict key features of the governance cycle out-of-sample. We also present results for the AI model on the same test data. This approach allows us to conduct a classical "test" of the models on new data and evaluate which of them is the more successful.

5 | *Analyzing Models of Government Formation and Survival*

We design and build any model so we can manipulate its moving parts, developing our understanding of the world by systematically exploring effects of changes in model inputs on substantively important outputs. For our model of government formation, key input parameters include:

- party strength (which could be measured in a number of distinct ways, ranging from seats in parliament to some measure of pivotality in winning coalitions);
- parties' issue positions and the relative issue saliences of these;
- party leaders' taste for perks rather than policy payoffs;
- party leaders' risk tolerance in relation to issues that are tabled during government formation;
- the extent to which members of a caretaker government (the reversion point if bargaining fails) derive less utility than a newly invested government identical in every other way.

Substantively important model outputs (dependent variables) include: the partisan composition of the government which forms, agreed cabinet issue positions, and the stability of the government.

Most theorists working on this topic, as we have seen, radically simplify so that they may achieve purely deductive results (de Marchi and Stewart 2020). The resulting highly stylized models are expressed as systems of equations, from which it is possible to map inputs into outputs by *deducing* the effect on output quantity y of a unit change in input quantity x. This mapping is often described as "comparative statics." It is undeniably good to be able to explore a model in this fashion but, as we have noted, this benefit comes at a cost. Decades of theoretical work in this tradition have yielded few robust empirical hypotheses. While there are of course exceptions (e.g., Laver and Shepsle 1996b, Fréchette, et al. 2005b, Martin and Vanberg 2014, 2020, Cox 2021), formal theories of government formation have for the most part had rather little to say about the empirical reality of government formation in parliamentary democracies.

In our view, interesting and empirically fruitful models of important political phenomena featuring sophisticated actors are likely to be deductively intractable and computationally demanding. This is especially true for the complex and high-stakes world of bargaining over government formation. We recognize that building more complex models presents a different challenge: These models are not amenable to the deductive approach used in traditional comparative statics. The solution, as with many areas of mathematics and the natural sciences, is to turn to computational methods. These allow us to step outside the constraints imposed by requiring purely deductive solutions so that we can analyze more realistic models.

There are, however, substantial similarities between computational and deductive methods of analysis and our work builds on the foundations of prior deductive work. In both cases, there are well-specified sets of actors, actions, and payoffs. As we showed in the last chapter, our approach yields an extensive form game (albeit a very, very large one). And, as noted in Technical Appendix A3, computational models are expressed in lines of computer code that are logically identical to the systems of equations which characterize deductive models. Rather than mapping inputs into outputs by analytically "solving" the model's system of equations, inputs are mapped into outputs by *computing* the effect on output quantity y of a unit move in some input quantity x. Many different values of x are chosen from known probability distributions, over many different trials, in what is known as a Monte Carlo experiment. With sufficient computational firepower, this mapping can be very detailed – quite detailed enough to reveal the general theoretical insights that are the ultimate objective of all modeling.[55] There is, therefore, no significant *epistemological* difference between analytical and computational mapping of inputs into outputs. There is simply a difference in the *method* used to generate these mappings.

There is, however, an important *substantive* difference between the two approaches. Computational methods allow for more complex theoretical models and can attack deductively intractable problems; this helps us generate empirical hypotheses for contexts that feature

---

[55] If the mapping is not detailed enough to allow us to draw confident conclusions, we simply run our simulations for longer, or deploy more computers.

complex strategic behavior involving highly motivated actors. This is why computational methods are four-square in the mainstream of most modern sciences, though political scientists are only recently beginning to apply them to important but unresolved substantive problems.

In what follows, we discuss three topics that explain the logic behind building and analyzing a formal model using a computational approach:

- How to choose values for parameters in the model?
- How to analyze a complex model?
- How these results differ from those produced by typical game-theoretic models?

At the end of this chapter, we turn to the analytical results generated by our ABM of government formation.

Choosing Parameter Values

Exactly like any formal model in the social sciences, our model of government formation depends on a large number of parameters. Some (such as the choice of bargaining protocol) are features of the model itself. Some (such as the number of parties) vary from setting to setting. Still others (such as the trade-off between perks and policy payoffs) vary from politician to politician. The model we specify in Chapters 2 and 3, however, has a parameter space that is especially "large" compared to existing formal models. In part, this is structural and arises from our desire to build a realistic model of government formation. Allowing multiple parties to make simultaneous proposals including both issue positions and perks allocations, and then allowing logrolling over these issue positions, adds substantial complexity compared to prior work which assumes sequential offers solely over perks. In part, the parameter space is large because our computational approach actually allows us to explore the impact of a large number of different inputs on model outputs.

Nonetheless, it is neither feasible nor sensible to map the entire logically possible parameter space into model-predicted outcomes. While 1,000-party systems are a logical possibility, it would be absurd to investigate what our model says about the coalitions that form in 1,000-party systems. We therefore specify empirically "reasonable" constraints on the parameter space.[56] We do this because, even if we had access to the world's most powerful supercomputers, we would still face a finite computational "budget" and would want to focus our resources on empirically realistic regions of the parameter space.[57]

Some of the key parameters in our model are *empirically observable*. We have noted, for example, that it is easy to count the number of parties in actual parliamentary party systems. Another key model parameter concerns the variance of legislative parties' seat shares over a series of elections, which we can also observe empirically. Setting parameter values for computational work within empirically realistic ranges is straightforward for such parameters. Others are not naturally observable, but can be estimated using standard measurement instruments. For example, as we will see, parties' stated issue positions and saliences are often estimated by political scientists using content analyses of party manifestoes or by using expert surveys.

Other parameters are *fundamentally unobservable*. Examples of fundamentally unobservable parameters include: negotiating politicians' trade-offs between perks and policy payoffs; their risk tolerance concerning tabled issues in the agreed government policy program; and the rate at which the value of a caretaker government is discounted relative to a newly installed government identical in every other respect. These are idiosyncratic psychological variables for individual politicians, whether they are consciously aware of them or not. They are also matters on which negotiating politicians may have strong strategic incentives to dissemble, thereby complicating measurement.

---

[56] While this is sometimes implicit, this is also typically the case with deductive comparative statics. There are highly regarded deductive models that confine themselves to at most three parties and at most two policy dimensions, for example. Real parliamentary democracies almost always have substantially more than three legislative parties, while real politicians' preferences are best described in rather high-dimensional issue spaces. What we need to do, therefore, is to exercise our models for sets of parameter values that are empirically realistic.

[57] The fact that we are able to explore much larger parameter spaces than a purely deductive model is important since all results – whether for deductive or computational models – are conditional on the assumptions used (Bendor and Moe 1985, Judd and Page 2004). To develop confidence in the results of a model, therefore, it is incumbent on researchers to investigate as much of the "realistic" parameter space as possible and not produce results which are over-reliant on particular parameter choices.

For these unobservable parameters, we do not pick specific values in most cases, even though this would simplify the model. While simpler models are, all else equal, preferred to more complex models, there is no guarantee that any particular set of parameter values leads to a good mapping between a model and the empirical reality it is meant to explain (de Marchi 2022).

We therefore borrow from the machine learning literature and resist committing to specific values for our unobservable parameters. Instead, as we show in the next section, we allow these unobservable parameters to vary in each trial of a Monte Carlo experiment, systematically exploring how these parameters map into key outputs of the model. Crucially, we divide our empirical cases of government formation into a training and a test dataset, where the training set provides evidence on which values for each parameter best explain empirical outcomes. Once we have chosen ranges for each parameter that lead to a good mapping to empirical reality, we test the model by making predictions for the cases in the out-of-sample test set. In our minds, this is the most scientifically sound approach to parameter selection in complex models and avoids potentially misleading findings arising from focusing on a single set of parameters, chosen for convenience.

Creating the Training Dataset

We selected a "calibration" or "training" set of government formations after twenty real-world elections, designed to be representative of the empirical universe which interests us – modern European parliamentary democracies. Creating a representative training set allows us to exercise our model in a way that relies on empirically realistic parameters, but it is very important to note that the analyses that follow in this chapter *are not empirical tests of model predictions*. We turn to the empirical evaluation of model predictions in Chapter 6, using completely new, out-of-sample, data (in machine learning parlance, a test dataset).

When selecting the twenty training cases, we first ensured these are representative of the empirical distribution of "legislative types," which have been shown to be both theoretically and empirically relevant to government formation in parliamentary democracies (Laver and Benoit 2015). Ranking legislative parties in order of size, and excluding legislatures in which one party has an overall majority, these types are:

Type B: "dominant party." The largest party can form a winning coalition with the third largest, but the second largest party cannot do this. Excluding the largest party therefore requires a three-party coalition. For example, in a 99-seat legislature, this happens with the weight vector (40, 25, 20, 8, 6). Laver and Benoit (2005: Table 2) found about 36 percent of minority legislatures in European parliamentary democracies were in this category.

Type B*: "system dominant party." A special case of Type B. The largest party can form a winning coalition with *any* other party. For example (44, 21, 20, 8, 6) in a 99-seat legislature. About 11 percent of minority legislatures fell into this category.

Type C: "top three" system. The second and third largest parties can form a winning coalition. Arithmetically, therefore, no party outside the top three can be *pivotal* in any winning coalition. For example (30, 26, 24, 15, 4) in a 99-seat legislature. About 12 percent of minority legislatures fell into this category.

Type D: "top two" system. The largest party can form a winning coalition with the second largest, but not with the third largest. The only two-party winning coalition comprises the two largest parties. For example (40, 35, 9, 8, 7) in a 99-seat legislature. About 22 percent of minority legislatures fell into this category.

Type E: "open" system. The largest party cannot form a winning coalition with the second largest. Winning coalitions must comprise three or more parties. For example (25, 24, 20, 17, 13) in a 99-seat legislature. About 19 percent of minority legislatures are in this category.

We also wanted training cases to represent, for each legislative type, the range of party system sizes observed in parliamentary democracies. Analyzing the replication dataset for Laver and Benoit (2015), which was based on the *European Representative Democracy* dataset,[58] we identified the distribution of the calibration cases between legislative types and party system sizes described in Table 5.1.

Our choice of training cases was also constrained by available empirical data. A widely used and authoritative source of data on party issue positions and saliences is provided by the series of Chapel Hill Expert Surveys (CHES),[59] from which we can derive estimates,

---

[58] Andersson, Staffan, Torbjörn Bergman, and Svante Ersson (2014). "The European Representative Democracy Data Archive, Release 3." Main sponsor: Riksbankens Jubileumsfond (In2007-0149:1-E), www.erdda.se.

[59] Bakker, Ryan, Liesbet Hooghe, Seth Jolly, Gary Marks, Jonathan Polk, Jan Rovny, Marco Steenbergen, and Milada Anna Vachudova. 2020. "1999–2019 Chapel Hill Expert Survey Trend File." Version 1.2. Available on chesdata.eu.

Table 5.1 *Number of calibration cases*
by legislative type and party system size

	Legislative type					
No. of parties	B	B*	C	D	E	Total
4		1	1			2
5	3	1	1			5
6	2		1	1		4
7	1			1	1	3
8	1			1	1	3
9				1	1	2
10					1	1
Total	7	2	3	4	4	20

for many countries, of party positions and saliences for fourteen different issue dimensions.[60] This is a reliable and widely used dataset of issue positions and saliences at a high enough dimensionality to allow us to model logrolling as part of the government formation process. The Laver–Benoit replication dataset runs to the end of 2010, and the expert survey series begins in 1999, so our selection of calibration cases comes from the intersection of these two periods – the twelve-year period between the beginning of 1999 and the end of 2010.

Reanalyzing the Laver-Benoit replication dataset, we, therefore, used a stratified case selection method, identifying postelectoral government formation cases satisfying the criteria for each cell in Table 5.1, for which expert survey data are also available on issue positions and

---

[60] These surveys used the same questions on many issues as the earlier expert survey fielded by Benoit and Laver (2006), which we therefore used for some of the calibration cases. For some countries in some years, the expert surveys did not include all fourteen issue dimensions. In these cases, we used the smaller set of issue dimensions which were in fact included in the survey. We also attempted to use data from the Comparative Manifestos Project (CMP). In theory, this should be a good source of information on high-dimensional issue positions and saliences. CMP data have been widely used to compute a one-dimensional left-right scale which aggregates twenty-six manifesto labeling categories. In practice, extracting high-dimensional data on party issue positions and saliences proved problematic. Many labeling categories in many manifestos were empty, leaving scale positions depending on them indeterminate or uninterpretable.

saliences. Sometimes there is only one relevant case, in which case we
selected this. Sometimes there are more cases than we need in some
cell of Table 5.1, in which case we selected cases in order to satisfy a
further constraint. This is for each of the twenty calibration cases, as
far as possible, to come from a different country, thereby maximizing
the empirical scope of our theoretical analysis. The resulting set of
twenty calibration cases thus comes from nineteen different countries
during the period 1999–2010.[61] There are twelve cases from western
and southern Europe and eight from central and eastern Europe. Party
systems investigated have between four and ten legislative parties.

Selecting *Observable* Model Parameters
for Theoretical Analysis

With the training data in hand, we exercise our model by systematically and repeatedly computing outputs implied by the model, varying
values of key input parameters. The most salient input parameters in
our model are listed in Table 5.2. The first three parameters in the
table are at least potentially observable features of party politics; the
latter three are fundamentally unobservable psychological variables.
We first examine how to instantiate the observable parameters.

Even when we confine ourselves to the observable model parameters of party weights, issue positions, and saliences, we still face an
immense number of possible ways to specify these. We might be able
to observe some particular *realized* party configuration *empirically*,
but *theoretically* mapping the gigantic universe of *possible* party
configurations into a space of possible outcomes would result in a
model that is computationally intractable.[62] For a particular government formation setting with n parties and m salient issue dimensions,
each case is specified by: a party weight vector, an $n \times m$ party issue
position matrix, and $n \times m$ party issue salience matrix. This is one
reason why theorists often limit models to a single policy dimension
(i.e., $m = 1$), given the resulting enormous reduction in the complexity of
the parameter space. The costs of such an approach, however, are also

---

[61] The full set of twenty cases was: AU1999, BEL2003, BG2001, CZ2006,
DEN2005, EST2007, FIN1999, GER2002, LAT2006, LUX2009, NL2010,
POL2007, PT1999, PT2002, ROM2008, SLVK2010, SLVN2000, SP2008,
SWE2006, and UK2010.
[62] As noted in Chapter 4, one solution to this is to coarsen the parameter space.

Table 5.2 *Summary of input parameters of interest*

Parameter	Meaning	Range
weight, w_i	Actor's legislative seat share.	$0 \leq w_i \leq 1$
issue position, p_{ij}	Actor's preferred position on issue j.	$p_{ij} \in [0, 1]$
issue salience, s_{ij}	Actor's relative salience for issue j.	$0 \leq s_{ij} \leq 1$
alpha, α_i	Actor's utility trade-off between perks and policy payoffs. Higher-α actors value perks more.	$0 \leq \alpha \leq 1$
tau, τ_i	Actor's tolerance/optimism about the uncertainty involved in tabling issues in the government program. Higher-τ actors are less optimistic/tolerant.	$0 \leq \tau \leq 1$
theta, θ_i	The reduction in utility for cabinet members of a caretaker government if the reversion point is reached.	$0 \leq \theta \leq 1$

obvious: Substantively important strategic behaviors such as logrolling are excluded from consideration.

Most possible parameterizations, however, are utterly unrealistic and, as noted above, we limit our efforts to empirically realistic values.[63] It is important to note that, in doing this, we do not consider any feature of the *outcomes* of government formation. Our concern is to identify a set of empirically plausible *input* party configurations, specified in terms of party weights, issue positions, and saliences, which allow us to draw *substantively* informative conclusions when we map inputs into outputs. How should we select plausible values for observable parameters in a systematic and replicable way? Rather than doing this intuitively, we calibrate our model *empirically* using the cases in our training dataset.

For each of the twenty training cases, we simulate fundamental uncertainty and/or unbiased measurement error in relation to parties' issue positions and saliences, using a method we developed in earlier work (de Marchi and Laver 2020). The CHES issue position

---

[63] Imagine, for example, a theoretically possible party configuration with fifteen parties and thirty key issue dimensions in which all parties had identical weights, and identical positions and salience vectors. With infinite resources, we could investigate everything in a nanosecond, but a finite budget of analytical resources can be much better employed NOT investigating such a setting.

and salience estimates are mean expert scores for each party on the relevant dimensions. For each calibration case and issue dimension j, we first linearly rescale party position scores to the [0, 1] interval. For each issue dimension and for each of 1,000 trials per case, we perturb this rescaled CHES issue score for each party by adding Gaussian noise with a mean of 0 and a standard deviation σ_p. We then map these perturbed scores to binary policies (i.e., 0 or 1). This generates perturbed binary positions, p'_{ij}, for each party i on each issue j. Based on our experience with the analysis reported in our earlier work, for each run repetition, we draw values of the "policy noise" parameter, σ_p, from a uniform distribution on the [0.25, 0.50] interval. We perturb party issue saliences for each run repetition in a directly analogous way, using a "saliency noise" parameter, σ_s. We do not round perturbed saliences to integers, but linearly rescale these to sum to unity across all issue dimensions for each party.

A more general feature of a party's issue positions, taken as a whole, is also clearly relevant to its prospects of getting into government. Parties with relatively extreme positions across the entire set of relevant issues are by construction less likely to share these with others, making it more difficult for them to agree to a joint program and more likely to face the need to make costly policy concessions in order to logroll a joint policy program. Accordingly, we generate a summary fourteen-dimensional measure of mean issue-eccentricity, $\hat{e}_i$, for each party. The CHES issue scales range from 0 to 10 and are centered on 5. For each of the fourteen CHES scales we use, we compute policy eccentricity for a party with a position p_{ij} as $e_{ij} = |p_{ij} - 5|$.[64] We then compute, for each party for each trial, the party's fourteen-dimensional issue eccentricity as its mean eccentricity, $\hat{e}_i$, across all issue dimensions.

Selecting *Unobservable* Model Parameters for Theoretical Analysis

The other three parameters in Table 5.1 (α_i, τ_i, and θ_i) are fundamentally unobservable parameters. For our computational experiments using the twenty calibration cases, therefore, we want our choices on these parameters to vary so that we can examine how this variance

---

[64] NB: for the EU policy scale, where the CHES scale center is 4 not 5, $e_i = 5 \cdot |p_i - 4| / 3$.

affects our results. This Monte Carlo approach is designed to ensure that values of parameters which cannot be calibrated empirically are represented as comprehensively as possible in our final results. Accordingly, we perform a suite of 1,000 trials for each of the twenty calibration cases. For each of the fundamentally unobservable psychological parameters, α_i, τ_I, and θ_i, for each trial, we pick values drawn from uniform distributions on the [0, 1] interval.

Analyzing Complex Models: "Computational Comparative Statics"

As we noted above, it is impossible to examine the complex models presented here using a purely deductive approach. Our goals, however, remain the same as those of any formal modeler. We want to understand the roles that our parameters play in generating analytical results that will help us understand government formation.[65]

To make things more concrete, consider the canonical formal model in the literature from Baron and Ferejohn (1989). The most salient results deduced in this paper are that the proposer has an advantage in bargaining, the first proposal made is passed without delay by a majority, and benefits are distributed to a minimum winning coalition. These results are, of course, *conditional* on a number of parameter choices, including the impatience of actors, stationarity, the exogenous mechanism that selects proposers in sequence with a given probability distribution, the reversion point of 0 for all actors, etc. In making choices for these different parameters, most of which we would categorize as unobservable, Baron and Ferejohn were guided by a desire to produce an equilibrium result which they contrast with the prior work "of social choice theory [which] yields no equilibrium" (p. 1199).

While we share the goal of rigorously connecting the inputs into our model with the results, we differ in our other goals. We do not want to choose particular values for key model parameters that we declare as theorists to be either realistic or convenient. Choosing values for

---

[65] Specifying an empirical model for a complex set of causes is difficult (Braumoeller 2003). Our approach here focuses on relatively low-hanging fruit, and we leave for future work an examination of interactive or nonlinear effects in our models.

the *observable* parameters is relatively straightforward.[66] The situation is more complicated, however, when it comes to choosing values for *unobservable* parameters. For example, it may be the case that senior politicians engaged in real-world government formation possess high values for α – they value perks more highly than policy. But the opposite may also hold. These parameters may vary from case to case, and there is no guarantee that any specific parameter value (or distribution) will provide a good description of the empirical feature of interest.

The traditional approach to selecting parameters can be haphazard and has avoided dealing with these issues directly. Specific parameter values may be chosen for analytical convenience (i.e., to produce a unique equilibrium) or based on particular case studies, or simply be based on the intuition of the researcher. Results may well then depend, possibly quite sharply, on the particular values chosen.

Our approach to calibrating model parameters is different and more closely approaches model calibration in many of the natural sciences. We explore large regions of the parameter space and identify which ranges of parameter values best map to empirical outcomes in our *training dataset*. These outcomes include the partisan composition of cabinets that form after elections in parliamentary democracies and the subsequent durations of these. Of the very large universe of models we could create, we seek a model that can predict these key empirical targets. *Using only our training dataset*, which does not feature in model testing, we choose parameter values that generate accurate predictions. This rigorous, systematic, and *replicable* process allows us to avoid making idiosyncratic choices for the values of fundamentally unobservable model parameters.

This process is made possible by using relatively simple applied statistical techniques that allow us to describe the relationship between the values of our input parameters and our dependent variables. Each of the 1,000 trials in each Monte Carlo experiment computes, for the particular case in question, how the perturbed vectors of model inputs, both observable and unobservable, map into the model-predicted outputs. We then combine all of these trials into a single dataset and explore the relationship between the model parameters and our

---

[66] There are conceptual issues involved, even with observable parameters. Taking the strength of each party as an example, it is not clear whether we should use the seats held by each party or instead rely on a pivotality measure (see Laver, de Marchi, and Mutlu 2011a).

primary dependent variables. Other than the inputs described above, we do not include any other case-specific information. For example, we ignore prior histories of government formation and duration, the presence of "pariah" parties, and so on. This is because we are aiming for a general model of government formation, not model-powered case studies.

All of this gives us a computed dataset of 20,000 observations based on the twenty calibration cases, which we use to explore the relationships between model inputs and model outputs. When reporting our main findings, we differ from purely deductive work by using regressions to explore the role of different parameters in producing results. The conditionality of these results is, as a consequence, very transparent. This is the computational analogue of deductive comparative statics.

Distributions of Predicted Outcomes, Not Point Predictions

A final difference between our approach and traditional analytical work deserves attention. We exercise our ABM using Monte Carlo experiments, which generate *distributions of predicted outcomes* rather than a single point prediction for any given set of inputs.[67] Model outputs from each trial can thus be aggregated into a *probability distribution* of model-predicted outcomes, across the set of all logically possible governments and agreed policies.[68] Producing probability distributions allows us to capture substantively important features of government formation that would be missed if we only made point predictions. In horse racing, for example, there are races where the field is wide open and others where a single horse is the heavy favorite. Similarly, in government formation, there are settings where bargaining power is distributed evenly across several parties and many potential coalitions are on the table, resulting in a relatively flat probability distribution across the set of possible coalition governments. There are other settings with a single dominant party and far fewer

---

[67] We could, of course, take the prediction with the maximum probability mass on it and return that result for each case, but this would lose crucial information about the bargaining context.

[68] The latter also allows us to compute the proportion of issues that are tabled in the agreed government program, which we use in Chapter 6 when modeling the vulnerability of the incumbent government to agenda shocks.

coalition options on the table, where we expect to be able to make much sharper predictions.

Government formation, like everything else in life, is subject to fundamental uncertainty. On top of this, key model parameters, such as parties' issue positions and saliences, are subject to inevitable measurement errors. Others, such as politicians' risk tolerances, are fundamentally unobservable. In real government formation settings, both practicing politicians and seasoned observers might well say that some outcome, *y*, is the most likely – even by far the most likely. Few, however, would ever say that outcome *y* will happen *with 100 percent certainty* and that no other outcome is even remotely possible.

When we examine the range of values of fundamentally unobservable parameters associated with "successful" model predictions in the training data, therefore, a successful prediction is one where the predicted distribution of outcomes produced by our model places greater probability mass on the government which actually forms in that particular setting.[69] As an illustration, Table 5.3 shows model-predicted outcomes of 1,000-trial Monte Carlo experiment for the calibration case of Austria in 1999. With only four pivotal legislative parties, this is the "simplest" case we consider in our analysis. There are only fifteen possible cabinet predictions, to which we add the prediction of no government or a cycle. Parties are labeled from 0 to 3 in order of size. The top panel of Table 5.3 shows the election result, and the bottom panel shows the frequency of trials with a model prediction that a particular proposed cabinet wins a majority vote in pairwise comparisons with all other proposals. Predictions in this case are distributed across seven of the fifteen possible cabinets – the other eight possibilities were predicted in none of the 1,000 trials. The most frequently predicted cabinet for Austria in 1999, with 34 percent of the probability mass, is a majority coalition between the Freedom Party (FPÖ) and the Peoples Party (ÖVP). As it happens, this is the cabinet that did actually form

---

[69] There are $2^n - 1$ coalitions with varying partisan compositions in an *n*-party system, including the grand coalition of all parties but excluding the null coalition of no party. In a seven-party system, for example, that means 127 different possible coalitions exist. One additional possibility is that the model predicts no winning cabinet proposal for the trial in question, making 2^n different possible model predictions. Given the number of potential coalitions, predicting the empirically realized outcome is a difficult task.

Table 5.3 *Election results and model-predicted cabinets: Austria 1999*

Party label	Party name	Seats
0	Social Democrats (SPÖ)	65
1	Freedom Party (FPÖ)	52
2	People's Party (ÖVP)	52
3	Greens (G)	14
Total		183

Predicted cabinet	No. of model predictions	%
(0, 1)	100	10.0
(0, 2)	21	2.1
(0)	128	12.8
(1, 2)	**342**	**34.2**
(1, 2, 3)	10	1.0
(1)	14	1.4
(2)	272	27.2
No govt/cycle	113	11.3
Total	1,000	100

in this case. Note also that the second most predicted government is a single-party ÖVP cabinet. While ÖVP and FPÖ both won the same seat totals, a single-party FPÖ cabinet is extremely unlikely to be predicted – which is intuitively unsurprising given its relatively extreme issue positions.

Austria in 1999 represents a case where we make relatively sharp predictions. In contrast, Sweden in 2006 is a much more difficult case. Seven pivotal parties exist (with minimum integer weights of one or greater) and our model puts positive probability mass on two dozen different proto-coalitions, with no coalition achieving more than 24 percent of the total probability mass.

Given a model-generated probability distribution of outcomes for each training case, and our observation of the actual outcome in this case, we can estimate the range of values of fundamentally unobservable model parameters associated with empirically successful model predictions. This allows us to calibrate the unobservable parameters of our model for the out-of-sample empirical analysis we report in Chapter 6.

When we combine the bargaining game set out in Chapter 2 with the behavioral rules set out in Chapter 3, our model predicts either *single-party* minority cabinets or majority coalitions. While these are the most common types of government in postwar European parliamentary democracies (Laver and Benoit 2015), we do sometimes observe *minority coalitions*. Nothing in our modeling architecture or government formation environment precludes these, but the particular greedy heuristic we investigate here assumes that party leaders do not consider minority coalitions, while nonetheless considering single-party minority administrations.[70] Since, for obvious reasons, we did not take into account the government which eventually formed when selecting our calibration cases, this means that our greedy heuristic makes zero correct predictions of the eventual cabinet when this is a minority coalition. We are in good company in this regard, since no formal model of government formation of which we are aware predicts minority coalitions.[71] However, our greedy formation heuristic may still make correct predictions about *individual party membership* in empirically observed minority coalitions, a matter to which we return in Chapter 6.

Summary of Monte Carlo Experiments Used to Exercise the ABM

The research design of our Monte Carlo experiments is, therefore, as follows:

1. Identify substantive output variables. These dependent variables will be the targets of the theoretical model.

[70] This raises an important point about our behavioral model for the ABM detailed in Chapter 3. While it is possible to write down, in a parsimonious way, the decision rules we employ, our model nonetheless relies on a great deal of computation by actors in much the same spirit as the hill-climbing algorithms utilized in Kollman, et al. (1992, 1998). Our rule of thumb was to limit the amount of computation required such that the model could execute comfortably on a single workstation for systems with up to twelve parties. This meant that we had constraints on the complexity of the decision rules. Allowing actors to search the entire set of minority coalitions was thus possible, but we did not consider this possibility in the present work given the computational burden it implied for actors.

[71] Dragu and Laver do predict minority or surplus majority coalitions, in an incomplete information setting in which actors have no perks preferences and one-dimensional policy preferences (Dragu and Laver 2017). And, as we will see in Chapter 6, our AI model does predict minority coalitions.

2. Create a training dataset. This allows us to debug/refine the model and make the parameter choices used to exercise it.
3. Use Monte Carlo methods, randomly sampling key inputs, to establish the mapping between input parameters and output variables. This helps us understand the dynamics of the model and leads directly to *analytical* results found in propositions 5.4–5.7 below.
4. Select values of the unobservable parameters that improve accuracy in predicting substantively interesting dependent variables. The parameter values selected lead to the *analytical* results found in propositions 5.1–5.3 below.
5. Generate predictions from the model for new cases in a test dataset. These predictions use parameter values selected in the preceding step. These *empirical* results are detailed in Chapter 6.

Analytical Results

We now report the general conclusions we derive from our ABM by using the approach described above. It is worth repeating that these *analytical* results are different in kind from the *empirical* predictions covered in Chapter 6; these concern, for new cases, how successfully our model predicts which governments form and how long these governments last.

While we could report results on a case-by-case basis, we have chosen instead to focus our efforts on more general findings based on the entire set of training cases. Calibrating the model on a case-by-case basis would be valuable if our intention was to get into the nitty-gritty of each case or to generate the most accurate predictions possible. But, our goal throughout this book is to produce a general model of the governance cycle, one which applies to the entire population of interest.

We summarize our theoretical findings below. These are based on analyses of model-generated data from our Monte Carlo experiments, using theoretically informed regressions. Additional detail for each result is presented in Technical Appendix A5.

Effects of Party Characteristics on Government Formation

Our first set of results focuses on the effects of particular unobservable party leader characteristics (α_i, τ_I, and θ_i), along with parties' issue eccentricities, on the process of government formation. Following the approach outlined above, which leverages our training data to identify empirically plausible ranges for each parameter of interest, we have the following propositions:

Proposition 1: Senior politicians tend to have high values of α (α_i > 0.6), valuing perks more than policy when engaged in government formation.

Proposition 2: Senior politicians tend to have low values of τ (τ_i < 0.3), assuming optimistically that tabled issues will not be forced onto the agenda or will turn out well for them if this happens.

Proposition 3: Senior politicians tend to have low values of θ (θ_i < 0.2), heavily discounting the continuation value of the outgoing government.

Proposition 4: Parties with more extreme issue positions (with higher eccentricity $\hat{e}_i$) are less likely to be predicted as members of any government.

Substantively, the first three findings indicate that when senior politicians negotiate over government formation, they are in general inclined to be:

- more concerned with getting into office than holding firm on their issue positions;
- not concerned about leaving contentious issues out of the joint program, but instead optimistic about their ability to keep these off of the government agenda;
- unwilling to allow an outgoing caretaker government to continue.

Proposition 4 confirms a straightforward intuition about government formation. Parties that are more "central" have greater numbers of possible partners in forming governments. All else equal these parties are expected to have a better chance to successfully navigate government formation after elections. This result is particularly strong in cases where single-party governments form; much of the time, this happens when there is a strong, central party.

In addition to providing some insight into unobservable features of the preferences of senior politicians negotiating over government formation, we use these findings in Chapter 6 to calibrate unobservable parameters of our model when we make *out-of-sample* predictions.

As we will see in Chapter 6, tuning the model in this way yields systematically better predictions. This in turn implies that the substantive interpretations of α_i, τ_i, and θ_i we suggested above are *prima facie* plausible.

Effects of Party System Characteristics on Government Formation

Our second set of results focuses on features of the party system:

Proposition 5a: Condorcet winners. Increased complexity, arising from higher dimensional issue spaces which allow for logrolling, increases the probability of Condorcet winners and reduces the probability of cycling.

Proposition 5b: Condorcet winners. Legislatures dominated by senior politicians who are risk acceptant about tabled issues have a higher likelihood of Condorcet winners.

Proposition 6: Single-party cabinets. Legislatures dominated by senior politicians who value perks and/or are risk averse about the future effects of tabled issues are more likely to produce single-party governments.

Proposition 7: Government survival. Legislatures dominated by senior politicians who value perks and are optimistic about the future effects of tabled issues tend to form cabinets that are less durable.

Propositions 5a and 5b deal with the same puzzle that motivated Baron and Ferejohn's research on legislative bargaining. This is that social choice models of legislative voting in minority legislatures imply there should be no majority rule voting equilibrium, and, therefore, no stable majority-preferred government – yet we do not observe this instability empirically. Baron and Ferejohn (1989) attacked this puzzle using the tools of noncooperative game theory. Our work suggests an alternative solution. Proposition 5a extends our earlier work (de Marchi and Laver 2020) and rests on the simple observation that our model frequently generates predictions of Condorcet winning cabinets. This implies that strategic complexity – captured by logrolling over issues positions in a high-dimensional issue space – can generate Condorcet winners and thereby avoid majority rule cycling.

Proposition 5b expands on this, showing that a key unobservable model parameter about the behavior of senior politicians, risk acceptance toward tabled issues, affects the success of logrolls and the likelihood that larger coalitions form. This optimism about the effects of future shocks also produces more Condorcet winners and reduces cycling.

Propositions 6 highlights the conditions under which we predict single-party minority governments to form. If senior politicians engaged in government formation care more about perks and less about policy, and if they are pessimistic about the effects of including tabled issues in the government program, then logrolling deals are harder to come by. In such contexts, a single powerful party, pivotal in a large number of winning coalitions, can govern alone because logrolling Condorcet winning *coalitions* is more difficult.

Proposition 7 shows that the durability of governments depends on unobservable characteristics of the decision rules used by senior politicians. When party leaders place little weight on policy and are more optimistic about the effects of future shocks, they can find themselves in a coalition that is fragile, because it tends to have a larger proportion of tabled issues. We return to this topic and provide additional empirical support for this proposition in Chapter 6.

For propositions 4 through 7, we set out the relevant evidence in Technical Appendix A5. For each of these propositions, we generate the result by using a regression to examine the data created by our Monte Carlo experiments. Taking proposition 6 on the probability of single-party governance as an example, we test the proposition using the following logistic regression:

$$\text{single-party govt } (0/1) = a + b_{1-4}(L_1 - L_4) + b_5 N + b_6 \alpha$$
$$+ b_7 \tau + b_8 \theta + \epsilon$$

The binary dependent variable captures whether or not a single-party government forms. Independent variables include legislative types $(L_1 - L_4)$ as controls, the number of parties in the system (N), the parties' trade-offs between perks and policy (α), attitudes toward tabled issues (τ), and attitudes toward the continuation value of caretaker cabinets (θ).

Conclusions

It bears repeating that we are not engaged in any empirical evaluation of our model in this chapter. We have conducted an empirically calibrated *theoretical* exercise of the model using computational comparative statics. This has three essential purposes. The first is *methodological* – mundane but vital. We want to ensure that both the model and its computational implementation are working as expected for the target universe of modern parliamentary democracies. We therefore coded the model and then exercised it with a series of Monte Carlo experiments on a training set carefully selected to represent modern parliamentary democracies. We set out prior intuitive expectations in Technical Appendix A5 about how the model should map inputs into outputs. These a priori expectations were vindicated in analyses of the datasets generated by the Monte Carlo experiments. This gives us comfort that the model is working as expected.

The second purpose is *substantive*. We want to learn from the model. The model's computational comparative statics have a number of implications of substantive interest. One of the more striking propositions concerns the likelihood of forming either a single-party minority government or a majority coalition in any particular setting. At a *system* level, the computational comparative statics confirm the informal intuition that minority governments are *more* likely when politicians tend to care *less* about perks and more about policy. This is because a minority government can only form with the support of parties which command a legislative majority but which get no perks at all – whereas policy payoffs go to all parties, whether they are in or out of government. In contrast, at a *party* level, the model predicts that it is parties who care *more* about perks and less about policy which, other things equal, are more likely to form single-party minority administrations. This is because they are more likely to make the policy concessions necessary for winning support in the legislature from nongovernment parties. This seems to us to be a substantively important and distinctive theoretical implication of our model.

The model also has distinctive implications concerning the tabling of issues in the government's joint policy program – a direct consequence of the modeled process of logrolling policy agreements in high-dimensional issue spaces. Politicians' tolerance for having tabled issues is captured by the τ parameter: high-τ politicians expect tabled issues to turn out badly; low-τ politicians expect them to turn out well. At a system level, the computational comparative statics confirm the informal intuition that if politicians tend to be high-τ, then they will tend, *ceteris paribus*, to favor single-party minority administrations, since these have no tabled issues. In contrast, if politicians tend to be low-τ, then they will be willing to accept coalition governments, caring less about the fact these are likely to have tabled issues in their logrolled joint programs.

Further implications from the model concern parties' fourteen-dimensional eccentricities in the issue space and their bargaining leverage. We demonstrate that high issue eccentricity sharply reduces the probability a party is a predicted member of the cabinet – strikingly so for single-party cabinets, which tend to be predicted as comprising centrist parties. Even controlling for the powerful predicted effects of bargaining leverage and policy eccentricity, however, it is striking that it is the more perks-oriented parties which are predicted by our model to be more likely to form single-party minority governments.

The third purpose of this chapter has been to calibrate our model for the out-of-sample empirical analyses reported in Chapter 6. We shortly return to this but, to recap briefly, our calibration exercise on the training set suggests that the model will perform best assuming that politicians tend to prefer perks over policy payoffs, to be relatively unconcerned about tabled issues, and to heavily discount the continuation value of the outgoing caretaker government. Given that this calibrated model makes better out-of-sample predictions, these seem to us to be interesting substantive findings about the fundamentally unobservable preferences of politicians in parliamentary democracies.

6 | Empirical Analyses of Government Formation and Stability

Empirical Approach

In Chapter 5, we used applied statistics to develop a better understanding of how key parameters of our ABM of the governance cycle map into substantively important features of the governments that are predicted to form. That was an essentially *theoretical* analysis. In this chapter, we bring our ABM and AI models to bear on an *empirical* analysis of the real world of democratic governance. We assess whether hypotheses derived from the models explain what we observe in the real world. Our approach involves the following steps.

i. In Chapter 5, we created a *training set* comprising a stratified sample of twenty cases that are representative of the population of interest – governments in postwar Europe. This includes "difficult" cases of newer democracies in Eastern Europe, minority governments, and surplus governments.

ii. We used this training set to *tune* our computational model in a limited way to identify "realistic" ranges of values for the fundamentally unobservable model parameters: α (the rate of trade-off between perks and policy payoffs), τ (tolerance for tabled issues), and θ (the discount applied to the value of the outgoing caretaker government). For each of these key parameters, we identified the best range of values for predicting, *within the training set*: (1) full partisan composition of the observed cabinet and (2) party-level membership of the observed cabinet (see hypotheses H1 and H2, below). We report the difference between out-of-sample results on the training set and the calibrated values to evaluate the extent to which model predictions are improved by this calibration.

iii. We now use two different out-of-sample *test sets of new cases* to evaluate how well our model predicts empirically observed government formation and duration in the real world. When using the model to analyze our test sets, we use the calibrated ranges of values for α, τ, *and* θ, derived as set out in (ii) above.

When using our theoretical model to predict empirically observed outcomes in the real world, we use only open-source inputs for observable model parameters: the number and seats shares of legislative parties[72] and the policy and salience vectors of each party.[73] In other words, we do not employ any case-specific information (no dummy variables, no "pariah parties," no history of elections). All the work is done by the formal model of the governance cycle set out in previous chapters: the institutional environment, behavioral rules for party negotiating politicians, and the scheduling algorithm. Our assumption is that these are largely the same across the case universe of interest to us and, therefore, that it makes sense to think of a general model of the governance cycle.

While we depend on observational data to test our empirical hypotheses, it is important to note that our model was written down and computationally exercised *before* conducting the empirical tests presented here. No setting of observable model parameters was informed by any information in our test datasets. While we are not using experiments (natural or otherwise) to evaluate causal mechanisms, we are nonetheless providing sharp out-of-sample tests of the causal mechanisms embedded in our model.[74]

Testing Predictions of Government Membership and Stability

The central purpose of this chapter is to compare theoretical model predictions of key features of the governance cycle with empirical observations of these: Which parties go into government together and how long do the governments they form tend to endure?

Our aim throughout has been to build a formal model of key processes in the governance cycle and then use this to generate empirical hypotheses about questions such as these. In common with all theorists, we have made assumptions about: the behavior of party leaders, the composition of their utility functions, and a scheduling

---

[72] Sourced from the ParlGov dataset, www.parlgov.org/
[73] Sourced from the CHES expert surveys, www.chesdata.eu/
[74] For a lengthier treatment of this topic, see Technical Appendix A5.

protocol specifying how offers are made and voted on. Our aim has been to produce a *computationally* tractable model that captures complex empirical phenomena which interest us. There is a price to be paid for this. Instead of a purely deductive model, we have a computational model written in computer code. Instead of deductive comparative statics, we use applied statistics to map model inputs into model outputs. Instead of a logical proof of our main results, we have a combination of statistical regularities generated by our model and near-Nash outcomes from our MCCFR refinement. The payoff is a complex model generating distinctive empirical implications that we can compare with empirically realized governments, to assess whether our theory is capturing important features of real political behavior. We successfully used this approach in previous work (de Marchi and Laver 2020), using a different but related model to predict postelectoral delays in government formation. Here, we evaluate the predictive success of the model with distinctive empirical implications summarized in three core hypotheses.[75]

H1: Full cabinet composition. The extensive form game described in Chapter 2 and the behavioral rules described in Chapter 3 (ABM) and Chapter 4 (AI) predict the full *partisan composition* of the cabinet in parliamentary democracies.

We set our models a very low bar if we require them to predict observed cabinets better than a random draw from the set of all logically possible cabinets. To the best of our knowledge, however, there is no other formal model of the high-dimensional governance process we analyze here. In other words, there is no "state of the art" baseline model with which to compare our own predictions. Nonetheless, we need an informative baseline against which to assess our empirical results. We distil this baseline from the many models of coalition government formation put forward over the decades since Riker which have incorporated his central argument in one way or another. This is that the coalition which forms should control enough weight to pass the *winning* threshold but be *minimal* in the sense of including

---

[75] We are, here, making the argument in H1–H3 that our underlying model of government formation and our behavioral models of party leaders must have a correspondence to real-world political phenomena given that we are able to predict outcomes.

no member which can be excluded while still leaving the coalition winning (Riker 1962). The prediction of MWCs, therefore, while in no sense state of the art, is at least a common denominator of many if not most models in the field. We therefore use a uniform random draw from the set of MWCs in each setting under investigation as our baseline, an informative null for comparison.[76]

Turning from predicting the partisan composition of the full cabinet to predicting the participation in government of individual parties, we have:

H2: Party-level membership of cabinet. The extensive form game described in Chapter 2 and the behavioral rules described in Chapter 3 (ABM) and Chapter 4 (AI) predict *cabinet participation of individual parties* in parliamentary democracies.

H2 shifts the case universe from whole cabinets to individual parties. It involves a more fine-grained set of predictions than H1 and allows "partial credit" for the model when it predicts *most* of members of the observed coalition correctly but adds or subtracts a single party, for example.

As we noted in Chapter 3, our model of the full governance cycle also deals with the *expected durations* of predicted cabinets.

H3: Cabinet durations. All else equal, incumbent governments tend to endure longer when: there are fewer predicted winning alternatives to the incumbent; there is a higher probability of chaotic cycling if the government formation process is re-triggered; there are fewer tabled issues in the joint program.

The empirical implications set out in H3 are particularly distinctive to our model. To the best of our knowledge, these implications are shared with no other published model of government duration. H3 therefore sets out a precise empirical test of our ABM, and we use the model to generate three measures that bear directly on it.

First, we measure the proportion, of the thousand trials involved in the Monte Carlo experiment for each case, of winning cabinets predicted by our model *which are not the empirically realized*

---

[76] We present an alternative, policy-based baseline model derived from the prior literature on this topic in Technical Appendix A6. For obvious reasons, we exclude empirical cases where a single party won a legislative majority, since all extant models of government formation make the effectively trivial prediction in such settings that this party will go on to form the government.

government. Given our random perturbation of key input parameters for every trial, each set of 1,000 trials can be seen as representing a set of different "shocked" realities for the case in question. Shocks that generate *model-predicted winning alternatives to the incumbent cabinet* are potentially destabilizing. As the proportion of these increases, the model-predicted durability of the incumbent decreases.

Second, we measure the proportion of trials for each case, each representing a shocked reality, in which *the model predicts there is no winning cabinet*, but rather a chaotic majority rule cycle. As the probability of chaotic cycling in the event the government formation process is retriggered increases, we expect an increase in the robustness of the incumbent government to random shocks. In effect, we assume that a majority of legislators choose the continuation of a cabinet they once preferred to all others, over the alternative of chaotic cycling.

Third, for reasons set out at length in Chapter 3, we expect that a government with more tabled issues in its joint program will be more vulnerable to agenda shocks. These shocks destabilize the incumbent government by forcing its member parties to agree a common position on a high-salience contentious issue on which they previously agreed to disagree.

Data

We could sit back and wait to test model predictions until the emergence of entirely new cases of government formation; parliamentary elections happen all the time. However, it would take years to gain a suitable sample size. Instead, we assemble two test sets, described below, which comprise historical data, but were not referred to in any way when we formulated and calibrated our models. These test sets, therefore, are effectively new data. We calibrate the parameters in our theoretical model based on our Monte Carlo experiments on the *training* data. We then conduct our out-of-sample empirical analysis using the "new" unanalyzed *test* sets.

One test set consists of recent cases from 2006 to 2019 and includes cases from Eastern Europe. The other test set consists of cases we used for a different purpose in earlier empirical work (de Marchi and Laver 2020) and includes largely older cases from 1986 to 2010. We thus have a chance to falsify empirical implications of our model by examining its predictions for "newer" democracies and more recent elections (test set 1) and for more established democracies and older cases (test set 2).[77] For both sets, we excluded elections where the parties and seats won by each party were ambiguous.[78] We also limited our case universe to settings with twelve parties or fewer, due to computational constraints.[79]

The first test set of more recent elections has thirty-five cases and the second test set has thirty-nine cases. The size of these test sets might seem small when compared to previous "large-n" work in comparative politics, so it is important to highlight two distinctive features of our empirical approach. The first is scientific. Much large-n work in comparative politics, for example, is concerned with inductively characterizing the features of a particular case universe, guided by expectations generated by some theory, whether formal or informal. Our work is concerned with a sharp empirical test of case-by-case model predictions, for which we need a representative set of cases, but not necessarily the entire case universe. This is directly analogous to researchers testing the null hypothesis that a new vaccine has no beneficial effect, using a sample of patients that is large enough to allow good representation of the target population, but small enough to be practicable. Concern with practicability motivates our second reason for the relatively small test sets. For every empirical case we investigate, we conduct a 1,000-trial Monte Carlo experiment, where each trial is a run of a complex model. This is a computationally intensive process. Once we have two representative test sets of cases, therefore, we prefer to budget inevitably finite computational resources by running more robust simulations than by adding additional cases. Table 6.1 provides a description of our three samples.

---

[77] We did not engage in selection that might have provided our model with a more consistent/homogeneous case universe. For example, we did not control in any way for case-specific features such as "pariah" parties.

[78] For example, we excluded the 2016 Irish case. The Parlgov database has six (of the ten) independent seats as part of an "independent alliance" – clearly, this is not a party and two of the members of this group voted against the government. Best practice would be to include each independent separately, but (a) it would be difficult to gather policy/salience information on these legislators and (b) that would inflate the number of parties to a point where our model would run into computational limits.

[79] Given the complexity of our ABM and MCCFR algorithms, cases with more than a dozen *pivotal* parties are difficult to run and we save these for future work. There is no reason to believe that the model will behave differently in settings with more than twelve parties than it does for twelve-party systems.

Table 6.1 *Composition of training and test datasets*

	N	Years	# Parties	Countries
Training set	20	1999 to 2010	4 to 10	Austria, Belgium, Bulgaria, Czechoslovakia, Denmark, Estonia, Germany, Finland, Latvia, Luxembourg, Netherlands, Poland, Portugal, Romania, Slovakia, Slovenia, Spain, Sweden, United Kingdom.
Test set 1	35	2006 to 2019	4 to 13	Austria, Bulgaria, Croatia, Czechoslovakia, Estonia, Germany, Finland, Hungary, Latvia, Lithuania, Luxembourg, Netherlands, Poland, Portugal, Romania, Slovakia, Slovenia, Spain, Sweden, United Kingdom.
Test set 2	39	1986 to 2010	4 to 9	Austria, Germany, Iceland, Luxembourg, Netherlands, Norway, Portugal, Sweden, United Kingdom.

If our model generates different levels of performance in the test sets compared to the training set, then, as in the machine learning literature, this is a sign of trouble. "Trouble" here means that our formal model is potentially over-fit to the training cases and does not generalize to new cases. While this represents a significant departure from the way theoretical models are typically tested in political science, we feel it is a good way to develop sharp out-of-sample empirical tests of our theoretical models of the governance cycle in parliamentary democracies.[80]

---

[80] There is a tradition of empirical work in this area, notably Martin and Stevenson (2001). The main idea of this work is to pin down empirical regularities to help guide theoretical models. For example, Martin and Stevenson test the effects of minority versus minimum winning coalitions on the likelihood of government formation. For a more recent attempt to engage in empirical work in this area, see Kayser, et al. (2019).

The first two hypotheses present a challenge to any theoretical model of government formation. There are 2^N-1 possible coalitions that could form in any given case. The large number of possibilities makes it difficult for models to stumble on the empirically realized outcome by chance alone. In what follows, therefore, we evaluate the success rate of model predictions against the null hypothesis, chosen for reasons we set out above, that the cabinet which we observe to form will be a random draw from a *uniform distribution across the set of minimum winning coalitions*.

Model Calibration and Predictive Success on Test Data

In order to provide a baseline for empirical work, we begin with results from our training dataset, chosen to be representative of our target case universe. These are shown in Table 6.2. Detailed case-by-case results are in Technical Appendix A6.

The first row of Table 6.2 shows mean predictive accuracy for the MWC baseline model, which we take as an informative null. Given the large number of possible coalitions, this null does a respectable job, with 13 percent of cases accurately predicted out-of-sample. We also, in Technical Appendix A6, present results from the prominent Laver and Shepsle (1996b) model of government formation, which has roughly the same performance as the MWC baseline. Theoretical models of government formation must clearly exceed this level of accuracy to merit further consideration.

As discussed in Chapter 3, we have two versions of our ABM, distinguished by their use of different search regimes: "alpha-branch" and "best-rule." The second and third rows of Table 6.2 show that predictive success rates for these models are nearly identical. Note that the *untuned* model is making cabinet predictions for the training set which are effectively out-of-sample and both versions of our ABM have an accuracy of 34 percent. This substantially improves the informative null hypothesis. In fact, with the huge amount of potentially relevant case-specific idiosyncrasies – personalities, local institutions, pariah parties, and much, much more – we see this as very encouraging.

Given the effectively identical performance of the two rule regimes in making out-of-sample predictions for the test set, we focus on what follows the *alpha-branch* regime. Recall that with these behavioral rules for partner search, more perks-oriented party leaders look for

Table 6.2 *Tuned and untuned ABM and AI model predictions of full cabinet composition and individual party membership in training data*

	Cabinet level (H1)	Party level (H2)
MWC baseline	0.13	0.61
ABM, alpha-branch, untuned	0.34	0.76
ABM, best-rule, untuned	0.34	0.75
ABM, alpha-branch, tuned	0.35	0.78
AI (MCCFR)	0.40	0.84

partners that allow them to form minimum winning coalitions, while more policy-oriented party leaders look for partners who have ideal policy positions close to their own. This partner search regime is simpler, requires less of actors in terms of the complexity of their behavior, and achieves the same performance as the computationally more intensive best-rule regime. It is, however, worth noting that, while both regimes have similar aggregate performance, there is intercountry variation. For example, the Denmark, Estonia, Finland, Romania, Spain, and the UK cases perform substantially better in the best-rule ABM, while Czechoslovakia, Slovakia, and Sweden perform better in the alpha-branch ABM. This suggests the possibility that key parameters of our ABM vary by case. For example, party leaders in some settings might have less tolerance for tabled issues or more of a taste for perks over policy. We leave such case-specific explorations for future work.

The next question concerns whether we can improve predictive accuracy by calibrating the ABM model. Can we tune fundamentally unobservable model parameters to achieve better predictions? These parameters are: α (the weight on perks versus policy in the utility function), τ (the anticipated policy loss associated with a tabled issue), and θ (the discount rate for the SQ government).

Using the training dataset, we calibrate these parameters using a simple grid search. Instead of using all the data, we choose ranges for each of the above parameters, truncating the training set accordingly, to improve predictive accuracy.[81] Obviously, once we engage in this

---

[81] For the three parameters of interest, we defined an initial bin size of 0.1 on each parameter to perform the grid search. This is reasonably coarse but appropriate to the sample size.

sort of calibration we are no longer engaged in an out-of-sample test *on the training data* for H1 and H2. It is, however, useful to see how tuning these model parameters affects predictive accuracy. In Table 6.2, therefore, we report both untuned model accuracy (which is effectively out-of-sample) and tuned accuracy for the alpha-branch ABM, based on calibrated parameter values. Table 6.2 shows that calibrating our parameters did not greatly improve the overall accuracy of the model. We moved from 34 to 35 percent accuracy, and it is important to keep in mind that the latter is now an *in*-sample analysis.[82]

Finally, Table 6.2 has results for our fully strategic AI model, based on the refined MCCFR algorithm described in Chapter 4.[83] In Chapters 3 and 4, we left it as an open question the matter of how strategic the actual behavior of negotiating politicians might be, given the complexity of the governance process. The out-of-sample performance of the AI model on the training dataset is a very encouraging 40 percent.[84] Performance is enhanced, it seems, by assuming that negotiating politicians are in fact quite sophisticated. While we can capture much of the signal with the far simpler behaviors specified in our ABM, moving to a computationally more complex and strategic model does enhance predictive accuracy. This has important implications for modeling the behavior of party leaders engaged in complex negotiations.

Analysis of the training set also generated encouraging results for H2, which focuses on whether our models accurately predict the cabinet membership of individual parties. Results are reported in the second column in Table 6.2. Following the same progression as above, our first result is for the informative null of MCWs. This achieves a respectable 61 percent accuracy. In comparison, the result for our untuned ABM improves to an out-of-sample accuracy of 75–76 percent. Unsurprisingly, calibration again achieves an improvement, albeit modest, to an in-sample accuracy of 78 percent. Finally, our

---

[82] As noted above in the comparison of the two versions of the ABM, the calibration process did reveal that large gains could be made by calibrating parameters case-by-case. This suggests that important differences exist between cases. That said, our goal here is to build a general model of government formation and we leave this topic for future work.

[83] As noted in Chapter 5, we leveraged the training set to tune parameters for the ABM. The AI model, however, does not rely on parameters tuned on the training set so this is, in effect, an out-of-sample test.

[84] As with the untuned ABM, the AI results on the training data are effectively out-of-sample since no tuning/calibration took place.

fully strategic AI model achieves an out-of-sample accuracy of 84 percent in predicting individual party membership of observed cabinets in the training dataset. We consider these results to be a successful preliminary test for our theoretical models' ability to explain real-world political phenomena.

Empirical Analysis of ABM Predictions Using of New Test Data

Having established benchmarks, we now turn to the key empirical tests of our ABM – out-of-sample tests on completely new data. As we noted above, test set 1 comprises more modern cases and includes "newer" democracies in Central and Eastern Europe. The results of comparing model predictions with observed outcomes are reported in Table 6.3. Similar results are reported for test set 2, comprised entirely of more established democracies. The use of two different test sets, with different mixes of cases, allows us in effect to conduct two independent out-of-sample tests of the model and differences in results between the test sets can be informative.

In evaluating results reported in Table 6.3, we first compare the out-of-sample accuracy scores against those in the training set. As in the machine learning literature, if there is a significant drop off in accuracy from training to test sets, this raises concerns about the *robustness* of the theoretical model. Since we have two very different types of test set – one more modern and diverse, one older and with more established

Table 6.3 *Calibrated ABM predictions of full cabinet composition, and party membership of the cabinet, in test sets 1 and 2*

	Test set 1		Test set 2	
	Cabinet level (H1)	Party level (H2)	Cabinet level (H1)	Party level (H2)
MWC baseline	0.08	0.58	0.15	0.60
ABM alpha-branch, tuned	0.28	0.78	0.42	0.78
AI (MCCFR)	0.31	0.78	0.41	0.78

democracies – we have a chance to see if there is a particular type of empirical setting that causes problems for our model. For H1, concerning predictions of full cabinet membership, there is a small dip (7 percent) in accuracy for test set 1 but an identical increase in accuracy for test set 2, possibly explained both by the relative diversity and by the larger party system sizes of test set 1, compared to the relative homogeneity of test set 2. Note that the null hypothesis, predicting MWCs, is actually *half* as accurate in test set 1 as in test set 2. In both test sets, our ABM was about three times more accurate in predicting full cabinet membership than the MWC baseline.

For H2, concerning model predictions of party-level cabinet membership, the model is 78 percent accurate for both test sets, essentially identical to the out-of-sample accuracy of party-level predictions for the training data. In all cases, four out of five model predictions about whether a party is on or out of government are accurate. Again, this is a substantially higher predictive accuracy than the MWC baseline.

We therefore conclude, in terms of predicting both the full partisan composition of the cabinet and party-level inclusion in this, that our ABM of the governance cycle is performing well across a universe of cases, which includes almost all European parliamentary systems from the 1980s onward.

Empirical Analysis of AI Predictions Using New Test Data

As with the ABM, our AI model continues to be accurate in out-of-sample tests. For the first test, accuracy is 31 percent for coalition-level predictions and 78 percent for party-level predictions. For the second, accuracy is 41 percent for coalition-level predictions and 78 percent for party-level predictions. The out-of-sample accuracies of the ABM and AI models are, therefore, quite similar, but this underestimates the performance of the AI model. As we discussed at the end of Chapter 4, one important difference between the two approaches is that, unlike the ABM, the AI model does not have a "win-stay, lose-shift" feature, but in effect allows parties to renegotiate every coalition afresh, without regard to whether or not the previous government continues to control a majority of seats in parliament.

Additional features of the AI results are worth noting. First, as we saw in Chapter 4, the AI model consists of sophisticated actors relying on mixed strategies. We exercise the model by allowing these actors to play the game multiple times, thereby producing a range of outcomes. That said, it is *not* the case that every potentially winning coalition is equally desirable to party leaders. As a result, party leaders' mixed strategies focus on a relatively small set of proto-coalitions.

Second, the AI model, unlike the ABM, does not confine parties to making Gamsonian perks proposals; party leaders can make *any proposal at all* with respect to perks and policy. Using Iceland 2009 as an example of the AI results, the most likely coalition identified by the model is the coalition that was empirically realized: a minimum winning coalition featuring the Social Democratic Alliance (twenty seats in parliament) and the Left-Green Movement (sixteen seats). Empirically, the Sigurðardóttir 1 government split perks as evenly as possible, with each partner receiving four ministries. When the AI model predicts the correct *cabinet composition* in Iceland 2009, it does so on the basis of a range of *different perks distributions*. The minimum AI-predicted perks share for the Social Democrats across the set of outcomes predicted by the AI model is 0.2, the maximum is 0.8, while the mean predicted perks-share for this party is 0.6.

Given this and the canonical status in the profession of Gamson's law, it is worth asking more generally if the AI model returns Gamsonian perks. We will return to this important matter in future work, but our preliminary findings are that, while the AI model does generate a distribution of predicted perk distributions, the mean perk shares for each coalition member (weighted by the probability mass returned by the model for each outcome) largely conform to Gamson's law. To the extent that parties are predicted to have super-proportional perks shares, they tend to be smaller or more centrally located (with lower multidimensional eccentricity).

Third, the ABM tends to make "flatter" predictions than the AI model across a number of different proto-coalitions.[85] For example, the ABM has an accuracy of 0.29 for predicting which coalition forms in the Iceland 2009 case, but there are other, very different coalitions predicted by the model across the 1,000 trials. In contrast, when it

---

[85] As discussed in Chapter 4, these outcomes are different in nature than the ABM. With the ABM, the variance in results is due to our fundamental uncertainty about parameter values and we treat these distributions as informative. With the AI, variance is due to allowing the actors to employed mixed strategies in independent plays of the game. Given this, we use the most likely outcome as our prediction.

comes to coalition predictions, the AI model places its "bet" on a single coalition and thus has accuracies of 0 or 1 for each case.

ABMs or AI Behavioral Models?

Across all three datasets taken together, the accuracy of the AI model is slightly better than that of the ABM. This is notable in light of the fact that, unlike the ABM, the AI model does not leverage knowledge of the *status quo* government. This is consistent with an interpretation that negotiating politicians engage in relatively sophisticated strategic reasoning about the complex process of government formation. That said, the AI algorithm relies on enormous amounts of computation, since it depends fundamentally on massively repeated self-play. Substantively, it seems unlikely that negotiating politicians negotiating in real time, even complemented by expert staffs, are relying on this type of algorithm.

Our ABM, on the other hand, has performance that compares well to that of the AI model and has two advantages. First, it is more transparent, in the sense that the behavioral rules for negotiating politicians outlined in Chapter 3 are much easier to understand than the AI algorithm detailed in Chapter 4. This transparency allows us to conduct computational comparative statics in Chapter 5, and this in turn, crucially, allows for *substantively interpretable* mappings of model inputs into model outputs. In this way, the ABM generates a series of substantive hypotheses, given the transparency of the parameters, which allow us to gain deeper insight into its mechanisms. In contrast, and in common with many AI models, our AI model is less transparent.[86] Even if it were to have a significantly higher level of predictive success, we would remain largely in the dark as to how this was achieved, and, therefore, would not expand our *casual* understating of the governance process.

Second, the ABM is much more efficient computationally. Substantively, this arguably makes it a more plausible description of senior politicians' decision-making in real time. Pragmatically, the ABM scales to settings with larger numbers of parties and allows both us and others to rerun

---

[86] To be concrete, the AI model returns mixed strategies for every actor. Given the sheer size of the extensive form game that is being played, substantively interpreting these strategies is a difficult task.

analyses using tweaks and changes to model assumptions, while requiring only modest amounts of computational power.

Given these advantages, we focus in what follows on empirical analyses of results generated by the ABM. For now, we note the impressive performance of the AI model and that this is to our knowledge the first deployment of an AI algorithm to resolve a complex political game. Given the large research program that this potentially opens up, however, we set this aside as something to which we will return in future work.

Empirical Tests of Model Predictions of Cabinet Durations

Hypothesis H3 concerns model-predicted durations of cabinets and leverages a key advantage of the ABM we noted above; the transparency of our model enables sharp empirical tests. When a new government is approved by any legislature, it is constitutionally liable to be voted out of office again by that same legislature at any point in time. While a majority of legislators must have preferred the incumbent to any alternative at the moment of formation, an unanticipated shock might change their minds. A key consideration for senior politicians in a parliamentary system is always whether, in the wake of some unanticipated shock, there is now a more compelling alternative cabinet to the incumbent. The insight provided by our model is that, in some settings, there may be shocked realities in which many good alternatives exist. In such settings, the incumbent government is, other things equal, more exposed to defeat in favor of some explicit alternative. In other settings, our model shows that there are fewer shocked realities generating good alternatives to the incumbent, increasing its model-predicted durability.

Our model suggests several measures of the robustness of the incumbent government to random shocks. Recall that the computational implementation of our model using Monte Carlo experiments is *stochastic*. Rather than making a single point prediction, it generates a *probability distribution of potentially winning cabinets* across the state space of possibilities. For any given setting, this probability distribution gives us important information about the potential stability of the incumbent. Our stochastic model of government formation returns the probability, in the simulated set of 1,000 perturbed states of the world we investigate, that the cabinet we empirically observe as the incumbent is predicted by the model as the winning outcome. It also returns two other important pieces of information. The first is the probability that *alternatives, or rivals, to the incumbent* are winning in different perturbed states of the world. Call this P_{rival}. This represents the likelihood that a random shock creates a situation in which there is at least one alternative cabinet that would prevail in a retriggered government formation process.

The second measure arises from the fact that a random perturbation may result in a setting in which *there is no winning cabinet*. When this happens, there will either be a chaotic majority rule cycle across a series of three or more alternatives or, more likely, some unmodeled cycle-busting mechanism. Call the probability that this is the case, in our set of 1,000 perturbed trials, P_{chaos}. As this measure increases, so does the likelihood that a random shock will generate a setting in which party leaders face a chaotic majority-rule voting cycle, with an unpredictable outcome.

Underlying both of these measures is the core dynamic of our stochastic model of government survival. How likely is it that some random shock leaves negotiating politicians preferring an alternative to the incumbent cabinet, if the government formation process we model is retriggered? The greater this likelihood, the less robust will be the incumbent cabinet to the stream of random shocks to which any incumbent government is inevitably subjected. H3, stated more precisely, says that the stability of the incumbent cabinet will tend to decrease in P_{rival} and increase in P_{chaos}, as well as decreasing in the number of tabled issues in the joint program.

In testing H3, we make some concessions arising from the relatively small size of the test sets. We merge all three of our datasets detailed in Table 6.1. Since *no model calibration is used to predict cabinet durations*, the data in the training and both test sets are effectively out-of-sample when it comes to predicting government durations.[87] The resulting sample size still remains quite small, however, so we use a simple model with relatively few parameters to test H3. Following the body of published work on government durations, this is a Poisson model. We include control variables for both the number of legislative parties and the legislative type, which have been systematically shown

---

[87] While we may be missing out from performance gains from calibrating on a test set with duration as a target, the loss in sample size would decrease confidence in our results.

Table 6.4 *Model-predicted*
government durations (N = 84,
bootstrapped standard errors)

Duration (days)	b	SE
P_{rival}	−0.48	0.03
P_{chaos}	1.24	0.04
Tabled issues	−5.02	0.69
n-parties	−0.05	0.00
Type B	0.19	0.01
Type C	−0.18	0.02
Type D	0.21	0.01
constant	7.09	0.00
(pseudo) R^2	0.12	

to affect government stability (Laver and Benoit 2015). The results are shown in Table 6.4.[88]

Table 6.4 shows that all relevant regression coefficients are substantial and in the predicted direction, providing strong support for H3. The coefficient for P_{rival} (the proportion of perturbed cases generating model-predicted winning alternatives to the incumbent) is negative, as predicted by our model. If a higher proportion of shocks generate model-predicted winning alternatives to the incumbent, then the incumbent does indeed tend to be less stable. The coefficient for P_{chaos} (the proportion of perturbed cases generating no model-predicted winning cabinet) is positive, also as predicted by our model. If a higher proportion of shocks generate chaotic cycling as an alternative to the incumbent, then it does indeed tend to be more stable.

Table 6.4 also shows that cabinets that are predicted by our model to have more tabled issues do systematically tend, empirically, to have shorter durations. According to our model, this is because

[88] Some of the prior literature has used a Cox proportional hazards model for government duration. Given that we have two *continuous* independent variables of theoretical interest and there is very little probability mass on counts under one hundred days, it would be difficult to demonstrate that the proportional hazards assumption holds. A log logistic AFT model was also used and had, in all cases, the same signs and comparable magnitudes as the Poisson model. Given the higher number of parameters in this model, however, significance on individual coefficients is somewhat worse.

agenda shocks are more likely to force onto the cabinet agenda the need for partners in government to resolve a salient issue on which they can neither agree nor logroll.

To sum up, three independent variables that are very distinctive implications of our model systematically predict out-of-sample cabinet durations, controlling for the number of legislative parties and the legislative type, both shown in prior work to have a strong systematic impact on government stability. We consider these three empirical findings to be extremely encouraging because they are so distinctively derived from our model, and so unlike predictions made by others who have previously modeled government durability.

Conclusion

We are very encouraged by these empirical results. We've done things differently from many previous empirical analyses in political science. We use our theoretical model to make explicit predictions about observed outcomes on a case-by-case basis in two out-of-sample test sets, rather than using regression models inductively to characterize relationships between independent and dependent variables. The predictions we make, furthermore, are very distinctive to our models – making it less likely that there are confounding explanations for our results. Using our model of government formation in a high-dimensional manifest issue space, we predict both the full membership of the cabinets likely to form and the participation in government of individual parties. We wish there were state-of-the-art baseline predictions with which to compare those of our model, but to the best of our knowledge there are not. Using the prediction of MWCs as a lowest-common-denominator baseline, our model predictions improve substantially on this. (We also show in Technical Appendix A6 that a policy-based model baseline derived from previously published work performed no better than the MWC baseline.)

We illustrated how to tune the computational model on a training dataset by identifying values of fundamentally unobservable model parameters that are associated with successful predictions. We learned two lessons from this. First, when parameters are tuned to enhance predictive accuracy across the entire country universe of test cases, there are benefits in out-of-sample predictive accuracy from doing this, though in our case they were modest. Second, we found evidence that tuning model parameters on a country-by-country basis would yield substantially bigger gains in predictive accuracy. This is substantively plausible, since unobserved country-specific features are likely to affect the mapping of model inputs into successful model predictions. Whether to tune a model for the entire case universe or on a country-by-country basis is an interesting and important methodological decision. We opted to tune for the entire country universe, because we are interested here in what we think of as theoretical comparative politics. If the maximand is the model's predictive accuracy, however, as opposed to deriving general substantive intuitions from the model, then tuning on a country-by-country basis is almost certain to be more successful.

We saw that the tuned ABMs made predictions about government membership in the out-of-sample test data that substantially improved on the informative baseline. And we also saw that our AI model, which learns how to navigate the government formation process strategically by massively repeated self-play, outperformed the ABMs in the training dataset and had similar predictive accuracy in the test datasets without leveraging information from prior elections. We think this is an important finding which opens up a whole new line of potential enquiry. Our AI model, the first of which we are aware in political science, attacks a problem that is too complex and intractable for traditional deductive game theory and generates results closely analogous to a game-theoretic solution, had one been available. Rather than using backward induction, the AI approach plays the game over and over again against simulated rational opponents – some doing exactly the same thing – and relentlessly learns the optimum mixed strategies for a huge and complex game tree.

Finally, we feel that our model's predictions of expected government durations are particularly impressive. Our stochastic approach to modeling cabinet survival precisely matches the mainstream view in political science that government stability is about robustness to an endless stream of potentially fatal random shocks. Simulating such shock streams, we show that three quantities distinctively derived from our model and no other – P_{rival}, P_{chaos} and the number of predicted tabled issues – significantly enhance the accuracy of our predictions of cabinet durations, over and above other features of each setting that have been shown to predict durations in prior published work. We said at the outset that finding empirical implications that are distinctive to our model and no other is the key to empirically evaluating our model, and we have now done this.

7 | Conclusions and Aspirations

What Have We Learnt about the Governance Cycle?

Substantively, this book is about the governance cycle in parliamentary democracies. We model component parts of this complex system and key interactions between these. Government formation is at the heart of the governance cycle. Not only is it triggered by an election, a government defeat, or government resignation, but the survival of any incumbent government depends fundamentally on the likelihood that some random shock now leaves a majority of legislators preferring some alternative government.

Modeling all of this rigorously would overwhelm traditional deductive methods, so we deploy two very different computational approaches. The first is a "bottom up" ABM. This is related to, but different from, notions of bounded rationality and behavioral economics. Substantively, this means we see seasoned and sophisticated politicians engaged in government formation as "functionally rational." They look for good solutions when they tackle hard problems for which the perfectly optimal solution is elusive. The second computational approach we deploy is a "top down" AI. This learns how to attack hard problems using massively repeated self-play of randomly selected paths through the game tree. This type of approach, which can beat the world's best human Poker, Go, and Chess players, has not to our knowledge been used to attack hard problems in political science.

So what have we learnt from all of this about the governance cycle? Building on our earlier work (de Marchi and Laver 2020), we have increased our understanding of why the hard job of forming a government can take so much time and effort. One of the most difficult parts of this process is wrangling a set of conflicting policy manifestos, each dealing with a huge number of issues, into an agreed government program. We describe this wrangling as logrolling, and model how functionally rational politicians might do this. This allows us to explore when politicians can – and when they can't – successfully wrangle an agreed policy program, even when their ideal issue positions diverge considerably at the start of the process. No other scholar, to our knowledge, has done this.

An important part of logrolling an agreed policy program is the plain fact that it is not necessary to include *everything* in this. Negotiators can "table" issues on which they agree to disagree. This seems to us to be eminently plausible substantively – implying that the set of issues covered in the government program is *endogenous* – yet missing in previous theoretical accounts of government formation.

Our stochastic modeling approach yields *probability distributions* of predicted government formation outcomes. Again, we feel that this is both substantively plausible yet missing from much previous theoretical work on government formation. No self-respecting "inside the beltway" analyst would in any circumstance say that the political future is 100 percent certain. Most, however, would indeed say that some outcomes are more probable than others. For the same reasons, we feel that our predicted probability distributions over the set of possible outcomes are a substantive improvement over previous models which make point predictions.

Another important substantive lesson from our modeling of government formation negotiations as logrolling is that stable predicted outcomes are possible, even in high-dimensional settings. Influential previous work on social choice theory (Schofield 1983, McKelvey and Schofield 1986, 1987) predicted chaotic cycling in such settings. Addressing this, influential previous work in noncooperative game theory predicted stable outcomes by assuming an exogenously imposed sequence of offers, with an advantage to the person selected to make the first offer (Rubinstein 1982, Baron and Ferejohn 1989, Baron 1991). Both accounts of government formation are substantively implausible, and what we have learnt here is that stable outcomes can emerge from a behavioral model of how seasoned politicians wrangle high-dimensional policy negotiations.

Turning to the detail of our model, we learnt that predictions of possible outcomes depend – we think plausibly – on underlying psychological characteristics of negotiating politicians. One of these is the trade-off (α) between the value of simply being in office, pure and simple, and the value of government policy positions. We take into account how different politicians may make different trade-offs and show how this affects government formation. Perks-oriented politicians tend to prefer single-party minority cabinets, in which their perks expectations are higher. Policy-oriented politicians tend to favor coalition cabinets, in which they can logroll policy outcomes closer to their ideal points. Calibrating our model to the training data, furthermore, we learnt that the model works best if we assume politicians tend to be perks - rather than policy - oriented. Since this underlying psychological parameter is fundamentally unobservable, this is a significant new substantive finding.

Another psychological factor that affects government formation concerns tolerance (τ) of tabled issues in the logrolled government program. Some politicians may be risk tolerant (or optimistic); others may be risk averse (or pessimistic). Other things equal, cautious politicians who dislike having tabled issues in the government program will obviously tend to prefer coalitions involving fewer tabled issues, and in particular to prefer single-party minority cabinets, in which there is no tabled issue. More optimistic or risk-tolerant politicians will be more open to coalitions, which are likely to involve at least some issues on which they agree to disagree, hoping that these are not forced onto the government agenda by some unexpected shock. Calibrating our model, we learnt that the model works best if we assume politicians tend to be optimistic rather than pessimistic about having tabled issues in the joint program – therefore, finding it easier to wrangle such a program. This is another matter not treated, as far as we are aware, by any previous work.

The third psychological parameter concerns how politicians feel about the continuation value of a caretaker government (θ) during stalled government formation negotiations. This captures the likely discounting of the value of cabinet portfolios held in a caretaker cabinet; substantively, these are likely to be valued less than the same portfolios held in a newly formed administration. Some politicians in some settings may be perfectly happy to continue in office on a caretaker basis; others may not. Calibrating our model, we learnt that the model works best if we assume politicians tend to discount the value of holding office in caretaker governments quite heavily. Since the value of the "reversion point" in the event of failure is critical to any understanding of bargaining and negotiation, we think this is another finding that is both substantively important and original.

Finally, we learnt a lot about the substantively important matter of government survival. While this is a subject that most previous scholars treated empirically by running regressions on large-n data, our stochastic modeling approach is ideally suited to giving us a *theoretical* understanding of government survival. This is because our model generates predicted *distributions* of what are in effect alternative realities. We can think of each of these alternative realities as coming into being following an unexpected shock that may leave a majority of legislators now preferring some alternative to the incumbent. Such shocks may also force tabled issues onto the government agenda, another source of potential instability. We learnt that this account of government survival added significantly to our ability to predict government durations, controlling for factors identified in previous work. Our successful predictions about government durability, furthermore, distinguish our model sharply from previous work and in this way add to our confidence in the substantive plausibility of our approach.

What Have We Learnt about Modeling Complex Social Interactions?

Moving beyond substantively important features of the governance cycle, we firmly believe that the type of computational analysis we develop here is part of the future of political science. This is already evident in various *empirical* political science research programs, such as those involving computational text analysis. Eggers and Spirling (2016), for example, use computational methods to analyze the official record of 856,405 House of Commons speeches made between 1832 and 1915, investigating the emergence of the British shadow cabinet. King, Pan, and Roberts (2013) collected and analyzed over 11 million social media posts in their investigation of social media censorship in China. Analyses such as these would have been inconceivable before political scientists had access to current levels of computational firepower. Despite their growing contribution to theoretical analysis in the natural sciences, and despite political science's aspiration to be a *bone fide* science, however, computational methods have had rather little impact on *theoretical* research programs in political science.

The past 60 or so years of formal theoretical analysis in political science has followed neoclassical microeconomics in relying heavily on the resolution of simple models using deductive logic.

The relentless progress of this research program over the years, which has evolved into a powerful subfield, reflects the fact that this approach has been a fertile source both of publishable theoretical results and useful insights. We wholeheartedly applaud the rigor and discipline that deductive modeling has brought to theoretical political science. A rigorous deductive proof is true forever – conditional of course on its assumptions. If the result is also *substantively* important, it is unambiguously valuable – as valuable, for example, as the result that the area of a circle, radius r, is $\pi \cdot r^2$.[89] However, while a rigorous formal proof can be elegant and beautiful, not everything that is elegant and beautiful is also useful. Theoretical political science should be more than an exercise in aesthetics; it should help us to understand the real world.

We have absolutely no desire to criticize those who came before us. Our models are built on foundations laid down by these theorists. Our aim is to try to map possible pathways for those who come after us. It does seem to us to be self-evident that computational methods will revolutionize theorizing in political science and will do this by allowing us to build more realistic models of complex political processes. No longer it is necessary to simplify models of the world so radically that, while we can solve them with a pencil and paper, they no longer plausibly refer to the world we seek to understand.

Computational methods will power a new type of formal modeling – and computational models are *quintessentially* formal models. There is nothing more formal than a model expressed precisely in code and resolved by a machine. The necessary rigor in computational modeling arises at two stages in the process. First, the computer code must scrupulously express the written description of the model presented to readers. Second, the computational experiments exercising the model must be carefully designed and analyzed, to allow model inputs to be mapped unambiguously into model outputs. These experiments generate "artificial data," and the mapping of inputs into outputs is carried out using modern methods of data analysis, rather than algebra.

The approach to mapping inputs into outputs that we use in this book makes our theoretical approach distinctive in two different ways. The first is that it involves computational experiments with

---

[89] Always assuming the circle is drawn on a plane and not, for example, on a sphere.

Monte Carlo parameterizations. We randomly select values of *unobservable* input parameters from substantively plausible ranges and then run the computer code to derive the logically implied outputs. While the randomization of input parameters is a stochastic process, our underlying ABM of government formation is deterministic, *for a given vector of input parameters*. A given vector of inputs implies a given vector of outputs. This is because our artificial agents are not randomizing in any way when they make decisions. A natural extension of the work we report above would be to assume, *behaviorally*, that key political decision makers randomize their choices of actions – in well-specified ways, in well-specified situations, for well-specified reasons.

There is a second feature of our modeling approach that is fundamentally stochastic, however. For each trial in our Monte Carlo experiments, we add parameterized Gaussian noise to *observable* agent characteristics – in our case to issue positions and saliences. We interpret this in two complementary ways. The first concerns the essential problem of measurement. Even if these "observable" parameters *theoretically* have "true" values, we can only *in practice* measure these with a degree of random error. The second is that these features of the world are subject to *fundamental uncertainty*. Making the comparison with Brownian motion in the physical world, we can think of a social world in which key features are continually subject to Gaussian shocks, each generating a potentially different reality. Some different realities may be associated with sufficiently different inputs that they generate different model-predicted outcomes. Over a large number of trials, therefore, a given (perturbed) vector of input parameters generates a *probability distribution of possible outcomes*.

This stochastic modeling approach sets us apart from much of the current mainstream modeling in political science, not least because our empirical prediction for any given out-of-sample empirical case is a *probability distribution over the set of possible outcomes*, not a point prediction of a single outcome. As would be the case with any rigorous real-life predictions, in some settings our prediction may focus on a very small number of possible outcomes, while in other settings the model may be compatible with a wider range of possible outcomes. Given what we believe to be the fundamental uncertainty of the social world, we see this as an eminently realistic consequence of our stochastic approach, not a drawback. This therefore has general implications for work, not only on the governance cycle, but on a wide range of important problems in political science.

Both our ABM and our AI approaches rely to a great extent on *reinforcement learning*. This is another huge area of scholarly effort that has powered major advances in other disciplines, but which has to date had little impact on theoretical political science. This is likely because formal deductive models of learning are very, very hard. It is no big thing, however, to specify, code, and run a learning model computationally. Confining ourselves to formal deductive methods, therefore, would isolate us from a considerable amount of very relevant wisdom about reinforcement learning which has developed in other fields. Sophisticated and seasoned senior politicians, according to many high-tech formal models of politics, are much less able to learn than baby rats. Our AI model is fundamentally built on learning, but our ABM also has an important "win-stay, lose-shift" component borrowed directly from the reinforcement learning literature. It seems to us to be self-evident that, behaviorally, many politicians will continue to do what they are already doing, as long as this is successful – even if a comprehensive strategic reanalysis of their situation at every single decision point might possibly, sometimes, yield a somewhat better option.

We conclude this discussion by drawing attention to our empirical method. This is much closer to modern approaches in machine learning than to the traditional approach in empirical comparative politics, which is to borrow or build a "large-n"[90] dataset of measures relevant to the problem at hand and then fit a regression model to this. The parameters of interest in such regressions are typically drawn, with varying degrees of rigor, from either a new theoretical model or informal conjectures derived from a survey of the existing literature. Our approach, in contrast, is first to exercise our model on a test dataset of relevant empirical data, using this phase of the analysis first to calibrate unobservable model parameters to empirical realities and then engage in the computational mapping of model inputs into model outputs.

Having developed theoretical expectations and calibrated unobservable parameters, we set aside the test data and turn to new

---

[90] Of course "large," for most political science research programs, would be "microscopically small" for most data science applications.

out-of-sample datasets. Our core empirical test is whether the model makes good out-of-sample predictions. While large datasets are typically better than small ones, with careful design we can still conduct rigorous tests of model predictions on relatively small out-of-sample datasets.[91] Our out-of-sample datasets are relatively small because, unlike most traditional empirical analyses in political science, we first make case-by-case predictions rather than predicting parameter effects *on average* and, second, run a computationally intensive 1,000-trial Monte Carlo experiment for every single case we investigate. Because we are not simply fitting a model to these data, however, but testing model predictions case by case and strictly out of sample, we can still draw informative conclusions from our empirical analysis. While ours is not a conventional method of empirical analysis in terms of old-school political science, we commend it to others as a way of leveraging insights from other fields concerned fundamentally with testing model predictions on out-of-sample empirical data.

What Next?

More Computational Power

The analyses reported in this book were implemented on a desktop workstation. This was powerful, but had nothing even approaching the power currently available via high-performance computing solutions. And it has nothing like the power that will be available on your very own desktop in a few years' time. We have three things to say about this. The first is that none of the findings we report in this book have been compromised by using "too little" computational firepower. Our published findings are *very* unlikely indeed to be reversed by running ever more simulations. The second is that we do not want to leave any reader with the view that the type of work we report here is open only to those with the access and know-how to code and run models on high-performance computers. In our view, you can make huge progress in computational social science using the machine already sitting

---

[91] If we are testing the null hypothesis that a six-sided dice is unbiased and throw it 50 times, and if it comes up six every time, then we can reject to null with a high degree of confidence. No statistician would tell us we need to throw it 1,000 more times before we can reach this conclusion.

on your desk. It's just a matter of deciding to do this. Our third point, however, is that we could push our work much further using more computational firepower.

Our AI model of government formation, for example, was coarsened until it was compatible with our computational budget. The computational load will scale up by orders of magnitude as we "uncoarsen" the model but, if we had the computational budget to absorb this, we would end up with a model that is closer to the empirical reality we are investigating. "More powerful AI" would be a welcome product of more powerful computing.

Another area in which we made compromises given our current computational budget was in our ABM of government survival. We did model the effects of preference and agenda shocks as part of our existing Monte Carlo experiments. We did not model the effect of opinion shocks – shocks to anticipated election results revealed, for example in public opinion polling. To do this would increase the computational load by an order of magnitude. This is because modeling the effect of a single opinion shock in a single case involves running a new 1,000-trial Monte Carlo experiment to estimate the model-predicted effect. If we wanted to estimate the effect of a distribution of, say, 1,000 potential opinion shocks, we are now looking at very large Monte Carlos per case. We do plan this as an avenue for future work.[92]

Perks as Well as Policy Negotiations

The essence of our model of government formation was to assume politicians negotiate agreed policy programs by logrolling but, as a behavioral short-cut, accept the folk-wisdom that perks allocations will be proportional to their legislative seat shares. We think there are good substantive justifications for this. The essence of all government formation negotiations, as least as these are reported, is coming up with a deal on policy, given sometimes radically divergent party manifestos. Only when agreed policy has been settled are the portfolios shared out. Indeed, the logic of the Laver–Shepsle portfolio allocation

---

[92] There are big potential efficiency gains when doing this, arising from ignoring shocks which do not change the decisive structure, and from binning shocks by the new decisive structures they generate.

model is that cabinet portfolios can only be allocated *after* the agreed policy program is known, since each cabinet minister is responsible for implementing policy in some particular area of the agreed program (Laver and Shepsle 1996b). It seems to us very unlikely that, after tiresome and complex policy negotiations have finally succeeded, the negotiating parties then turn their attention to a fight over the portfolio shares they will command. It seems far more likely that these policy negotiations are conducted in the shadow of the assumption that, setting aside who gets which particular portfolio, portfolio shares at the end of the day will be proportional.

However, we also assumed that some negotiating politicians do care more about perks and some care more about policy, capturing this in the alpha parameter in each politician's utility function. This implies that perks-oriented politicians might be motivated to make policy concessions to policy-oriented coalition partners in exchange for more perks, while policy-oriented coalition partners might be equally interested in agreeing to such a trade. While the Gamson's law regressions reported many times in the literature are very robust, there may nonetheless, *on the margin*, be deals to be done like this. If this is the case, then outliers getting a higher perks share than predicted by Gamson's law should be more perks-oriented, and those getting a lower than predicted perks share should be more policy-oriented. Since the value of alpha, the perks-policy trade-off, is a fundamentally unobservable quantity for any given politician, this will not be an easy matter to investigate empirically.

Alternatively, we might modify the model's agent decision rules to allow politicians to make perks offers that are not perfectly proportional. Our experiments with models that allowed politicians to propose *absolutely any* perks allocation resulted, essentially, in very unstable predictions – as might be expected from the fact the perks allocation under such rules is a divide-the-dollar game. However, it is possible to imagine decision rules under which rational deviations from Gamson's law on the margin might be achieved, while still being compatible with empirically observed patterns. For example, a perks-oriented party might propose to a policy-oriented party that it receives one more cabinet portfolio than would be proportional, in exchange for conceding on a number of high-salience contested issues that would otherwise be tabled. This model extension, if true, should better predict government formation.

Predicting Government Policy

We have so far left a very important feature of our model's predictions on the table when it comes to empirical research – the content of the agreed government policy program. This prediction, arising out of high-dimensional logrolling between the partners in government, is particularly distinctive to our model. The agreed policy program of the government that eventually forms, furthermore, is something which is to the best of our knowledge rarely predicted, as opposed to being assumed, by other models of government formation.[93] We do in fact use one feature of the agreed government policy program in the empirical work we report here. This is the predicted number of tabled issues in the program, which we use, with some success, to predict observed government durations. We have yet to test our model predictions of the substantive content of the joint program.

The core problems in doing this will be methodological. In contrast to the situation with party policy positions, there is much less available data on the substance of agreed government policy programs – which tend to differ considerably from case to case in terms of form and content. Indeed, it is only very recently that authoritative collections of the raw texts these programs have been assembled (Klüver and Bäck 2019). Analyzing these texts in a manner allowing the results to be compared with model predictions, and then rigorously performing such comparisons, will be a substantial empirical research program – a matter to which we will return in future work.[94]

---

[93] Exceptions include Laver and Shepsle (1996b), Dragu and Laver (2017, 2019).

[94] Once the collection of joint program texts is released into the public domain, analyze each text to estimate its position in the fourteen-dimensional issue space generated by the CHES expert survey data. (Klüver and Bäck report analyzing these using human coders and the CMP's 56-category coding scheme, which as we report above does not generate stable high-dimensional common spaces.) Use human coders (experts or crowd workers) to label, for positions in the fourteen CHES issue dimensions, the subset of government programs arising from settings in the training set. Train a suitable supervised machine learning algorithm using these human labels. Use the trained algorithm to label the out-of-sample government programs. The result will be a dataset on the issue positions of agreed government programs that can be compared data on the issue positions of government members. Specify, for any given case, a measure of the fit between the observed fourteen-dimensional government issue vector, and the distribution of 1,000 predicted issue vectors for the case in question. Summarize this fit for the full set of out-of-sample cases. Norm these findings, though there is no baseline against which to measure them. For all of these reasons, we feel this is a substantial research program best left for future work.

Incomplete Information

Perhaps the most fundamental item on a "to do" list in this area concerns incomplete information. Along with almost all who have come before us, our model of the governance process assumes everything about all politicians' preferences is common knowledge. In other words, each politician knows every other politician's "data": their preferred issue positions and saliences, their trade-offs between perks and policy, their tolerance of tabled issues, and so on.[95] Not only is the common knowledge assumption unrealistic, but common sense tells us that *uncertainty about the preferences of potential counter-parties is part of the essence of bargaining*. Most formal "bargaining" models involve the unilateral making of offers which others can either accept or reject. They do not describe what most civilians would think of as bargaining, the back and forth *haggling* that characterizes real-world bargaining and negotiation. This lacuna stems directly from the unrealistic assumption of complete information. When I make an offer to you, according to existing formal bargaining models, I know *exactly* what you will and will not accept and make my offer accordingly. Most real-world bargaining, however, happens *precisely because I don't know exactly what you will accept*. I test the waters by making you a lowball offer. You test me back with a highball response. We haggle, slowly moving toward a resolution. In a real world of incomplete information about the preferences of others, *we learn from rejected offers*.

While we model policy negotiations over government formation as logrolling in high-dimensional issue spaces, we freely admit that the complete information version of the model we propose here is but a first step along the road. As with all real-world bargaining and negotiation, it seems to us very likely that logrolling issue positions will also involve haggling. When I am haggling with you over policy, I might have a reasonable idea of your issue *positions*, since these at least are publicly stated. But the *salience* of each issue for you, fundamental to logrolling, is far less knowable by me. If this were not the case, then real-world government formation negotiations would not take as long as they do. Negotiating politicians could in effect read off their best

---

[95] Exceptions, involving incomplete information models of government formation, include Dragu and Laver (2017) and Dragu and Laver (2019).

viable offer from the common knowledge database. Our intuition is that it is haggling that takes time and that haggling in a world of incomplete information involves a trial-and-error, time-consuming, process of learning about potential counter-parties' preferences.

One thing we know for sure. Political science in particular, and the social sciences in general, will not be the same in twenty or thirty years' time. One way forward is already quite clear. In relation to empirical analysis, the collection, wrangling, and analysis of vast datasets will be transformed by ever-increasing computational firepower and constantly improving methods. We foresee a similar evolution in theoretical analysis. Without doubt, smart people will continue to prove substantively important new deductive results. Also, without doubt in our view, computational methods will power rigorous new theoretical analyses of complex but substantively important problems that overwhelm deductive solutions. Whether or not these include the types of method we put forward in this book remains to be seen. But we hope we have shown this to be a future with great promise.

Technical Appendix A2

Here we set out in more precise terms the baseline model of the governance cycle in parliamentary democracies described in Chapter 2. Throughout, vectors are in bold-face.

Actors

The negotiators are leaders, or their proxies, of N disciplined legislative parties $(1 \ldots i \ldots N)$, with relative weights $(w_1 \ldots w_i \ldots w_N)$ specified by their parties' seats in the legislature. Q is the quota required for a coalition $c \in C$ to win: $\Sigma_{i \in c} w_i \geq Q$. In our model, each legislature has a simple majority decision rule for choosing governments.

It is possible, in our model, to use different measures of parties' power instead of their legislative seat shares. For example, various pivotality measures – including Shapley values, Banzhaf power indices, or minimum integer weights (MIWs) – are all implemented in our code and our data files by default have both raw weights w and MIWs.[96] For intuition about pivotality, consider the case of a legislature with three parties and the following seats: (3, 3, 1). With $Q = 4$, no single party is winning and any two parties can form a minimum winning coalition. What we want is an equivalence class that expresses the relative pivotality of each party in the set of winning coalitions, also known as the "decisive structure." MIWs do this by replacing the vector of raw party weights with the vector comprising the smallest integers which generate the same decisive structure. The MIW representation of the (3, 3, 1) legislature is therefore (1, 1, 1). Many different legislatures are equivalent in the sense they have a "decisive structure" in which

---

[96] There are other measures of power, notably Shapley and Banzhaf values. While all of these pivotality measures are similar, MIWs have the most traction current in the literature. See Ansolabehere, et al. (2005), Laver, et al. (2011b), Martin and Vanberg (2014).

there are three parties, any two of which are essential to a winning coalition. For example, legislatures with (10, 10, 2), (49, 48, 2), and (25, 24, 23) seat vectors all have the same MIW representation of (1,1,1).[97]

Negotiators' Issue Preferences

There is an m-dimensional discrete space of binary preferences on each of a large set of issues expected to require action by any incoming cabinet. Negotiator i's ideal position is given by an issue vector p_i of size m, with each element p_{ij} reporting i's binary preference on issue j. The relative salience of each issue for politician i is given by a vector s_i of size m. Element s_{ij} shows the relative salience of issue j to politician i: $0 \leq s_{ij} \leq 1$ and $\sum s_{ij} = 1$. For all $i \in N$, p_i and s_i are common knowledge. There is also the question, common to all theoretical models in the area, of what the "right" size of p_i is. If bargaining over governments concerns only perks (i.e., $m = 0$), we expect endlessly cycling results due to the nonexistence of a Condorcet winner. As m increases and logrolling comes into play, the size of the uncovered set and the likelihood of a Condorcet winner can increase, depending on the particular behavioral and scheduling rules that are employed (Penn 2006, de Marchi and Laver 2020).

Government Policy Position and Perks Allocation

There is a fixed set of commonly valued government perquisites (perks), g, of which each party gets a share ($g_1 \ldots g_i \ldots g_n$). If party i is not in the government, then $g_i = 0$. For a proposed governing coalition $c \in C$, the cabinet is specified by:

- an issue vector p_c, the elements of which, p_{cj}, state the cabinet position on issue j
- a perks vector, g_c, the elements of which, g_{ci}, state party i's share of cabinet perks.

The set of parties in coalition c are those receiving some government perks. In the model, we use Gamsonian perks. That is, we fix

---

[97] Cutler, et al. (2014) show that MIWs matter more for bargaining during government formation but the raw seats w matter more for the distribution of perks postformation.

perks allocations for each party i in c as proportional to its share of seats w_i in the coalition (Gamson 1961). An extension of the model that is not implemented here is to allow perks to be negotiated along with policy. Our preliminary explorations of this extension suggest it renders government formation negotiations chaotic; the assumption of Gamsonian perks allocations adds some stability to this process. Indeed, this induced stability maybe an underlying reason why real politicians negotiating over government formation almost always seem at least reconciled to accepting Gamsonian perks allocations.

Negotiators' Utility

The utility U_{ci} derived by politician i from coalition c decreases linearly in the salience-weighted Hamming distance between cabinet policy and politician i's ideal point: $\sum s_{ij} * 1_{p_{ij} = p_{cj}}$.

Negotiators may agree to table an issue in the government program if they cannot agree a to position on it. The salience-weighted expected value of any tabled issue, $|p_{ij} - p_{cj}| = \tau_i$, appears in each agent's utility function in precisely the same way as for any other issue.

Negotiators' utility functions are a convex combination of separable utilities derived from policy and perks. Specifically, U_{ci}, the utility of negotiator i for coalition c, is a convex combination:

$$U_{ci} = \alpha \left(g_{ci} \right) + \left(1 - \alpha \right) \left(\sum s_{ij} * 1_{p_{ij} = p_{cj}} \right)$$

where $\alpha, 0 \leq \alpha \leq 1$, measures the relative importance of perquisites and policy. We implement versions of our model where α is either indexed by actor i or constant across all actors within each trial.

Sequence of Play

Without loss of generality, we start our description of the recursive governance cycle with a general election to the lower house of the legislature.

1. *General election.* Each party i publishes its issue (p_i) and salience (s_i) vectors in a manifesto. We treat elections as black boxes and do not model the endogenous evolution of party issue positions and saliences; doing so is a possible extension of the baseline model. The election generates a new vector of party weights at time t, w_t,

by applying unbiased Gaussian noise to the seat vector at $t{-}1$, and normalizing the perturbed weights to sum to the size of the legislature. We do not model the endogenous evolution of the party system – party births, party deaths, party splits, and fusions.

2. *Government formation.* Once parties have published their p_i and s_i, and the new w_t has been declared from the election results, there is a government formation process using these parameter vectors as inputs to the bargaining process. Negotiations over government formation take place between party leaders or their proxies. While there may or may not be some superficial institutional structuring of these negotiations, we model government formation as a "freestyle" process in which, whatever the formal rules of the game, negotiating politicians are free to say whatever they want, to whomever they want, whenever they want. Their objective is to propose a new cabinet, c, specified by a perks vector, g_c and a policy vector, p_c.

   2.1 If a new government is (explicitly or implicitly) approved by a majority vote in the legislature, subject to institutional details we elaborate in the next chapter, the process moves to the support and survival phase at 3 below.

   ELSE: the government formation process is restarted at 2.1 above.

   2.2 If this process goes into an infinite loop because no proposal is approved, EITHER the incumbent government continues in office; OR a new election is called. The process moves to 1 above.

3. *Government support and survival.* Immediately following its investiture, the incumbent government is subjected to a (parameterized) stream of shocks. These perturb:

   3.1 Politicians' preferences. Referring to the utility function for negotiating politicians set out above, these shocks perturb: issue positions, p_i, and saliences, s_i; risk tolerances, τ_i; willingness, α_i, to trade of perks against policy.

   3.2 The political agenda. An agenda shock randomly forces a government policy of either 0 or 1 on an issue that was tabled in the government program. Following this resolution, party leaders reconsider their support for the government, in effect rerunning 2 above.

4. *Constitutionally mandated elections.* A constitutionally mandated election forces the governance process to 1 above, regardless of the wishes of party leaders.

Parameterizations

While the above game is fully specified, it is much more complex than most game-theoretic accounts of bargaining over government formation. This is an active research area with a number of excellent models (e.g., Morelli 1999, Banks and Duggan 2006, Martin and Vanberg 2020), but most are relatively simple games due to the limitations of deductive theory. The canonical bargaining model in this area (Baron and Ferejohn 1989) is based on the Rubinstein tradition and depends on a number of parameters to produce an equilibrium. Notably, their model – and most that follow – makes the following common assumptions:[98]

i. *Bargaining over government formation is independent of elections and governance (and most often, policy).* As noted in Chapter 1, existing models ignore the inputs to and the outputs from coalition formation.
ii. *There is a strict sequence of play where an exogenous, uniform selection mechanism selects a single party that is able to propose a coalition at each point in time.*
iii. *There is a reversion point of 0 for all players if negotiations fail.* Again, there are a number of reasonable assumptions including the status quo government, a discounted version of that government as caretaker, etc.
iv. *Stationarity.* This assumes that history does not matter and that strategies remain constant in each stage. While game-theoretic models aim to avoid a focus on behavior, assumptions like this are very strong constraints on the ability of actors to engage in strategic action and are essentially an ad hoc approach to bounded rationality.
v. *Homogenous weights.* Homogeneous games have the property that all MWCs are of equal voting weight and relaxing this assumption causes a surprising amount of havoc in formal models (see Ansolabehere, et al. 2005, Snyder, et al. 2005 and the follow-up work by Laver, et al. 2011b).

There are other assumptions, but the above list gives one the flavor of the problem. All models in this area, even those that aspire to be

---

[98] This list is adapted from de Marchi and Stewart (2020).

purely deductive, depend on a particular set of choices from a very large parameter space for their results. Changing any of the above parameters would have a large impact on results. As we have noted, it is not feasible to do this deductively – there are simply too many possible parameterizations to work through.

While all models, formal or empirical, depend on parameters, we should be concerned about this. We would like to know, for example, which parameters are dispositive and how they influence the results. As Binmore and Samuelson show, it is easy to make broad claims about a particular model and find out later that sensible changes to the parameter space produce quite different results (Binmore and Samuelson 1992). The solution, in our minds, is straightforward and leverages a unique benefit of computational modeling. Any researcher can take our model and our data and change the assumptions/parameters we rely on. Using the tools of applied statistics, it is then possible via Monte Carlo methods to investigate the relationship between our parameters and the results of our model. And, by keeping an eye on empirically realized governments as a target, one can focus on the small subset of models that produces a systematic mapping to real-world politics. To be clear, all theorists aim for general results and we all fall short to one degree or another. Computational work is simply one approach that makes it easy to investigate different parameter settings in a rigorous way.

Brief Statement on Our Philosophy of Science

Theorists should build models that capture the relevant empirical phenomena and, if possible, exercise the model deductively. If that is impossible, instead of simplifying the theory, turn to computation and use applied statistics to examine the parameter space involved. Ideally, fit these parameters with the help of a training dataset, as in the machine learning literature. In either approach, test the model by generating a dispositive empirical test – in this case, the governments that form in actual PR systems are our target (de Marchi 2005). A new theory must both perform better on the known cases and generalize to a reasonable set of unknown cases. Otherwise, without any new data, it is too easy to "curve fit" a theory.

General theories also require general tests. Contexts with elite, strategic actors or those that involve multiple, potentially interactive treatments may not allow an experimental (natural or laboratory) approach. Experiments offer the advantage of more precise control over treatments, but often at the expense of generality; for example, natural experiments are typically limited to a particular context (i.e., both with respect to place and time). Observational data allow less control, but offer the potential of more general tests across multiple contexts. If a theory is specified *ex ante* and subjected to repeated tests against new cases, we develop confidence in the theory even if these tests rely on observational data.

Technical Appendix A3

Behavior and Theoretical Models

The material in this chapter might seem to be a departure from the traditional norm for many theorists. Theoretical models in political science often adopt an approach that plays down the importance of behavior and relies on backward induction as an algorithm to solve games without modeling important political interactions (Diermeier and Krehbiel 2003).[99] In contrast, we focus on behavior, given the "difficult" recursive process of democratic governance we model here, we cannot analyze this in the traditional way by assuming actors use backward induction on an extensive game form. Backward induction does not scale well to complex games (de Marchi 2005). As emphasized in the computer science literature on algorithmic game theory: "Non-cooperative game theory provides a normative framework for analyzing strategic interactions. However, for the toolbox to be operational, the solutions it defines will have to be computed" (Conitzer and Sandholm 2002).

Theorists in the social sciences have largely sidestepped this problem by focusing on simple games. Studying two-actor models with few strategic options and simplifying matters further by assuming stationarity, algorithmic complexity is not a problem. The cost, as we have noted, is that an over-reliance on simple models gives us deductive solutions via backward induction but at the cost of being unable to

---

[99] Their position is, however, contradictory. Formal theorists often make use of equilibrium refinements and assumptions, like stationarity, that are essentially statements about behavior. Assuming actors "tremble," or forget the past, are simply decision rules (no more, no less). For example, Baron and Ferejohn argue that nonstationary strategies (i.e., those which depend on past histories of play) are implausible because it seems unlikely to them that "new members are ... able to know the whole history of play when they enter and to find it in their interests to act on that history" (Baron and Ferejohn, 1989, p. 1190).

generate empirically testable hypotheses. "If an equilibrium concept is not efficiently computable, much of its credibility as a prediction of the behavior of rational agents is lost .... Efficient computability is an important modeling prerequisite for solution concepts. In the words of Kamal Jain, 'If your laptop cannot find it, neither can the market.'" (Papadimitriou 2007).

If our goal is to specify a theoretical model of the governance process in parliamentary democracies, therefore, and if we want to say something about real-world governments, then we need a more complex behavioral model than is traditional fare. And as part of that, we must consider how key actors find solutions to the decision problems they face. The literature from computer science cited above has shown conclusively that finding Nash equilibria is an NP-hard[100] problem and that, as a result, we should not fetishize equilibrium. This is why we focus on assumptions about actual behaviors, rather than some idealized notion of backward induction.

We are by no means the first to concern ourselves with these issues. For example, a canonical graduate game theory text (Osborne and Rubinstein 1994) devoted considerable time to the complexity of solutions of (infinitely) repeated games. Relying on their notation, a finite state machine is implemented for a game with players $i \in N$ and sets of actions A_i as: $\langle Q_i, q_{0,i} \in Q_i, f_i: Q_i \to A_i, \varepsilon_i: Q_i \times A_i \to Q_i \rangle$. Q_i is the set of states, $q_{0,i}$ is the initial state/action taken by player i, f_i is a mapping of states to actions, and ε_i is a mapping of the action by player i and response from her opponent to a new state. The complexity of a machine is the cardinality of Q_i.[101]

To gain intuition, consider the iterated prisoner's dilemma and the famous tit-for-tat strategy often suggested as an option. The machine for tit-for-tat is shown in Figure A.3.1. The initial state q_0 is represented with a double circle and indicates the player will choose to cooperate on the first iteration of the game. The edges in the game correspond to the function ε and are the actions taken by the opponent. Qualitatively, then, the strategy represented by the machine is to cooperate as long as

---

[100] Loosely, NP-hard problems are likely not solvable in polynomial time. If one can prove the contrary, a million-dollar prize waits! (www.claymath.org/millennium-problems/p-vs-np-problem)

[101] As Osborne and Rubinstein note, this is a naïve measure (e.g., it does not account for the number of edges).

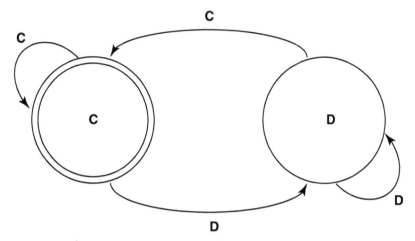

Figure A3.1 Tit for tat as a finite state machine

the other player also cooperates. If the other player defects, then one commits to defecting for at least one iteration of the game and returns to cooperating once the opponent cooperates again.

For Osborne and Rubinstein, the complexity of the above machine is low – it has only two states in Q. Given the folk theorem and a desire to avoid a large or infinite set of equilibria, their argument is that lower complexity strategies should be preferred to higher complexity strategies. This scratches the same itch as our approach in the sense that we are relying on a rule-based ABM that can "solve" government formation in a reasonable time frame – an algorithm that finishes just shy of the heat death of the universe is of little use.[102] Put a different way, we believe that all theorists are actually dealing with behavior, albeit in different ways, by simplifying their models via assumptions, by building finite state machines and limiting their complexity, or by building sets of decision rules and exercising these via a Monte Carlo. The utility of each approach depends on the context. For complex games of the sort we analyze here, we favor either decision heuristics deployed in an ABM or AI-based approaches. With this in mind, we elaborate on the fine details of our behavioral model.

---

[102] For this reason, we may not be interested in Nash but rather solutions that are "near-Nash." Or alternately, we may be most interested in solutions that match what real-world experts do.

Table A3.1 *ABM algorithm pseudo code*

ABM algorithm: (simplified) Win-Stay, Lose-Shift

Input: seats w, policies p_i, saliences s_i
An **offer** is a coalition c, policies p_c, and perks partition g_c
if SQ government maintains legislative majority, stay with SQ (win-stay)
else (lose-shift)
    for i in N **do**
        if offer $\langle(i), p_c = p_i, g_c = (g_i = 1; g_{n/i} = 0)\rangle > R$, add this proposal to
            agenda A
          elif $\alpha > .5$, search for minimal weight majority coalition c
            with $\langle$(min weight), logroll(p_c), Gamson(g_c)$\rangle > R$ for all i
            in c and add to A
          elif $\alpha \leq .5$, search for minimal policy distance majority
            coalition c with $\langle$(min policy distance), logroll(p_c),
            Gamson(g_c)$\rangle > R$ for all i in c and add to A
legislature **votes** on proposals in agenda A; majority required to supplant R
end

Win-Stay, Lose-Shift Algorithm for Government Formation

We present the nitty-gritty details of our decision rules in two formats. First, we show a – necessarily simplified – pseudo code version of the main algorithm in Table A3.1.

This is a parsimonious representation of the main algorithm and shows the various branches of the search actors engage in. As an alternative, we also present this same algorithm verbally. The behavioral model for political actors consists of the following steps.

Win-stay

If there is an outgoing majority government that maintained its legislative majority, or an outgoing minority government that increased its seat share, then all agents repeat the behavior which caused this government to form. Else:

Lose-Shift

1. Pick partner(s)

We start with what we take to be the uncontroversial assumption that party leaders most of all want to be prime ministers in a single-party cabinet in which their party controls every cabinet portfolio and enacts its ideal policy position. Therefore:

1.1 *Check if a single-party minority cabinet led by you is majority preferred to* **R,** the (discounted) value of the current incumbent government.

    1.1.1 Check whether a proposal of your ideal point, with your party getting all the perks, is majority preferred to **R**. If yes, this is your minority government proposal.

1.2 *Pick a majority proto-coalition of which you are a member.*[103]

We can specify two different partner search algorithms and two different rule "regimes" for parties searching for a coalition proposal. The two partner search rules are:

min-distance: using some measure of inter-party proximity on issue positions, pick coalition partners in order of the proximity to you, until the combined seat share of the proposed coalition exceeds the winning threshold.

min-size: pick coalition partners such that the combined seat share of the proposed coalition exceeds, but is as close as possible to, the winning threshold.

The two rule regimes for deploying these are:

alpha-branch. High-α party leaders use the **min-size** rule to search for minimum weight winning coalitions. Low-α: leaders use the **min-distance** rule to search for coalitions that minimize policy differences.

best-rule. Party leaders use both **min-size** and **min-distance,** picking the proposal they most prefer, if this is also preferred to **R** by all its members and by a legislative majority.

2. Make a proposal to your selected proto-coalition partners

A proposal is specified by a vector of *perks* shares to proto-coalition members, G_c, and a vector of proposed cabinet *policies* on salient issues, P_c.

---

[103] Note that this ignores *minority coalitions*. Empirically, these are the rarest, and shortest-lived, form of government. For now, we assume that politicians engaged in government formation never actively seek these. As a refinement, 1.2 could state "pick a proto-coalition preferred by a legislative majority to **R**" – which might be such that the members receiving perks do not themselves control a majority.

2.1 *Propose a perks vector, G_c,* which allocates perks between coalition members according to Gamson's law.

2.2 *Propose policy vector, P_c.* Policy proposals are generated by logrolling (following de Marchi and Laver 2020).

    2.2.1 Identify all contested issues for which one proto-coalition member is a unique outlier, with a position opposite to that of all other members. A change of position by the unique outlier results in unanimous agreement between coalition partners.

    2.2.2 Mark contested issues with no unique outlier as "tabled," since no simple trade can resolve these. Mark other contested issues as "tradable."

    2.2.3 Treating the ordering of issues as exogenous and recalling that we randomize this order over many trials in our Monte Carlo, consider negotiator A, the unique outlier on the first tradable issue, x. Negotiator A looks down the list of tradable issues for which other members are unique outliers, looking for the first such issue, y, with a unique outlier, B, from one of the $n-1$ other parties, such that A values y more than x, but B values x more than y. If there is such an issue, and there may not be, then A and B trade positions on issues x and y.

    2.2.4 Iterate the logrolling process, moving down the list of tradable issues until no such trade is possible.

    2.2.5 The residual set of contested issues for which no simple logroll is available is tabled by the coalition partners with costs τ.

There are several assumptions and parameters in the above algorithm. Our strategy for validating how reasonable these are turns on how well the model's empirical predictions fare against real-world government outcomes and also how similar the results are to an AI-based approach.

From Formal Model to Computer Code

Our complete theoretical model of government formation consists of the extensive form game described in the last chapter and the decision rules for behavior in this chapter. Solving this, as we have noted, requires building a suite of simulations with Monte Carlo parameterizations. This approach is relatively novel for social scientists and, to build intuition, a brief example of what this looks like in computer code is given here.

All of our code and data are online and modifiable by readers. Recent advances in computing make it easy both to replicate what we have accomplished and to extend this research. Using tools like Google Colab[104], for example, it is possible for researchers to share code and provide a complete runtime environment. This means that no one will have to install software, libraries, etc., to match the original conditions the code was written with. It is provided online and original code can be run out of a browser.

We recommend using python 3.x for social scientists conducting this type of research. Support for both machine learning and applied statistics is excellent and the language is expressive, parsimonious, and flexible. There is obviously a performance hit compared to compiled languages such as Fortran or C/C++, but the advantages in readability are worthwhile for most applications.

As a brief example of the difference between the mathematical expression of our model and the downstream code, consider our utility function for actors:

$$U_{ci} = \alpha \left(g_{ci} \right) + \left(1 - \alpha \right) \left(\sum s_{ij} * 1_{p_{ij} = p_{cj}} \right)$$

The corresponding version written in python is shown in Box 3.1:

Box 3.1:   Python code implementing our assumptions about politicians' utility functions

```
def evaluate(pnum, tcoal, tpro, t_loss):
    # now evaluate for player pnum, coaltion tcoal, and
proposal tpro the utility

    # calculate total votes in proposal
    pro_sum = 0
    for i in tcoal:
        pro_sum = pro_sum + parties[i]['w']
```

---

[104] https://colab.research.google.com/notebooks/intro.ipynb

```
        # first calculate payoff due to bargaining using Gamson's law
        # one could also use the proportion of MIWs instead
        perqs = 0.0
        if pnum in tcoal: perqs = parties[pnum]['w'] / float(pro_sum)

        # second calculate loss from policy distance weighted by salience
        poldis = 0.0

        for i in range(0,M):
            if tpro[i]!='*': poldis = poldis - parties[pnum]['s'][i] *
(parties[pnum]['pol'][i]-tpro[i]) * (parties[pnum]['pol'][i]-tpro[i])
            # if parties failed to logroll on an issue, deal with status quo
            elif tau_switch == 0: poldis = poldis - parties[pnum]['s'][i] *
(t_loss) * (1)
          # t_loss is random.uniform(0, 1) which comes from the sq_loss
variable in the main function
            elif tau_switch == 1: poldis = poldis - parties[pnum]['s'][i] *
parties[pnum]['tau'] * (1)
          # this substitutes the party-specific tau rather than using sq_loss

        # last, combine two types of utility and arrive at total util
        # util ~ alpha * perquisites + (1-alpha)*distance, where
distance is constrained to be negative
        pu = 0.0
        pu = parties[pnum]['alpha'] * perqs + (1-parties[pnum]
['alpha']) * poldis
        return pu
```

Comments in the code begin with the "#" character and are meant to explain to other researchers (or jog the memory of the authors) what the code does. The above block is our *evaluate* function and it accepts the following arguments:

- pnum: in our formal model, actor i
- tcoal: a proposed coalition c
- tpro: a policy vector for the coalition p_c
- t_loss: the value of a tabled issue τ_i.

The function computes (with Gamsonian perks) the utility of player i for a given proposal. While it may look complex, it is a one-to-one mapping of the formal setup from this manuscript. The main difference, of course, is that our fully implemented model consists of ~3,000 lines of python code. As a result, it is impossible to deductively interrogate the model. Running the code does, of course, throw errors if there is anything that does not parse, but much like complex proofs, there may still be logical errors in the code. The only remedy to this problem is the same as for any modeling. Multiple researchers working in the same area must replicate and extend earlier work.

Technical Appendix A4

CFP MCCFR Pseudo Code and Rationality Issues

The algorithm for our AI based approach is straightforward and the pseudo code is shown in Table A4.1. As noted above, our two main contributions to deal with the size of the search space for the government formation game are to: rely on constrained fictitious play (CFP) for the less pivotal players and; alternating play using the full MCCFR algorithm for the two most pivotal parties.

One important question which arises is that, if we fully model *only* the largest party with MCCFR, we generally find a solution with that party in the government. If we alternate between the largest and second largest in our alternating play algorithm, we get a "better" answer (given that the second largest sometimes forms governments), but substantially slow down convergence due to the increase in search costs. The question, of course, is what happens if we model all players as fully strategic via the MCCFR algorithm? In smaller cases (with, say, five parties), that is possible.

Table A4.1 *Pseudo code for CFP MCCFR algorithm*

CFP MCCFR algorithm

Input: seats w, policies p_i, saliences s_i
for $t = 1,2,3 \ldots$ do
    if i in max(w), use MCCFR for player i; add i's proposal to agenda A
    elif (CFP)
        for j in N_V do
            find MWCs containing player j, *coals*
            pick uniform draw c in *coals*
            if payoff(c) > R
                add c to agenda A as player j's proposal
legislature **votes** on proposals in agenda A; majority required to supplant R
end

If all parties are modeled as fully rational, then as a general rule we do *not* find a single Condorcet winner and probability mass is spread across many different proposals. Intuitively, given prior results in the formal theory literature, this should not come as a surprise – as parties become more rational, the likelihood of finding alternatives to any given proposal is very high. Other players would be able to adapt to any fixed strategy, by focusing on lower utility members of any proposed coalition, luring them away with outsized offers to disrupt the current leading proposal.

We thus have something of a conundrum. Limiting the behaviorally assumed strategic capacity of actors makes a difference if we want a model that maps to real-world outcomes. Given how much our assumptions about behavior matter, this brings to the fore our argument throughout this manuscript. As much as we might wish otherwise, behavior – even in strategic games played by elite political actors – is squarely at the center of the theoretical enterprise.

Fictitious Play and CFP MCCFR

Define a game (N, A_i, U_{ci}), where N is the set of players and for $i \in N$, A_i is the set of actions, and U_{ci} is a von Neumann and Morgenstern utility function as defined in Chapter 3. Following Berger, consider a two player repeated game with $i, j \in N$, time $t \in N$, and BR() is a best response function (Berger 2007). Alternating fictitious play is a sequence $(a_{it}, b_{jt}) \in A$:

$$a_{it+1} \in \text{BR}\left(y(t)\right) \text{ and } b_{jt+1} \in \text{BR}\left(x(t)\right)$$

with beliefs $x()$ and $y()$:

$$x(t) = \frac{1}{t}\sum_{s=1}^{t} a_{is}, \, y(t) = \frac{1}{t}\sum_{s=1}^{t} b_{js}$$

Clearly, a straightforward implementation of alternating fictitious play is infeasible in our government formation game given limits on computation and convergence. Instead of averaging over prior play $s = [1 \dots t]$, we rely on a simpler version where less pivotal players rely on the heuristic-based approach detailed in the chapter. This means that less pivotal players select strategies with a large stochastic component to prevent corner solutions from dominating. Pivotal players are modelled as fully rational, take up the vast majority of compute time, and play against the expected strategies of the heuristic-based opponents.

Technical Appendix A5

Monte Carlo Setup

The research design for our Monte Carlo experiments is straightforward. As noted in the chapter, we have two distinct sets of parameters for each case. The first are empirically observable:

i. Party seats w_i (or some other power measure; e.g., minimum integer weights);
ii. Party policy positions p_i (primarily from CHES);
iii. Party policy saliences s_i (primarily from CHES).

The second are fundamentally unobservable psychological parameters for each decision maker:

iv. Politicians' utility function trade-offs between perks and policy, α;
v. Politicians' optimism/pessimism about the outcome of tabled issues, τ;
vi. Politicians' discount rates for payoffs arising from caretaker governments, θ.

Parameters iv–vi can be specified to vary by party or, on aggregate, by party system. For the results presented in the chapter, system-level expectations were estimated using Monte Carlo experiments with system-specific parameter values. Party-level expectations were estimated using Monte Carlos with party-specific values. Both approaches, however, yield very similar results, especially when it comes to the empirical results of Chapter 6.

Results from Monte Carlos depend on statistical evidence and are not mathematical proofs. That said, Monte Carlos allows us to gather as much model-generated data as needed to test our propositions and the evidence is, as a consequence, quite strong.

Estimation

We use two types of empirical models in this book. The first analyzes output of Monte Carlo experiments. We therefore have an abundance of data, limited only by our patience and available computing power. In the event, we conducted 1,000 randomly parameterized model runs per training case but could if this had proved necessary have conducted many more. Datasets analyzed in this chapter, therefore, have 20,000 observations, each representing an outcome predicted by the model in one of the twenty training cases. The second type of dataset is analyzed in Chapter 6 and focuses on predicting government formation and duration for specified empirical settings. We therefore have relatively few observations of actual observed cases – just under one hundred.

For either type of model, we want to have confidence our findings are robust, to guard against the perils of significant but tiny effects where we have an abundance of artificial "data," and significant but spurious effects where we have relatively small samples. We therefore rely on the nonparametric bootstrap for all of our models. This is an easy way to gain intuition about the robustness of our estimates and is in some ways analogous to k-fold cross validation. While it is not foolproof (a nonrepresentative sample or large swings in estimates based on a few observations will cause trouble), it does help us understand the quality of our results in these models. For an overview, see Shalizi (2010).

Causal Claims

To understand the workings of our model, we rely in this chapter on data produced by Monte Carlo experiments. To test our model in Chapter 6, we rely on observational data from outcomes in real political systems. We are neither performing experiments ourselves nor searching for some natural experiment. In this respect, we are somewhat at odds with the causal inference movement in economics and political science. At some risk of simplifying the issues involved, the causal inference movement has (rightly) been concerned with identifying causal effects. This is distinct from the standard practice of running a regression and telling a story based on the estimated coefficients:

The aim of standard statistical analysis, typified by regression, estimation, and hypothesis testing techniques, is to assess parameters of a distribution from samples drawn of that distribution. With the help of such parameters, one can infer *associations* [emphasis added] among variables ... These tasks are managed well by standard statistical analysis so long as experimental conditions remain the same. Causal analysis goes one step further; its aim is to infer not only beliefs or probabilities under static conditions, but also the dynamics of beliefs under *changing conditions*, for example, change induced by treatments ... (Pearl 2009, p. 99).

Association and causation are obviously distinct concepts, and our aim is always to capture causation. If we want an *interpretable* forecast of some outcome of interest, perhaps to evaluate programs or make policy interventions, we need estimates of causal effects. When we model the governance cycle, however, we model the behavior of seasoned and sophisticated senior politicians in a complex environment. Even the simplest bargaining models of such matters are quite complex. More generally, the informative analysis of "bargaining over government formation" is not feasibly reducible to a single treatment variable or even small set of treatments. It is not an accident that most of the models in the causal inference tradition, given the limitations of the methods employed, focus on single treatments and do not produce general knowledge. These models are instead focused on a particular time and place where it is possible to identify a causal effect and for the most part do not deal with strategic action on the part of actors. This raises an obvious question: What are the empirical models we set out here actually telling us? Put bluntly, are we estimating no more than mere associations? Our answer is that we do in fact capture causal effects because we proceed in the following way:

  i. We specify a theoretical model of government formation without any empirical content beyond our general understanding of the politics of parliamentary systems, of the behavior of party leaders, reports of government formation in specific cases, and so on.
 ii. We examine the main mechanisms in our model using a computational version of comparative statics. This relies on synthetic data and establishes that our (relatively complex) theory is doing what we intuitively expect.
iii. For unobservable model parameters such as the trade-off between perks and policy in the utility function, we calibrate our model

using a representative training set of twenty cases. Based on these training data, furthermore, we conclude that model predictions are not sharply sensitive to choices of these parameters.

iv. In Chapter 6, we test our theory by using our calibrated model to make case-by-case empirical predictions of the governments expected to form in nature as a function of party seats, policy, and salience. We include nothing else; there are no case-specific controls. The goal is to capture the general dynamics of bargaining over government formation rather than to optimize case-by-case.

Our theory of government formation is by no means a complete characterization of all that transpires when governments form. As we will see, we capture about 40 percent of the variance in the outcomes of interest. And, it is also possible our theory may be wrong going forward, either because our sample is biased or because exogenous shocks permanently alter the character of governance in parliamentary systems. That said, we adopt the view that specifying the model first, calibrating this using training data, and then using the calibrated model to make out-of-sample case-by-case predictions of observed outcomes, buys us something substantial in terms of the scientific knowledge that is produced. If our model were plain wrong or purely correlational, it is extraordinarily unlikely that it would produce high-quality predictions in multiple datasets across very different contexts.

Exercising the Model

It can be difficult to build intuition about complex models. When we create a model that attempts to capture a complex strategic environment as well as behavioral algorithms designed to function well in this environment, there are many moving parts to consider. Here, we motivate our analysis with "common sense" intuitions about the main dynamics in our model and test these intuitions using applied statistics. Since our model is complex, however, and our intuitions are informal, we will not be completely surprised if these intuitions are not realized in the results. This sort of work is essential, however, in revealing the dynamics at work in a complex model.[105]

---

[105] This is also useful during debugging a computational model. Surprises are expected and generating novel findings are one of the reasons we create theoretical models in the first place. But, surprises can also be bugs!

These analyses are also used to support propositions 4 through 7. Our Monte Carlo gives us an abundance of data, but it is important to remember our goals in this exercise. We want a computational analog of deductive comparative statics – to understand the moving parts of our model by rigorously mapping the relationship between model inputs and model outputs. Unlike a purely deductive model, our model is so complex that we use applied statistics to investigate these relationships. We are *not*, in this chapter, *making predictions about real-world political outcomes*, a matter to which we turn in Chapter 6.

Note also that in Chapter 3 we propose two different "rule regimes" for finding potential partners in government. These differ in terms of how actors deploy, on the one hand, a "min-distance" rule that looks for partners who are close in the issue space and, on the other hand, a "min-size" rule that looks for the smallest possible winning coalition. The first rule regime is "alpha-branch": High-α politicians prefer perks, so use the min-size rule to enhance perks expectations; low-α: leaders prefer policy, so use the min-distance rule to reduce the need for policy compromises between coalition partners. The second rule regime is "best-rule": All politicians compute the effects of both rules and submit the resulting proposal they prefer.

We run two separate 1,000-trial Monte Carlo experiments for each of the twenty calibration cases, one for each rule regime. For each proposition, we first lay out our expectations conceptually and then turn to the results of regressions designed to test these expectations.

Support for Proposition 4: Eccentricity

Following the vast body of the literature on government formation, our expectations are that a *party's issue positions* are relevant to its prospects of getting into government. We explore the impact of multidimensional issue position eccentricity on the membership of particular parties in any predicted government. Proposition 4 is expressed in E 4.1 with the following logistic regression:

$$\text{E 4.1: Party in cabinet } (0/1) = a + b_1\alpha + b_2\tau + b_3\text{eccentricity} + \epsilon$$

Parties with relatively extreme positions are less likely to share these with others, making it more difficult for them to agree on a joint program. The results for this model are below in the section on party-level regressions.

Support for Propositions 5A and 5B: Condorcet Winners

As noted in the chapter, this proposition replicates the main finding of de Marchi and Laver (2020). For Proposition 5a, the bargaining model and behavioral rules for our ABM once again produce Condorcet winning cabinet proposals, though the proportion of these varies across cases. Proposition 5b concerns the role of τ: When senior politicians are risk acceptant and, therefore, more likely to engage in logrolling, we see an increased likelihood of Condorcet winning coalitions. Proposition 5B is expressed in E 5.1 as a logistic regression using party-level data:[106]

$$E\ 5.1:\ \text{Condorcet winner}\ (0/1) = a + b_1\tau + \epsilon$$

Results match expectations, showing that b_1 is negative, statistically significant, and that the overall model fit is good.

Support for Proposition 6: Single-Party Governments

We have the following expectations about whether single party or MWCs form:

E 6.1 Predictions of single-party minority governments are more likely in legislatures with a *"system dominant" party*, which can form a majority coalition with any other party. Predictions of MWC governments are more likely in legislatures with no system dominant party.

E 6.2 Predictions of single-party minority governments are more likely in legislatures dominated by low-α senior politicians, who tend to value policy over perks. Predictions of MWC governments are more likely legislatures where senior politicians tend to value perks more than policy.

Our intuition on these matters arises because lower-α parties care more about policy and must find a coalition where logrolling is possible. Conversely, higher-α parties will be more willing to make the policy compromises necessary to get into power.

---

[106] System-level regressions treat the setting as the case and mean levels are used for the independent variables of interest. Party-level regressions treat the party as the case and use individualized values for the independent variables.

E 6.3 Predictions of single-party minority governments are more likely in legislatures dominated by high-τ senior politicians, who are pessimistic about the effects of tabling issues. Predictions of MWC governments are more likely in low-τ legislatures, where senior politicians believe they can keep contentious issues off of the agenda.

Our intuition on this matter arises because higher-τ parties are systematically more likely to expect tabled issues to turn out badly and single-party minority cabinets have no tabled issues. Conversely, lower-τ parties are more optimistic and accordingly have an easier time creating MWCs that involve tabled issues.

We summarize Expectations E6.1 to E6.3, about the formation of single-party and MWC governments, using system-level logistic regressions that map model parameters into outputs:[107]

$$\text{Single-party government } (0/1) = a + b_{1-4}(L_1 - L_4) + b_5 N$$
$$+ b_6 \alpha + b_7 \tau + b_8 \theta + \epsilon$$

$$\text{Coalition government } (0/1) = a + b_{1-4}(L_1 - L_4) + b_5 N$$
$$+ b_6 \alpha + b_7 \tau + b_8 \theta + \epsilon$$

Note that we have two distinct dependent variables given the possibility that no government is predicted to form.

Tables 5.4–5.5 report coefficients from the two regression models, for each rule regime, together with the relevant bootstrapped standard errors. Given the large number of trials, most coefficients are highly "significant" statistically, though this means much less in large volumes of simulated data than it does with analyses of limited real-world empirical data.[108] Note also that, since our research design involves intentionally adding a considerable amount of random noise to each simulation run, we do not expect the fit of these regression models to be particularly high. What concerns us are systematic patterns in this noisy environment: the signs and magnitudes of the relevant regression coefficients.

---

[107] $L_1 - L_4$ are legislative types B*, B, C, and D, respectively. Type E, an open legislature in which no two-party coalition is winning, is the omitted category.

[108] In computational work such as this, it is typically possible to derive "statistically significant" results simply by increasing the number of trials until this is achieved. We therefore pay no attention our interpretation of these results to significance levels, focusing instead on the much more informative signs and relative magnitudes of the relevant regression coefficients.

Table A5.1 shows that Expectations E6.1 to E6.3, concerning the likelihood of single-party minority cabinets, are confirmed by the simulation results. Single-party minority cabinets are more likely to be predicted in legislatures with system dominant parties, in lower-alpha legislatures where party leaders care more about policy than perks, and in higher-tau legislatures where party leaders expect tabled issues to turn out poorly. These findings are similar for each rule regime, although most of the relevant coefficients, as well as the percentage of variance explained, are larger for the "best-rule" regime. This gives us comfort that the model as coded is working as expected.

Table A5.2 shows essentially complementary results for MWCs. These findings are again similar for each rule regime, although most of the relevant coefficients, as well as the percentage of variance explained, are now smaller for the "best-rule" regime.

In a nutshell, if negotiating politicians use the best-rule regime to pick coalition partners, then the model tells us they are more likely to form single-party governments, whereas if they pick partners according to their trade-off between perks and policy, they are more likely to form coalitions. This finding emerged from our analysis, and we did not include it in our intuitive a priori expectations, but it seems to us to be plausible. Politicians using the best-rule regime pick a proposal that focuses exclusively on their own utility, which seems to indicate a preference for single-party governments. Politicians using min-distance may pick larger coalition partners, consuming a greater share of the perks in any proportional allocation – resulting in coalition proposals that are more likely to be approved by other parties.

Note that the model is most likely to predict coalitions, and least likely to predict single-party administrations, in Type E "open" legislatures (the omitted category in these regressions), where even the two largest parties cannot command a legislative majority between them. This is consistent with the empirical finding, reported by Laver and Benoit (2015) that, despite being found in about a quarter of all minority legislatures in parliamentary systems, single-party governments are by far the least likely to form, being observed in only 5 percent of relevant cases, in legislatures where no two-party coalition is winning. The bottom-line conclusion is that the model is working as expected, judged in terms of the confirmation of the a priori intuitive expectations set out above.

Table A5.1 *Mapping model parameters into predicted single-party minority governments (E6.1–E6.3: bootstrapped standard errors)*

Single-party govt	alpha-branch regime		best-rule regime	
	b	SE	b	SE
type B*	2.95	0.09	3.49	0.09
type B	1.09	0.05	1.59	0.07
type C	1.48	0.07	1.77	0.09
type D	0.82	0.06	1.08	0.07
n-parties	0.04	0.01	–0.00	0.01
alpha	–0.58	0.06	–1.06	0.06
tau	4.80	0.13	4.65	0.13
theta	–0.13	0.12	–0.50	0.12
constant	–3.85	0.13	–4.15	0.14
(pseudo) R^2	0.14		0.18	

Table A5.2 *Mapping model parameters into predicted coalition governments (E6.1–E6.3: bootstrapped standard errors)*

Coalition govt	alpha-branch regime		best-rule regime	
	b	SE	b	SE
type B*	–2.29	0.08	–1.65	0.08
type B	–0.76	0.04	–0.76	0.05
type C	–0.98	0.07	–0.75	0.07
type D	–0.45	0.04	–0.40	0.05
n-parties	–0.09	0.01	–0.07	0.01
alpha	0.87	0.05	0.34	0.06
tau	–4.62	0.12	–3.56	0.11
theta	0.06	0.10	–0.62	0.11
constant	2.81	0.11	2.05	0.12
(pseudo) R^2	0.11		.07	

Support for Proposition 7, Government Duration

Turning to tabled issues, recall that the number of tabled issues in the government program is an important feature of our model of government survival, measuring the incumbent's vulnerability to agenda

Table A5.3 *Mapping model parameters into predicted number of tabled issues (E7.1–E7.2: bootstrapped standard errors)*

	alpha-branch regime		best-rule regime	
N. *of tabled issues*	*b*	*SE*	*b*	*SE*
type B*	–0.005	0.000	–0.010	0.000
type B	0.000	0.000	–0.002	0.000
type C	–0.005	0.000	0.005	0.000
type D	–0.002	0.000	–0.002	0.000
n-parties	–0.004	0.000	–0.005	0.000
alpha	0.002	0.000	0.004	0.000
tau	–0.012	0.001	–0.014	0.000
theta	0.001	0.000	0.010	0.000
constant	0.041	0.000	0.059	0.000
(adj.) R^2	0.373		0.654	

shocks, which force it to take a position on tabled issues. The number of tabled issues in the government program is not only an output of our model of government formation but also an input to our model of government survival.

E 7.1   Predicted governments are more likely to have tabled issues in legislatures dominated by high-α senior politicians, who value perks more than policy.

Our intuition on this matter arises because higher-α parties care less about policy payoffs, including anticipated payoffs from tabled issues. Other things equal, therefore, they should be less likely to oppose proposed governments with higher numbers of tabled issues.

E 7.2   Predicted governments are likely to have fewer tabled issues in legislatures dominated by high-τ senior politicians, who are less optimistic about the effects of tabling issues.

Our intuition on this matter arises because higher-τ parties are systematically more likely to expect tabled issues to turn out badly. Other things equal, therefore, proposals with higher numbers of tabled issues should be less likely to be supported.

Expectations E7.1 and E7.2 are summarized using the following system-level linear regression:

$$n\text{-tabled-issues} = a + b_{1-4}\left(L_1 - L_4\right) + b_5 N + b_6 \alpha + b_7 \tau + b_8 \theta + \epsilon$$

Table A5.3 shows that the model, as expected, predicts fewer tabled issues in higher-τ legislatures (where the expected penalty for tabled issues is higher). It is also more likely to predict tabled issues in higher-α legislatures (in which senior politicians attach less weight to issue payoffs). While the results are essentially the same for each rule regime, the regression coefficients, and proportion of examined variance, are all higher for the best-rule regime. The interactions in the model are complex, but our conjecture here is that this arises from the tendency of politicians using the best-rule regime to favor single-party minority governments, which by construction have no tabled issue.

Party-Level Analysis

We can also examine the above propositions with the party as the unit of analysis. Since the relevant regressions concern the predicted participation in government of individual parties, we add two measures of each party's bargaining strength as controls. These are the party's raw seat share and its minimum integer weight (MIW) – the latter a measure of its bargaining power, given the set of possible winning coalitions (Snyder, et al. 2005, Freixas and Molinero 2009, Laver, et al. 2011a). This is because we are interested in how our model predicts parties' participation in government, *over and above their raw bargaining power*. Table A5.4 reports coefficients from these regression models for both rule regimes, with bootstrapped standard errors.

Expectations 6.1 through 6.3 concern predicted party participation in single-party minority cabinets. For the subset of cases in which such predictions were made, the results reported in Table A5.4 show that our expectations are largely realized for both rule regimes. When single-party governments are formed, these are more likely to comprise higher-α, more perks oriented, parties. Such parties are more prepared to make the policy concessions necessary to win the support of non-government parties for a single-party government in which they do not participate.

Our expectation on the role of τ is realized for parties using the alpha-branch rule regime but not for the best-rule regime. Given the complex interactions involved, we don't have a clear intuition of why this might be the case. Higher-τ parties, *in or out of office*, have a

Table A5.4 *Mapping model parameters into party participation in governments (E4.1–E4.3: bootstrapped standard errors)*

	Party in single-party cabinet (E4.1–4.2)				Party in any cabinet (E4.3)			
	alpha-branch regime		best-rule regime		alpha-branch regime		best-rule regime	
Variable	*b*	*SE*	*b*	*SE*	*b*	*SE*	*b*	*SE*
alpha	0.30	0.08	0.21	0.07	-0.05	0.03	0.10	0.03
tau	0.70	0.15	-0.02	0.14	-0.26	0.06	-0.04	0.06
theta	-0.39	0.15	-0.09	0.14	-0.03	0.06	-0.07	0.06
eccentricity	-15.20	0.32	-14.70	0.25	-3.13	0.07	-3.69	0.07
seats	0.32	0.16	-0.41	0.30	-2.43	0.13	-3.43	0.14
n-parties	0.02	0.01	0.04	0.01	0.11	0.01	0.14	0.01
MIW	8.42	0.44	8.60	0.40	5.14	0.17	6.16	0.18
constant	-2.76	0.17	-2.31	0.15	-1.30	0.07	-1.64	0.07
(pseudo) R^2	0.62		0.604		0.100		0.12	

greater dislike for having tabled issues in the joint program and, therefore, prefer single-party minority governments, other things equal, since these have no tabled issues. This does not necessarily imply they themselves are more likely to form single-party minority governments.

Expectation 4.1 concerns party membership in *any* cabinet and is also confirmed in simulation results. Parties with more "eccentric" (off-center) policy positions are much less likely, for straightforward reasons, to be predicted as members of any cabinet. A feature of these results, however, is that the effect of party policy eccentricity is much greater for single-party cabinets. Increasing policy eccentricity dramatically reduces the likelihood a party is predicted to form a single-party cabinet, a result that is intuitively plausible and gives us further comfort that our model is working as expected. Single-party cabinets, according to our model, are very likely to be centrist.

Another feature of the results in Table A5.4 concerns the relative impact of the two different measures of party weight, used as control variables. Replicating a prior finding by Cutler, et al. (2014), it is a party's bargaining leverage, measured by MIWs, rather than its raw seat share, which drives model predictions of cabinet membership. While MIWs sharply predict participation in both single-party and coalition cabinets, the coefficient for seat shares is either barely significant, or negatively signed. Given that seat shares are likely negatively correlated with eccentricity (more eccentric parties probably tend to be smaller), it is difficult to disentangle the detailed interactions here, but the bottom line is that seat shares contribute little to model predictions of party participation in government, controlling for the sharp effects of policy eccentricity and MIWs (pivotality in the set of winning coalitions).

Given these effects, it is striking that a distinctive feature of our model, the psychological trade-off, α, between perks and policy payoffs, has such a robust effect, anticipated a priori, in these training data. More perks-oriented parties are systematically predicted to be more likely to form single-party minority governments, being more inclined to make policy concessions to nongovernment parties in exchange for control of the full sack of perks.

Technical Appendix A6

Detailed Results for Hypotheses H1 and H2

Below, we report the case-by-case results for our models. Table A6.1 shows the coalition-level results and Table A6.2 the party-level results for the training set. Table A6.3 shows the full results for test set 1, and Table A6.4 has these results for test set 2.

Baseline Models and Policy Dimensionality

Currently, we use a uniform draw of minimum winning coalitions as our baseline model. As noted in the text, it is important to have an informative baseline model. Otherwise, given the large number of possible coalitions, it would be too easy to declare success for a relatively poor model.

MWCs, however, are not a perfect reflection of current scholarship on this topic, leading us to consider the possibility of an appropriate policy-based baseline theoretical model. Any policy-based theory, however, must resolve the fundamental problem of the dimensionality of any *empirical* analysis. As Benoit and Laver note:

How many ... dimensions ... do we need to describe and analyze the political problem at hand without destroying "too much" information? Not surprisingly, this problem is much easier to ask than to answer. This is because the appropriate "dimensionality" of some political space depends on the political problem at hand. There is no general "dimensionality" that is applicable to any conceivable question regardless of context, but rather a range of possibilities that depend on which question we seek to answer (Benoit and Laver 2012: p199).

To build a policy-based baseline, therefore, we must fix the dimensionality of the policy space. Prior work has given quite different answers to this question.

Table A6.1 *Uncalibrated and calibrated ABM and AI model predictions of full cabinet composition in training data*

Case	Year	Parties	Coalition type	Coalition: Null/MWC	Coalition: Untuned	Coalition: Tuned	Coalition: MCCFR
Austria	1999	4	mwc	0.33	0.00	0.00	0.00
Belgium	2003	10	mwc	0.02	0.00	0.00	0.00
Bulgaria	2001	4	mwc	0.33	0.31	0.31	1.00
Czechoslovakia	2006	5	minority	0.00	0.09	0.19	0.00
Germany	2002	5	mwc	0.33	1.00	1.00	1.00
Denmark	2005	8	minority	0.00	1.00	1.00	1.00
Estonia	2007	6	mwc	0.11	0.02	0.00	0.00
Finland	1999	10	surplus	0.00	1.00	1.00	1.00
Latvia	2006	7	surplus	0.00	0.00	0.00	0.00
Luxembourg	2009	6	mwc	0.20	1.00	1.00	1.00
Netherlands	2010	10	minority	0.00	0.00	0.00	0.00
Poland	2007	6	mwc	0.25	0.26	0.53	0.00
Portugal	1999	6	minority	0.00	1.00	1.00	1.00
Portugal	2002	5	mwc	0.25	0.17	0.20	0.80
Romania	2008	5	mwc	0.33	0.08	0.18	0.00
Slovakia	2010	6	minority	0.20	0.16	0.00	0.00
Slovenia	2000	10	mwc	0.05	0.00	0.00	0.00
Spain	2008	10	minority	0.00	0.45	0.11	0.25
Sweden	2006	7	mwc	0.08	0.00	0.08	0.00
UK	2010	10	mwc	0.20	0.26	0.33	1.00
Mean accuracy				0.13	0.34	0.35	0.40

Table A6.2 Uncalibrated and calibrated ABM and AI model predictions of individual parties' cabinet membership in training data

Case	Year	Parties	Coalition type	Party: Null/MWC	Party: Untuned	Party: Tuned	Party: MCCFR
Austria	1999	4	mwc	0.67	0.75	0.75	0.75
Belgium	2003	10	mwc	0.60	0.68	0.68	0.75
Bulgaria	2001	4	mwc	0.67	0.81	0.80	1.00
Czechoslovakia	2006	5	minority	0.50	0.71	0.83	0.80
Germany	2002	5	mwc	0.73	1.00	1.00	1.00
Denmark	2005	8	minority	0.53	1.00	1.00	1.00
Estonia	2007	6	mwc	0.54	0.47	0.53	0.59
Finland	1999	10	surplus	0.52	1.00	1.00	1.00
Latvia	2006	7	surplus	0.51	0.37	0.40	0.58
Luxembourg	2009	6	mwc	0.63	1.00	1.00	1.00
Netherlands	2010	10	minority	0.55	0.79	0.82	0.90
Poland	2007	6	mwc	0.71	0.80	0.83	0.83
Portugal	1999	6	minority	0.83	1.00	1.00	1.00
Portugal	2002	5	mwc	0.65	0.79	0.78	0.96
Romania	2008	5	mwc	0.73	0.64	0.72	0.80
Slovakia	2010	6	minority	0.47	0.40	0.28	0.48
Slovenia	2000	10	mwc	0.67	0.76	0.78	0.90
Spain	2008	10	minority	0.55	0.88	0.92	0.93
Sweden	2006	7	mwc	0.50	0.44	0.43	0.57
UK	2010	10	mwc	0.60	0.83	0.95	1.00
Mean accuracy				0.61	0.76	0.78	0.84

Table A6.3 *Calibrated ABM predictions of full cabinet composition, and party membership of the cabinet, in test set 1*

Case	Year	N	Coalition type	Coalition: Null/MWC	Coalition: Tuned	Party: Null/MWC	Party: Tuned
Austria	2017	5	mwc	0.33	0.00	0.73	0.60
Austria	2019	5	mwc	0.25	0.63	0.65	0.80
Bulgaria	2014	8	minority	0.00	0.00	0.49	0.57
Bulgaria	2017	5	mwc	0.25	0.08	0.65	0.72
Croatia	2016	13	minority	0.00	0.00	0.54	0.90
Czechoslovakia	2013	8	mwc	0.04	0.00	0.54	0.65
Czechoslovakia	2017	9	minority	0.00	0.00	0.62	1.00
Estonia	2015	6	mwc	0.11	0.07	0.57	0.65
Estonia	2019	5	mwc	0.20	0.00	0.52	0.60
Finland	2015	9	mwc	0.04	0.00	0.56	0.80
Finland	2019	10	surplus	0.00	0.00	0.58	0.57
Germany	2013	4	mwc	0.25	0.09	0.56	0.53
Germany	2017	6	mwc	0.09	1.00	0.48	1.00
Hungary	2006	5	mwc	0.25	1.00	0.65	1.00
Latvia	2014	6	mwc	0.08	1.00	0.53	1.00
Latvia	2018	7	surplus	0.00	0.00	0.50	0.55
Lithuania	2012	9	surplus	0.00	0.00	0.57	0.67
Lithuania	2016	11	mwc	0.03	0.73	0.56	0.90
Luxembourg	2013	6	mwc	0.17	0.30	0.53	0.52
Luxembourg	2018	7	mwc	0.17	1.00	0.57	1.00
Netherlands	2012	11	mwc	0.01	0.23	0.50	0.87

Table A6.3 (cont.)

Case	Year	N	Coalition type	Coalition: Null/MWC	Coalition: Tuned	Party: Null/MWC	Party: Tuned
Netherlands	2017	13	mwc	0.00	0.00	0.53	0.77
Poland	2011	6	mwc	0.20	1.00	0.67	1.00
Portugal	2015	5	minority	0.00	0.13	0.65	0.72
Portugal	2019	9	minority	0.00	0.38	0.50	0.90
Romania	2012	10	surplus	0.00	1.00	0.60	1.00
Romania	2016	7	mwc	0.14	0.00	0.67	0.80
Slovakia	2016	8	mwc	0.04	0.00	0.52	0.59
Slovenia	2014	9	surplus	0.00	0.00	0.61	0.77
Slovenia	2018	11	minority	0.00	0.00	0.54	0.47
Spain	2016	12	minority	0.00	0.00	0.55	0.87
Sweden	2014	8	minority	0.00	0.00	0.56	0.70
Sweden	2018	8	minority	0.00	0.00	0.52	0.75
UK	2010	9	mwc	0.06	0.59	0.53	0.97
UK	2017	9	minority	0.00	0.50	0.78	0.95
Mean accuracy				0.08	0.28	0.58	0.78

Table A6.4 Calibrated ABM predictions of full cabinet composition, and party membership of the cabinet, in test set 2

Case	Year	N	Coalition type	Coalition: Null/MWC	Coalition: Tuned	Party: Null/MWC	Party: Tuned
Austria	1986	4	mwc	0.33	0.00	0.67	0.50
Austria	1990	4	mwc	0.33	1.00	0.67	1.00
Austria	1994	5	mwc	0.33	1.00	0.73	1.00
Austria	1995	5	mwc	0.33	1.00	0.73	1.00
Austria	2002	4	mwc	0.25	1.00	0.56	1.00
Austria	2006	5	mwc	0.14	0.10	0.49	0.56
Germany	1987	4	mwc	0.25	1.00	0.56	1.00
Germany	1990	5	mwc	0.25	1.00	0.65	0.74
Germany	1994	5	mwc	0.25	1.00	0.65	1.00
Germany	1998	5	mwc	0.25	0.15	0.65	0.72
Germany	2005	5	mwc	0.14	0.00	0.49	0.73
Germany	2009	5	mwc	0.25	0.00	0.65	0.60
Iceland	1987	7	mwc	0.06	0.00	0.58	0.59
Iceland	1991	5	mwc	0.25	0.00	0.65	0.78
Iceland	1995	6	mwc	0.17	0.00	0.58	0.67
Iceland	1999	5	mwc	0.25	1.00	0.60	1.00
Iceland	2003	5	mwc	0.33	1.00	0.73	1.00
Iceland	2007	5	mwc	0.25	0.00	0.65	0.60
Iceland	2009	5	mwc	0.20	0.29	0.56	0.88
Luxembourg	1989	7	mwc	0.17	1.00	0.62	1.00
Luxembourg	1994	5	mwc	0.20	1.00	0.56	1.00

Table A6.4 (*cont.*)

Case	Year	N	Coalition type	Coalition: Null/MWC	Coalition: Tuned	Party: Null/MWC	Party: Tuned
Luxembourg	1999	6	mwc	0.20	0.00	0.63	0.67
Luxembourg	2004	5	mwc	0.25	0.00	0.65	0.60
Netherlands	1989	9	mwc	0.10	0.00	0.58	0.78
Netherlands	1998	9	surplus	0.00	1.00	0.55	1.00
Netherlands	2003	9	mwc	0.08	0.00	0.63	0.77
Norway	1989	7	minority	0.00	0.00	0.55	0.20
Norway	1993	8	minority	0.00	0.05	0.64	0.89
Norway	1997	8	minority	0.00	0.00	0.48	0.55
Norway	2001	8	minority	0.00	0.00	0.56	0.70
Norway	2005	7	mwc	0.07	0.00	0.54	0.67
Norway	2009	7	mwc	0.13	1.00	0.59	1.00
Portugal	2009	5	minority	0.00	0.38	0.52	0.89
Sweden	1988	6	minority	0.00	0.85	0.69	0.95
Sweden	1991	7	minority	0.00	0.00	0.46	0.18
Sweden	1994	7	minority	0.00	0.80	0.73	0.92
Sweden	1998	7	minority	0.00	0.27	0.54	0.78
Sweden	2002	7	minority	0.00	0.50	0.57	0.93
Sweden	2010	7	minority	0.00	0.00	0.48	0.48
Mean accuracy				**0.15**	**0.42**	**0.60**	**0.78**

Perks Payoffs, No Policy, and MCWs

Though Riker didn't have a formal model, his explicit verbal argument referred to a constant sum, divide-the-dollar, game (Riker 1962). If perks payoffs are cabinet portfolios, the core assumption is that different portfolios may well have different values, but the same portfolio has the same value for each negotiating politician. There can be no gain from trade. The theoretical leap from this assumption to an expectation that MCWs should form is uncontroversial, unchallenged for sixty years, and baked into many later models. Absent additional assumptions, this involves an unambiguous baseline prediction of cabinet composition: a uniform distribution across the set of MCWs and we use this as our current baseline.

Policy, No perks

The idea that policy matters rather than perks has a slightly earlier pedigree (Black 1958). This, however, is a committee-by-committee, issue-by-issue argument that does not speak directly to government formation. On our assumption that a government must one way or another settle the whole raft of salient issues, we get the Kadane (1972) "division-of-the question" result which powered Laver and Shepsle's approach (Laver and Shepsle 1996b). This assumes, as we also do implicitly, that policy preferences are *separable* across dimensions. In our context, the utility from government position p on dimension x doesn't depend on the government position on any other dimension, y.

In other words, theoretically, there is a straight line from Black through Kadane to Laver–Shepsle (hereafter LS). Combined with the substantive assumption that cabinet ministers *de facto* set policy in their jurisdictions, we could rely on a baseline model by predicting the formation of the dimension-by-dimension median (DDM) cabinet in each case.[109] The logic of this prediction rests on the assumption (which has been contested in the substantive literature) *that cabinet ministers effectively set policy.* Thus, the LS model explicitly predicts

---

[109] The LS approach also has the possibility of predicting "strong" party minority cabinets. A strong party has an ideal point in the winset of the DDM and can therefore veto the DDM. We will, however, set this aside since the empirical likelihood of strong parties falls rapidly as dimensionality increases. The strong party concept is dependent on dimensionality, while the DDM is not.

cabinet membership and the DDM is unique. In other words, this is a deterministic model with a point prediction.[110]

Underlying the DDM prediction is a subtle concept that relates to the size of parties. Which particular party is median on some dimension is, in most empirical datasets, *much more a matter of size than of position on the policy dimension*. Further, the probability of a party being median on an arbitrary dimension is, precisely, its Shapley value. A system dominant (B*) party is, by construction, median on every dimension in which it is not at one of the two most extreme positions. A merely dominant (type B) party is still *much* more likely to be median than other parties. Here, nearly 50 percent of our data are B or B*. The bottom line, for any level of dimensionality, given at least one or two relatively large parties, is not only that there will be far fewer median parties than most scholars intuitively expect but also that much of the information about median party status is contained in the party weight vector.

Turning to the matter of dimensionality, there are three main issues. First, concerning theory, there is a brief and speculative, but substantively relevant, discussion in Chapter 12 of LS of both "complex" (more than one issue per portfolio) and "endogenous" (issue allocation to portfolios is strategic) policy jurisdictions. Both play on the same idea: There is no "one true dimensionality" ... substantive dimensionality is endogenous.

Second, concerning empirics, there is a great deal of work on correlations between actors' positions on different issue dimensions and the various plausible inductively implied low-dimensional representations of these (discovered using latent variable models such as PCA). The number of dimensions in this empirical work is most often one, two, or three, with one-dimensional representations typically privileged given their role in simplifying formal theoretical work. LS, for example, assumes that many salient issues (e.g., economic) are grouped together in one portfolio (e.g., the finance ministry) and opted for either two- or three-dimensional empirical analyses. Their choice depended on whether there was a statistically significant difference in rankings by experts of the importance of the second and third most salient cabinet portfolio in an expert survey

---

[110] Once more, this sets aside strong parties. And, it is worth noting that Laver and Shepsle (1998) subsequently jittered policy positions and saliences as we do here. Given computational resources as the time, they relied on two cases as a proof of concept.

(Laver and Hunt 1992). This representation enables their model to make empirical predictions of *party-level* membership of cabinets that could be single-party minority, minority coalitions, or MWCs.[111]

Finally, in the work presented here, our *theoretical model* is n-dimensional. Our *empirical realization* is fourteen-dimensional, for no good reason other than the availability of CHES data. We needed reliable high-dimensional data on party-specific issue positions and saliences, and this was the only show in town. CHES often deployed more dimensions in a given country-year; the number fourteen emerged because this was the number of issue dimensions CHES deployed widely across space and time. This is a pragmatic decision, and we believe a good one, but there is nothing either theoretically or methodologically privileged about it.[112] In all cases, predictions may in fact depend on the choice of dimensionality.

In search of a policy-based baseline theoretical model of government formation, therefore, we compute DDM cabinet predictions derived from a fourteen-dimensional implementation of the LS model. This model is based purely on policy motivations (as opposed to our assumption of politicians motivated by a convex combination of perks and policy payoffs) and can predict single-party minority cabinets, minority coalitions, and majority coalitions. Setting aside strong parties, the LS model always also predicts a DDM cabinet and the underlying proofs involve no constraint on dimensionality. We therefore take the predicted cabinet comprising the set of party medians on the fourteen dimensions in our test datasets. One possible concern is that allowing fourteen policies may, in many cases, push the DDM to predict a supermajority or even unity government which would perform worse than our MWC baseline. It is our opinion, however, that we should choose our tests *ex ante* and not based on what we expect the outcomes to be. We recognize the possibility that a "better" estimate of dimensionality might exist for the DDM-based approach but that is a matter for future research. The important point is that the DDM

---

[111] The Laver–Shepsle model also predicts surplus majority cabinets in some relatively arcane circumstances, but set this aside.

[112] It is worth noting that de Marchi and Laver (2020) use a quite different approach to dimensionality. In that work, they start with a lower-dimensional space and jitter/expand these dimensions to arrive at very high-dimensional spaces. Theoretically, this allowed their model to focus on logrolling and explain the bargaining that occurs over party manifestos.

baseline is a reasonable policy-based comparator for our work, derived from a research tradition on this topic stretching back to Black.

There is the issue where for a few cases in which there are blocking coalitions or multiple parties with identical policy positions, some of the policy dimensions may not have a unique party at the median. In these cases, we generate a prediction based on a uniform distribution across the relevant possibilities.

Digression: Minimum Connected Winning Coalitions

Axelrod's one-dimensional minimal connected winning coalition (MCW) theory was informal ... and logically incoherent (Axelrod 1970). If, as Axelrod assumes, all that matters is one dimension of policy, then Black's argument should apply and the prediction is a single-party minority cabinet at the median. The "winning" part of MCW must imply that perks are also important. But if perks are also important, then the inclusion of (perks consuming) nonpivotal parties within the range of the MCW, as Axelrod does, does not follow deductively. The prediction should have been the MCW with minimal ideological range. We therefore do not consider MCWs to be a suitable predictive baseline.

DDM Baseline Results

The results of deploying the fourteen-dimensional DDM baseline model on the training set are presented in Table A6.5.

The mean accuracy of the cabinet-level prediction is 0.10, and the party-level prediction is 0.69. In comparison, the MWC baseline has a coalition-level accuracy of 0.25 and a party-level accuracy of 0.61. Descriptively, the mean number of parties predicted to form a coalition in the DDM model is, as expected, quite high at 3.6; the MWC baseline has a mean of 2.4 parties. Qualitatively, while the coalition-level predictions of the DDM model are not terribly good compared to the MWC baseline, the party-level predictions are superior.

Clearly, there is interesting signal here that is distinct from the MWC baseline model – and there are any number of ways we could enhance the DDM or MWC baseline. For example, adding a "win-stick" rule to the DDM model improves performance at the coalition level to 0.25. But, as with all such modeling endeavors, we should be careful

Table A6.5 *Fourteen-dimensional DDM baseline predictions*

Setting	DDM	Empirical coalition	DDM cabinet accuracy	DDM party accuracy
Austria 1999	(1, 2)	(1, 2)	1	1
Belgium 2003	(0, 1, 3, 4)	(0, 1, 2, 3)	0	0.8
Bulgaria 2001	(0, 1, 2, 3)	(0, 3)	0	0.5
Czech 2006	(0, 1, 2, 3, 4)	(0,)	0	0.2
Denmark 2005	(0, 1, 2, 3, 7)	(0, 3)	0	0.625
Estonia 2007	(0, 2, 4, 5)	(0, 2, 3)	0	0.5
Finland 1999	(0, 1, 2, 3, 5, 6)	(0, 2, 3, 4, 5)	0	0.7
Germany 2002	(0, 1, 2)	(0, 2)	0	0.8
Latvia 2006	(0, 1, 2)	(0, 2, 4, 5)	0	0.57
Lux 2009	(0, 2, 4)	(0, 1)	0	0.5
Neths 2010	(0, 1, 2, 3, 4) or (0, 1, 2, 3, 4, 8)	(0, 3)	0	0.65
Poland 2007	(0, 2) or (0, 2, 3) or (0, 2, 4) or (0, 2, 3, 4)	(0, 3)	0	0.67
Portugal 1999	(0, 1)	(0,)	0	0.83
Portugal 2002	(0)	(0, 2)	0	0.8
Romania 2008	(0, 1)	(0, 1)	1	1
Slovakia 2010	(0, 2, 3) or (0, 2, 3, 4)	(1, 2, 3, 4)	0	0.67
Slovenia 2000	(0, 1, 2, 4)	(0, 2, 3)	0	0.625
Spain 2008	(0, 4, 5) or (0, 4, 5, 6)	(0,)	0	0.69
Sweden 2006	(0, 2, 3, 4) or (0, 1, 2, 3, 4)	(1, 2, 3, 4)	0	0.79
UK 2010	(0, 1, 2)	(0, 2)	0	0.83

at this point of mixing and matching parts of different models to optimize performance on the now fixed training data. We have a great deal of information about these cases and the performance of different models. Future research must judge results against new cases. And at this point, the baseline model should be our agent-based model or artificial intelligence models given their superior performance across all three datasets in this chapter.

References

Aksoy, Deniz. 2012. "Institutional Arrangements and Logrolling: Evidence from the European Union." *American Journal of Political Science* 56: 538–52.

Aldrich, John H., Jacob M. Montgomery, and David B. Sparks. 2014. "Polarization and Ideology: Partisan Sources of Low Dimensionality in Scaled Roll Call Analyses." *Political Analysis* 22: 435–56.

Alvarez, R. Michael. 2016. *Computational Social Science.* Cambridge: Cambridge University Press.

Andersson, Staffan, Torbjörn Bergman, and Svante Ersson. 2014. "The European Representative Democracy Data Archive, Release 3." Main sponsor: Riksbankens Jubileumsfond (In2007-0149:1-E), www .erdda.se.

Ansolabehere, Stephen, James M. Snyder, Aaron B. Strauss, and Michael M. Ting. 2005. "Voting Weights and Formateur Advantages in the Formation of Coalition Governments." *American Journal of Political Science* 49: 550–63.

Axelrod, Robert. 1997. "The Evolution of Strategies in the Iterated Prisoner's Dilemma." In *The Complexity of Cooperation: Agent-Based Models of Competition and Collaboration,* ed. Robert Axelrod. Princeton: Princeton University Press. 14–29.

1980a. "Effective Choice in the Prisoner's Dilemma." *Journal of Conflict Resolution* 24: 3–25.

1980b. "More Effective Choice in the Prisoner's Dilemma." *Journal of Conflict Resolution* 24: 379–403.

1970. *Conflict of Interest.* Chicago: Markham.

Axelrod, Robert, and William D. Hamilton. 1981. "The Evolution of Cooperation." *Science* 211: 1390–96.

Bäck, Hanna. 2003. "Explaining and Predicting Coalition Outcomes: Conclusions from Studying Data on Local Coalitions." *European Journal of Political Research* 42: 441–72.

Bakker, Ryan, Catherine De Vries, Erica Edwards, et al. 2015. "Measuring Party Positions in Europe: The Chapel Hill Expert Survey Trend File, 1999–2010." *Party Politics* 21: 143–52.

Bakker, Ryan, Liesbet Hooghe, Seth Jolly, et al. 2020. *2019 Chapel Hill Expert Survey.* Chapel Hill: University of North Carolina.

Banks, Jeffrey S., and John Duggan. 2006. "A General Bargaining Model of Legislative Policy-Making." *Quarterly Journal of Political Science* 1: 49–85.

Baron, David. 1991. "A Spatial Bargaining Theory of Government Formation in Parliamentary Systems." *American Political Science Review* 85: 137–64.

Baron, David, and John Ferejohn. 1989. "Bargaining in Legislatures." *American Political Science Review* 83: 1182–202.

Bassi, Anna. 2013. "A Model of Endogenous Government Formation." *American Journal of Political Science* 57: 777–93.

Bednar, Jenna, and Scott E. Page. 2018. "When Order Affects Performance: Culture, Behavioral Spillovers, and Institutional Path Dependence." *American Political Science Review* 112: 82–98.

Bendor, Jonathan, and Terry M. Moe. 1985. "An Adaptive Model of Bureaucratic Politics." *American Political Science Review* 79: 755–74.

Bendor, Jonathan, and Piotr Swistak. 2001. "The Evolution of Norms." *American Journal of Sociology* 106: 1493–545.

Benoit, Kenneth, Drew Conway, Benjamin E. Lauderdale, Michael Laver, and Slava Mikhaylov. 2016. "Crowd-Sourced Text Analysis: Reproducible and Agile Production of Political Data." *American Political Science Review* 110: 278–95.

Benoit, Kenneth, and Michael Laver. 2012. "The Dimensionality of Political Space: Epistemological and Methodological Considerations." *European Union Politics* 13: 194–218.

2006. *Party Policy in Modern Democracies.* London: Routledge.

Benoit, Kenneth, Michael Laver, and Slava Mikhaylov. 2009. "Treating Words as Data with Error: Uncertainty in Text Statements of Policy Positions." *American Journal of Political Science* 53: 495–513.

Berger, Ulrich. 2007. "Brown's Original Fictitious Play." *Journal of Economic Theory* 135: 572–78.

Billings, Darse, Neil Burch, Aaron Davidson, et al. 2003. "Approximating Game-Theoretic Optimal Strategies for Full-Scale Poker." Paper presented at the IJCAI.

Binmore, Ken. 1998. "The Complexity of Cooperation." *Journal of Artificial Societies and Social Simulation* 1.

Binmore, Kenneth G., and Larry Samuelson. 1992. "Evolutionary Stability in Repeated Games Played by Finite Automata." *Journal of Economic Theory* 57: 278–305.

Black, Duncan. 1958. *The Theory of Committees and Elections.* Cambridge: Cambridge University Press.

Bowler, Shaun, Gail McElroy, and Stefan Müller. 2022. "Voter Expectations of Government Formation in Coalition Systems: The Importance of the Information Context." *European Journal of Political Research* 61: 111–33.

Braumoeller, Bear F. 2003. "Causal Complexity and the Study of Politics." *Political Analysis* 11: 209–33.

Brown, Noam, and Tuomas Sandholm. 2019. "Superhuman AI for Multiplayer Poker." *Science* 365: 885–90.

2017. "Libratus: The Superhuman AI for No-Limit Poker." Paper presented at the IJCAI.

Browne, Eric, and John Frendreis. 1980. "Allocating Coalition Payoffs by Conventional Norm: An Assessment of the Evidence from Cabinet Coalition Situations." *American Journal of Political Science* 24: 753–68.

Browne, Eric, John Frendreis, and Dennis Gleiber. 1986a. "An Exponential Model of Cabinet Stability: The Durability, Duration, and Survival of Cabinet Governments." *American Journal of Political Science* 30: 628–50.

1986b. "The Study of Governmental Dissolutions in Western Parliamentary Democracies." *Legislative Studies Quarterly* 11: 619–28.

Budge, Ian, Hans-Dieter Klingemann, Andrea Volkens, et al. 2001. *Mapping Policy Preferences: Parties, Electors and Governments: 1945-1998: Estimates for Parties, Electors and Governments 1945-1998.* Oxford: Oxford University Press.

Budge, Ian, David Robertson, and Derek Hearl. 1987. *Ideology, Strategy and Party Change: Spatial Analyses of Post-War Election Programmes in 19 Democracies.* Cambridge: Cambridge University Press.

Carrubba, Clifford J., and Craig Volden. 2000. "Coalitional Politics and Logrolling in Legislative Institutions." *American Journal of Political Science* 44: 261–77.

Chiba, Daina, Lanny W. Martin, and Randolph T. Stevenson. 2015. "A Copula Approach to the Problem of Selection Bias in Models of Government Survival." *Political Analysis* 23: 42–58.

Conitzer, Vincent, and Tuomas Sandholm. 2002. "Complexity Results about Nash Equilibria." *arXiv preprint cs/0205074.*

Converse, Phillip E. 1964. "The Nature of Belief Systems in Mass Publics." In *Ideology and Discontent.*, ed. David E. Apter. London: Free Press of Glencoe. 206–61.

Cox, Gary W. 2021. "Nonunitary Parties, Government Formation, and Gamson's Law." *American Political Science Review* 115: 917–30.

Cutler, Josh, Scott de Marchi, Max Gallop, Florian M. Hollenbach, Michael Laver, and Matthias Orlowski. 2016. "Cabinet Formation and Portfolio Distribution in European Multiparty Systems." *British Journal of Political Science* 46: 31–43.

de Marchi, Scott. 2022. "The Complexity of Polarization." *Proceedings of the National Academy of Sciences* 119: e2115019119.

2005. *Computational and Mathematical Modeling in the Social Sciences.* Cambridge: Cambridge University Press.

de Marchi, Scott, Spencer Dorsey, and Michael J. Ensley. 2021. "Policy and the Structure of Roll Call Voting in the US House." *Journal of Public Policy* 41: 384–408.

de Marchi, Scott, and Michael Laver. 2020. "Government Formation as Logrolling in High-Dimensional Issue Spaces." *The Journal of Politics* 82: 543–58.

de Marchi, Scott, and Scott E. Page. 2014. "Agent-Based Models." *Annual Review of Political Science* 17: 1–20.

de Marchi, Scott, and B. Stewart. 2020. "Wrestling with Complexity in Computational Social Science: Theory, Estimation and Representation." In *The SAGE Handbook of Research Methods in Political Science and International Relations*, eds. Curini, Luigi, and Robert Franzese. London: Sage Publications. 289–310.

Denzau, Arthur T., and Douglass C. North. 2000. "Shared Mental Models: Ideologies and Institutions." In *Elements of Reason: Cognition, Choice, the Bounds of Rationality*, eds. Chong, Dennis, and James H. Kuklinski. Cambridge: Cambridge University Press. 23–46.

Diermeier, Daniel, Hülya Eraslan, and Antonio Merlo. 2003. "A Structural Model of Government Formation." *Econometrica* 71: 27–70.

Diermeier, Daniel, and Keith Krehbiel. 2003. "Institutionalism as a Methodology." *Journal of Theoretical Politics* 15: 123–44.

Diermeier, Daniel, and Antonio Merlo. 2000. "Government Turnover in Parliamentary Democracies." *Journal of Economic Theory* 94: 46–79.

Diermeier, Daniel, and Randy Stevenson. 2000. "Cabinet Terminations and Critical Events." *American Political Science Review* 94: 627–40.

1999. "Cabinet Survival and Competing Risks." *American Journal of Political Science* 93: 1051–68.

Diermeier, Daniel, and Peter Van Roozendaal. 1998. "The Duration of Cabinet Formation Processes in Western Multi-Party Democracies." *British Journal of Political Science* 28: 609–26.

Döring, Holge, and Philip Manow. 2020. "Parlgov. Parliaments and Governments Database: Information on Parties, Elections and Cabinets in Modern Democracies." www.parlgov.org/.

Dragu, Tiberiu, and Michael Laver. 2019. "Coalition Governance with Incomplete Information." *The Journal of Politics* 81: 923–36.

2017. "Legislative Coalitions with Incomplete Information." *Proceedings of the National Academy of Sciences* 114: 2876–80.

Druckman, James N., and Paul V. Warwick. 2005. "The Missing Piece: Measuring Portfolio Salience in Western European Parliamentary Democracies." *European Journal of Political Research* 44: 17–42.

Ecker, Alejandro, and Thomas M. Meyer. 2019. "Fairness and Qualitative Portfolio Allocation in Multiparty Governments." *Public Choice* 181: 309–30.

Eggers, Andrew C., and Arthur Spirling. 2016. "Party Cohesion in Westminster systems: Inducements, Replacement and Discipline in the House of Commons, 1836–1910." *British Journal of Political Science* 46: 567–89.

Fortunato, David, et al. 2021. "Attributing Policy Influence under Coalition Governance." *American Political Science Review* 115: 252–68.

Fowler, James H., and Michael Laver. 2008. "A Tournament of Party Decision Rules." *Journal of Conflict Resolution* 52: 68–92.

Fréchette, Guillaume, John H. Kagel, and Massimo Morelli. 2005a. "Behavioral Identification in Coalitional Bargaining: An Experimental Analysis of Demand Bargaining and Alternating Offers." *Econometrica* 73: 1893–937.

2005b. "Gamson's Law versus Non-Cooperative Bargaining Theory." *Games and Economic Behavior* 51: 365–90.

Freixas, Josep, and Xavier Molinero. 2009. "On the Existence of a Minimum Integer Representation for Weighted Voting Systems." *Annals of Operations Research* 166: 243–60.

Friedman, Milton. 1953. "The Methodology of Positive Economics." In *Essays in Positive Economics*, ed. Freidman, Milton. Chicago: University of Chicago Press.

Gallagher, Michael, Michael Laver, and Peter Mair. 2012. *Representative Government in Modern Europe* (5th ed.). Maidenhead: McGraw-Hill.

Gamson, William A. 1961. "A Theory of Coalition Formation." *American Sociological Review* 26: 373–82.

Ganzfried, Sam, and Tuomas Sandholm. 2008. "Computing an Approximate Jam/Fold Equilibrium for 3-Player No-Limit Texas Hold'em Tournaments." Paper presented at the Proceedings of the 7th International Joint Conference on Autonomous Agents and Multiagent Systems-Volume 2.

Gibson, Richard G., Neil Burch, Marc Lanctot, and Duane Szafron. 2012. "Efficient Monte Carlo Counterfactual Regret Minimization in Games with Many Player Actions." Paper presented at the NIPS.

Gigerenzer, Gerd, and Wolfgang Gaissmaier. 2011. "Heuristic Decision Making." *Annual Review of Psychology* 62: 451–82.

Gigerenzer, Gerd, and Reinhard Selten. 2002. *Bounded Rationality: The Adaptive Toolbox*. Cambridge, MA: MIT Press.

Golder, Sona N. 2010. "Bargaining Delays in the Government Formation Process." *Comparative Political Studies* 43: 3–32.

Guo, Rongxing. 2019. "Win-Stay, Lose-Shift: A Survival Rule." In *Human-Earth System Dynamics*, ed. Guo, Rongxing. Singapore: Springer. 1–21.

Heinrich, Johannes, and David Silver. 2014. "Self-Play Monte-Carlo Tree Search in Computer Poker." Paper presented at the Workshops at the Twenty-Eighth AAAI Conference on Artificial Intelligence.

Hoffmann, Robert. 2000. "Twenty Years on: The Evolution of Cooperation Revisited." *Journal of Artificial Societies and Social Simulation* 3: 1390–96.

Jenke, Libby. 2022. "Introduction to the special issue: Innovations and current challenges in experimental methods." *Political Analysis* 30.S1: S3–S7.

Johanson, Michael, Neil Burch, Richard Valenzano, and Michael Bowling. 2013. "Evaluating State-Space Abstractions in Extensive-Form Games." Paper presented at the Proceedings of the 2013 International Conference on Autonomous Agents and Multiagent Systems.

Judd, Kenneth, and Scott E. Page. 2004. "Computational Public Economics." *Journal of Public Economic Theory* 6: 195–202.

Kadane, Joseph B. 1972. "On Division of the Question." *Public Choice* 13: 47–54.

Kahneman, Daniel, and Amos Tversky, eds. 2000. *Choices, Values and Frames*. Cambridge: Cambridge University Press.

Kayser, Mark A., Matthias Orlowski, and Jochen Rehmert. 2019. "Coalition Inclusion Prob-Abilities: A Party-Strategic Measure for Predicting Politics and Policy." Working Paper. Hertie School of Governance, Berlin.

Keohane, Robert. 1999. "Ideology and Professionalism in International Institutions: Insights from the Work of Douglass C. North." *Alt, J., M. Levi y E. Ostrom [ed](1999)*: 228–46.

King, Gary. 2003. "The Future of Replication." *International Studies Perspectives*. In Bueno de Mesquita, Bruce, Nils Petter Gleditsch, Patrick James, Gary King, Claire Metelits, James Lee Ray, Bruce Russett, Håvard Strand, and Brandon Valeriano. "Symposium on replication in international studies research." *International Studies Perspectives* 4: 72–107.

1995. "Replication, Replication." *PS: Political Science & Politics* 28: 444–52.

King, Gary, Jennifer Pan, and Margaret E. Roberts. 2013. "How Censorship in China Allows Government Criticism but Silences Collective Expression." *American Political Science Review* 326–43.

King, Gary, James E. Alt, Nancy Elizabeth Burns, and Michael Laver. 1990. "A Unified Model of Cabinet Dissolution in Parliamentary Democracies." *American Journal of Political Science* 34: 872–902.

Klingemann, Hans-Dieter, Richard I. Hofferbert, and Ian Budge. 1994. *Parties, Policies, and Democracy, Theoretical Lenses on Public Policy.* Boulder: Westview Press.

Klingemann, Hans-Dieter, Andrea Volkens, Judith Bara, Ian Budge, and Michael McDonald. 2006. *Mapping Policy Preferences II: Estimates for Parties, Electors, and Governments in Eastern Europe, European Union and OECD 1990-2003.* Oxford: Oxford University Press.

Klüver, Heike, and Hanna Bäck. 2019. "Coalition Agreements, Issue Attention, and Cabinet Governance." *Comparative Political Studies* 52: 1995–2031.

Kollman, Ken, John Miller, and Scott Page. 1998. "Political Parties and Electoral Landscapes." *British Journal of Political Science* 28 139–58.

1992. "Adaptive Parties in Spatial Elections." *American Political Science Review* 86: 929–37.

Lanctot, Marc, Kevin Waugh, Martin Zinkevich, and Michael H. Bowling. 2009. "Monte Carlo Sampling for Regret Minimization in Extensive Games." Paper presented at the NIPS.

Laver, M. 2003. "Government Termination." *Annual Review of Political Science* 6: 23–40.

Laver, Michael. 2020a. *Agent-Based Models of Polarization and Ethnocentrism.* Cambridge: Cambridge University Press.

2020b. *Agent-Based Models of Social Life: Fundamentals.* Cambridge: Cambridge University Press.

Laver, Michael, and Kenneth A. Benoit. 2015. "The Basic Arithmetic of Legislative Decisions." *American Journal of Political Science* 59: 275–91.

2003. "The Evolution of Party Systems between Elections." *American Journal of Political Science* 47: 215–33.

Laver, Michael, and W. Ben Hunt. 1992. *Policy and Party Competition.* New York: Routledge.

Laver, Michael, Kenneth A. Benoit, and John Garry. 2003. "Estimating the Policy Positions of Political Actors Using Words as Data." *American Political Science Review* 97: 311–31.

Laver, Michael, Scott de Marchi, and Hande Mutlu. 2011a. "Negotiation in Legislatures over Government Formation." *Public Choice* 147: 285–304.

2011b. "Negotiation in Legislatures over Government Formation." *Public Choice* 147: 285–304.

Laver, Michael, and Norman Schofield. 1998a. *Multiparty Government: The Politics of Coalition in Europe.* Ann Arbor, MI: University of Michigan Press.

1998b. *Multiparty Government: The Politics of Coalition in Europe.* Ann Arbor paperback ed. Ann Arbor, MI: University of Michigan Press.

Laver, Michael, and Ernest Sergenti. 2012. *Party Competition: An Agent-Based Model, Princeton Studies in Complexity.* Princeton: Princeton University Press.

Laver, Michael, and Kenneth A. Shepsle. 1998. "Events, Equilibria and Government Survival." *American Journal of Political Science* 42: 28–54.

　1996a. *Making and Breaking Governments: Cabinets and Legislatures in Parliamentary Democracies*. Cambridge: Cambridge University Press.

　1996b. *Making and Breaking Governments: Cabinets and Legislatures in Parliamentary Democracies*. Political Economy of Institutions and Decisions. New York: Cambridge University Press.

　1994. *Cabinet Ministers and Parliamentary Government*, Political Economy of Institutions and Decisions. Cambridge [England]: New York: Cambridge University Press.

Lowe, Will, Kenneth Benoit, Slava Mikhaylov, and Michael Laver. 2011. "Scaling Policy Preferences from Coded Political Texts." *Legislative Studies Quarterly* 36: 123–55.

Lupia, Arthur, and Kaare Strom. 1995. "Coalition Termination and the Strategic Timing of Parliamentary Elections." *American Political Science Review* 89: 648–65.

Martin, Lanny, and Georg Vanberg. 2020. "Models of Coalition Politics: Recent Developments and New Directions." *The SAGE Handbook of Research Methods in Political Science and International Relations*: 244.

　2015. "Coalition Formation and Policymaking in Parliamentary Democracies." In *Routledge Handbook of Comparative Political Institutions*, eds. Gandhi, Jennifer, and Rubén Ruiz-Rufino. London, New York: Routledge.

　2014. "Parties and Policymaking in Multiparty Governments: The Legislative Median, Ministerial Autonomy, and the Coalition Compromise." *American Journal of Political Science* 58: 979–96.

　2011. *Parliaments and Coalitions: The Role of Legislative Institutions in Multiparty Governance*. Oxford: Oxford University Press.

　2003. "Wasting Time? The Impact of Ideology and Size on Delay in Coalition Formation." *British Journal of Political Science* 33: 323–32.

Martin, Lanny W., and Randolph T. Stevenson. 2001. "Government Formation in Parliamentary Democracies." *American Journal of Political Science* 45: 33–50.

McKelvey, Richard D., and Norman Schofield. 1987. "Generalized Symmetry Conditions at a Core Point." *Econometrica* 55: 923–33.

　1986. "Structural Instability of the Core." *Journal of Mathematical Economics* 15: 179–98.

Miller, John H., and Scott Page. 2009. *Complex Adaptive Systems*. Princeton, NJ: Princeton University Press.

Morelli, Massimo. 1999. "Demand Competition and Policy Compromise in Legislative Bargaining." *American Political Science Review* 93: 809–20.

Müller, Wolfgang C., and Kaare Strøm. 2003. *Coalition Governments in Western Europe*. Oxford: Oxford University Press.

2000. *Coalition Governments in Western Europe.* New York: Oxford University Press.

Munger, Michael C. 2020. "Ideology and the Direction of Causation in the Acquisition and Maintenance of Shared Belief Systems." *Kyklos* 73: 392–409.

Neller, Todd W., and Marc Lanctot. 2013. "An Introduction to Counterfactual Regret Minimization." Paper presented at the Proceedings of Model AI Assignments, The Fourth Symposium on Educational Advances in Artificial Intelligence (EAAI-2013).

Nowak, Martin A. 2006. *Evolutionary Dynamics: Exploring the Equations of Life*: Cambridge, MA: Harvard University Press.

Nowak, Martin A., and K. Sigmund. 1993. "A Strategy of Win-Stay, Lose-Shift That Outperforms Tit-for-Tat in the Prisoners' Dilemma Game." *Nature* 364: 56–58.

Osborne, Martin J, and Ariel Rubinstein. 1994. *A Course in Game Theory*: Cambridge, MA: MIT Press.

Ostrom, Elinor. 2010. "Beyond Markets and States: Polycentric Governance of Complex Economic Systems." *American Economic Review* 100: 641–72.

Page, Karen, and Martin Nowak. 2002. "Unifying Evolutionary Dynamics." *Journal of Theoretical Biology* 219: 93–98.

Page, Scott E. 2008. *The Difference: How the Power of Diversity Creates Better Groups, Firms, Schools, and Societies-New Edition*: Princeton, NJ: Princeton University Press.

Papadimitriou, Christos H. 2007. "The Complexity of Finding Nash Equilibria." *Algorithmic Game Theory* 2: 30.

Pearl, Judea. 2009. *Causality*: Cambridge: Cambridge University Press.

Penn, Elizabeth Maggie. 2006. "Alternate Definitions of the Uncovered Set and Their Implications." *Social Choice and Welfare* 27: 83–87.

Riker, William H. 1962. *The Theory of Political Coalitions*. New Haven: Yale University Press.

Rogers, Alex, Rajdeep K. Dash, Sarvapali D. Ramchurn, Perukrishnen Vytelingum, and Nicholas R. Jennings. 2007. "Coordinating Team Players within a Noisy Iterated Prisoner's Dilemma Tournament." *Theoretical Computer Science* 377: 243–59.

Rubinstein, Ariel. 1982. "Perfect Equilibrium in a Bargaining Model." *Econometrica* 50: 97–109.

Schelling, Thomas. 1971. "Dynamic Models of Segregation." *Journal of Mathematical Sociology* 1: 143–86.

Schmid, Martin, Neil Burch, Marc Lanctot, Matej Moravcik, Rudolf Kadlec, and Michael Bowling. 2019. "Variance Reduction in Monte Carlo Counterfactual Regret Minimization (Vr-Mccfr) for Extensive

Form Games Using Baselines." Paper presented at the Proceedings of the AAAI Conference on Artificial Intelligence.

Schofield, Norman. 1983. "Generic Instability of Majority Rule." *Review of Economic Studies* 50: 695–705.

Shalizi, Cosma. 2010. "The Bootstrap: Statisticians Can Reuse Their Data to Quantify the Uncertainty of Complex Models." *American Scientist* 98: 186–91.

Shu, Feng. 2020. "A Win-Switch-Lose-Stay Strategy Promotes Cooperation in the Evolutionary Games." *Physica A: Statistical Mechanics and Its Applications* 555: 124605.

Simon, Herbert. 1955. "A Behavioral Model of Rational Choice." *Quarterly Journal of Economics* 69: 99–118.

Slapin, Jonathan B., and Sven-Oliver Proksch. 2008. "A Scaling Model for Estimating Time Series Policy Positions from Texts." *American Journal of Political Science* 52: 705–22.

Smith, Alastair. 2004. *Election Timing*. Cambridge, UK; New York: Cambridge University Press.

Snyder, James M., Michael Ting, and Stephen Ansolabehere. 2005. "Legislative Bargaining under Weighted Voting." *American Economic Review* 95: 981–1004.

Spoon, Jae-Jae, and Heike Klüver. 2017. "Does Anybody Notice? How Policy Positions of Coalition Parties Are Perceived by Voters." *European Journal of Political Research* 56: 115–32.

Stokes, Donald E. 1963. "Spatial Models of Party Competition." *American Political Science Review* 57: 368–77.

Strøm, Kaare, Wolfgang C. Müller, and Torbjörn Bergman. 2008. *Cabinets and Coalition Bargaining: The Democratic Life Cycle in Western Europe*: Oxford: Oxford University Press.

Von Neumann, J. and Morgenstern, O. 2007. "Theory of Games and Economic Behavior." In *Theory of Games and Economic Behavior*, eds. Kuhn, H. W., von Neumann, J., Morgenstern, O. and Rubinstein, A. Princeton: Princeton University Press.

Warwick, Paul. 1994. *Government Survival in Parliamentary Democracies*. New York: Cambridge University Press.

Warwick, Paul V., and James N. Druckman. 2006. "The Portfolio Allocation Paradox: An Investigation into the Nature of a Very Strong but Puzzling Relationship." *European Journal of Political Research* 45: 635–65.

2001. "Portfolio Salience and the Proportionality of Payoffs in Coalition Governments." *British Journal of Political Science* 31: 627–49.

Waugh, Kevin, David Schnizlein, Michael H. Bowling, and Duane Szafron. 2009. "Abstraction Pathologies in Extensive Games." Paper presented at the AAMAS (2).

Index

CAMBRIDGE STUDIES IN COMPARATIVE POLITICS

For EU product safety concerns, contact us at Calle de José Abascal, 56–1°, 28003 Madrid, Spain or eugpsr@cambridge.org.